1750/N

The Planning-Programming-Budgeting Approach to Government Decision-Making

PRAEGER SPECIAL STUDIES IN
U.S. ECONOMIC AND SOCIAL DEVELOPMENT

The Planning-Programming-Budgeting Approach to Government Decision-Making

Harold A. Hovey

Foreword by
Senator William Proxmire

FREDERICK A. PRAEGER, Publishers
New York · Washington · London

The purpose of the Praeger Special Studies is to make specialized research monographs in U.S. and international economics and politics
available to the academic, business, and government communities. For
further information, write to the Special Projects Division, Frederick
A. Praeger, Publishers, 111 Fourth Avenue, New York, N.Y. 10003.

FREDERICK A. PRAEGER, PUBLISHERS
111 Fourth Avenue, New York, N.Y. 10003, U.S.A.
5, Cromwell Place, London S.W.7, England

Published in the United States of America in 1968
by Frederick A. Praeger, Inc., Publishers

Library of Congress Catalog Card Number: 68-55007

Printed in the United States of America

FOREWORD
By
Senator William Proxmire

The fact that government programs--at all levels--have
a significant impact on many phases of contemporary political,
social, and economic life is not startling. But as the size and
scope of government continues to increase, the role Congress
plays as the nation's "overseer" grows in difficulty. It is
imperative that members of Congress not only know costs of
government programs but also possess better information
about the real effects of these programs.

The need for improved methods of program analysis is
dire. Already approximately 30 per cent of national income
flows through federal, state, and local government accounts--
and of that amount, 80 per cent can be attributed to the federal
government. At the same time, programs at differing government levels and within disparate agencies with similar policy
goals often appear to compete with, rather than complement,
each other in attempting to attain their objectives.

For example, government concern with estuaries--the
wide mouths of rivers where they meet the sea--would, at
first glance, seem to be minimal, certainly not calling for
attention by more than a few offices. But when the Department
of the Interior instituted planning-programming-budgeting
(PPB) analysis, it discovered seven bureaus within the
Department dealing with estuaries.

This example may be extreme, yet again it may not. It
definitely points up the need within government for better
information-gathering and analysis techniques.

If we view the budget as a system in itself, we note the
importance of information inputs in the decision-making
process. Bad inputs lead to bad outputs, and bad outputs
cause serious resource misallocations within the budgetary

system. The application of PPB methods should prove a valuable advance for the better direction, coordination, and control of government budgetary concepts.

Although PPB systems represent a synthesis of evolving control techniques, the combination of a number of proved methods now gives policy-makers a more rational basis for choosing among various alternative programs. As such, the PPB system is an extension and adaption of many congressional and executive recommendations for improving government effectiveness.

However, the system does not lack critics. Some claim that PPB advocates are nothing but a new type of technocrat-- technicians who resort to the computer to segregate decision-making and politics. Thus they charge that congressional power is being usurped and that legislators eventually will be replaced by mathematicians. They accuse PPB of overcentralizing decision-making within executive departments; they say PPB methods tend to stifle healthy dissent. Critics point out that as long as the future is uncertain, it is foolish to plan and program in five-year time horizons.

Indeed, some of these complaints may prove valuable if Congress and other government officials are tempted to let PPB techniques assume the position of the ultimate decision-making factor. To retain effectiveness, PPB must always be viewed as a replacement for that process. Furthermore, it must be remembered that federal government PPB utilization is still relatively new; it has been less than three years since President Johnson issued a directive ordering all federal agencies to apply PPB techniques.

With the recognition that improved government management rates a high priority, congressional interest in PPB systems has been growing over the past eighteen months. Two major congressional committees, the Senate Government Operations Committee and the Congressional Joint Economic Committee, have held, and continue to conduct, extensive PPB investigations. As chairman of the Joint Economic Committee and of its Subcommittee on Economy in Government, I presided over a four-day hearing in the autumn of 1967 resulting in a subcommittee report, "The Planning-Programming-Budgeting System:

Progress and Potentials," released in December, 1967. The report concluded with this general statement:

> The subcommittee is of the firm opinion that PPBS represents a substantial forward step in budgetary techniques. At the same time, it is our opinion that much more work is needed in the definition of national objectives and the determination of priorities in the allocation of public funds. If the Nation had a little clearer notion of its goals and national priorities (bearing in mind that they are apt to be continuously shifting in a society like ours), it would ease the task of PPBS inasmuch as it would give rise to definable objective programs which could then be subjected to a systems approach.

> This subcommittee recommends to the Joint Economic Committee that the full committee conduct an inquiry into the possibilities for a clearer definition of Federal program objectives than now exists and develop information on possible conflicts, overlaps, or lack of coordination in our present goals and on ways of setting priorities in the allocation of Federal funds.

> As a general guide to improved budgeting, the subcommittee feels it appropriate to restate some of the proposals set down by the committee previously which emphasize basic economic principles. Among the recommendations made in the 1957 report of the Subcommittee on Fiscal Policy entitled "Federal Expenditure Policy for Economic Growth and Stability," and the 1963 report of the Subcommittee on Economic Statistics entitled "The Federal Budget as an Economic Document," the following have particular relevance to this study:

> (1) Economy in Government should be measured by the relative benefits and costs of each program. While quantitative evaluation of many Federal programs directed at social problems is admittedly difficult, the priority of these

programs must be weighted by careful consideration of their relative costs.

(2) Federal programs aimed at supporting or improving the economic position of particular groups or industries should be constantly re-evaluated in light of changing circumstances.

(3) The alternative-resource-use test also should be applied to Federal programs which involve no significant Federal expenditures. Federal enterprise activities and programs for insurance and guarantee of private loans may involve only small net budget expenditures, but exert a powerful influence on the allocation of resources.

(4) Recognizing that economic considerations may not always prevail in determining Federal expenditure programs emphasizes the need for carrying out these programs at minimum real cost.

(5) Federal expenditure policies closely geared to the Nation's economic growth objectives must provide for as rapid adjustment as possible in spending programs in response to changing demand and supply. Rigidities in Federal spending programs may limit significantly the economy's growth potential.

(6) The scope and character of Federal spending programs should reflect, wherever possible, the comparative economic advantages of the Federal, State, and local governments and of private enterprise in achieving program objectives.

(7) Federal participation in activities shared by State and local governments and private enterprise should be aimed primarily at improving the effectiveness of these activities and should avoid merely transferring responsibility for them to the Federal Government.

(8) The budgetary process should show how the various activities of the Federal Government are related to each other on a program basis, and how these programs are related to similar activities outside of the Federal Government.

(9) Budget decisions should be based upon a clear recognition of the longer range prospects for Government programs in terms of their costs and benefits. Specifically, the budget for each year should be presented in the context of a longer run set of budgetary projections, probably covering a 5-year period; and regular periodic revisions of budgetary estimates should be provided, on at least a quarterly basis.

This book by Dr. Harold A. Hovey stands as a major contribution to the growing field of PPB analysis. It describes the PPB approach in terms most readers will find relatively easy to understand, and it uses valuable examples from current government activities. Dr. Hovey examines in Part I the problems arising from budgetary procedures that fail to show the total impact of government action, problems which have long concerned me particularly as a result of my experience in preparing the aforementioned report "The Federal Budget as an Economic Document" while serving as chairman of the Subcommittee on Economic Statistics of the Joint Economic Committee.

From my standpoint as a member of Congress, an immediate and critical problem is that of tailoring PPB methods to government evaluation procedures. Part II of this book examines this problem and focuses on the difficulties involved in establishing goals through the political process. One area of immense importance is the evaluation of water resource projects, in which discounting techniques now used tend to create huge economic dislocations. Dr. Hovey offers a fine analysis of this controversy, and he dissects strategies often employed to justify low discounting rates.

The book confirms my belief that PPB systems contain enormous potential for upgrading government-program evaluation and administration. PPB techniques promise significant advances in government efficiency and, as such, merit serious attention. Dr. Hovey performs a useful service by increasing our understanding of PPB's potentials and problems.

PREFACE

Governments need better ways to decide what they should do, how they should do it, and what it should cost.

Although the need has long been recognized, the combined efforts of scholars, citizens, and political leaders have failed to find widely accepted ways to evaluate government programs. This book examines one approach to the problem-- the approach of planning-programming-budgeting. The approach encompasses many concepts: Cost-benefit analysis, cost-effectiveness analysis, program analysis, systems analysis applied to government, economic analysis, planning-programming-budgeting, program budgeting, and marginal analysis are all terms that have been used to describe the approach. Much effort has been expended in seeking to provide precise, widely accepted definitions for each of these terms. The effort has not been successful.

As Presidential Assistant Joseph Califano has put it, "The name is not important. The approach is."[1] In this book, attention is centered upon the thrust of the total planning-programming-budgeting (PPB) approach. Little attempt is made to attach rigid meanings to many of the terms which--because it has become fashionable in governmental circles to use them--have lost any precise meanings they may have had before they became so popular.

The analytical techniques currently being applied in the U.S. federal government and advocated for use elsewhere are designed to assist decision-makers in making choices. As a result, they bear considerable resemblance to traditional concepts of the logic and psychology of choice. For example, the staff of a congressional committee reviewing planning-programming-budgeting commented that cost-benefit analysis seems to have begun in the Garden of Eden (to eat or not to eat the apple), and noted that "the problem from the outset has been to avoid an underestimation of costs and an overestimation of benefits."[2] Even if the definition of cost-benefit analysis is construed somewhat less broadly, the analytical procedures can be traced as far back in history as 1667.[3] In the United States, economic analysis was used to consider proposed federal public works as early as 1902. Long-range planning, budgeting, and seeking the least costly way to achieve objectives all date back to days when man first began to think ahead and to realize that his resources were insufficient to permit him to do everything he wanted to do.

If the analytical techniques are so old, why, it may legitimately be asked, should so much attention be devoted to economic analysis now? The answer is to be found in the combination of sharply increased demand for better advice on government programs coupled with increased know-how to provide that advice.

The demand for better analysis of government programs has proceeded apace with the sharp growth of those programs. Federal government expenditures approximately doubled from fiscal 1958 to fiscal 1968.[4] State and local expenditures grew at an even faster rate.[5] Some of the increase in government activity reflects new programs in fields such as health, higher education, urban transportation systems, and pollution control. In addition to direct expenditure increases, government regulatory activities have become increasingly important in many fields. This combination of the expanding scope and higher costs of government would, even in the absence of other factors, create greater demand for analysis of government programs.

Other factors have also had an impact. It is not surprising that many of the early applications of cost-effectiveness analysis have been in the military field. Striking advances in the technology of war have sharply increased the lead-times for weapons systems. This increase has reduced the importance of the commander's field decisions and increased the importance of the weapon systems designer and military planner.

The "new economics" has changed some important ground rules of budgeting for federal agencies. So long as budgets had to be balanced each year, budgeting could be accomplished by adopting a total figure and allocating ceilings among agencies. Such an allocating method meant that the budget decision-making process obscured many issues about optimal levels of expenditures by forcing debate into questions of what could be squeezed under a given agency's ceiling. Once the concept of an annually balanced budget gives way to one of a flexible fiscal policy, the discipline of balancing short-term income and outgo disappears. To replace that discipline of the balanced budget, economic analysis is a useful tool. As former Budget Director Charles Schultze testified before a congressional committee, "A 'new' approach to expenditure evaluation is, I am convinced, a necessary corollary to the 'new' fiscal policy."[6]

In addition to these factors, the increasing complexity of the interrelationships among governments at state, local, and federal levels, and the multiplicity of interactions among government agencies and between government and private business have made the task of the government decision-maker increasingly difficult to understand and master. The natural response of busy decision-makers to these problems was to "call in the experts." But what experts were there to call? Scientists and engineers were ready with designs for roads, dams, and missiles; architects stood by with plans for buildings, city planners with plans for cities, and citizens with demands for action. Yet the expertise of the architect and the engineer did not tell the decision-maker whether a road or missile should be built or bought. Where was the expert to say that a road was or was not worth its price? An exploding technology made it technically feasible to do things man had never before dreamed of doing, yet clearly not all could be done.

The traditional disciplines of "administrative sciences" offered little to the decision-maker seeking substantive program advice. The budget officer offered no rigorous logic of choice and had for years been concerning himself with such questions as the proper floor space, number of secretaries, and travel allowance for a government division of one hundred people. He had not developed methods to advise the decision-maker as to whether the people were necessary at all. Experts in administrative management had much to say about both the organization of work within an office and the organizational arrangements within bureaus and departments. However, they had little to say about what policy should be pursued. Public administration specialists had much to say about how a decision should be made--the process of planning and budgeting--but little about what that decision should be.

The demand for "expertise" in the decision-making process did find a small supply of individuals who were helping governmental decision-makers face questions of choice. Prominent among these were the operations research specialists employed by the nation's military departments. During and after World War II, they were applying quantitative methods (and, equally important, facing the need for rigorous approaches to problem-solving, which are necessitated by the desire to quantify) to problems of military operations such as convoying procedures and logistical support. Both the analysts and their military sponsors began to realize that analysis could be applied not only to questions of operations, logistics, and equipment design but also to weapons systems concepts themselves. Thus, as early as 1954, analysts at the Rand Corporation had applied their expertise to recommending on the selection and use of strategic air bases.[7]

Some government civilian agencies have for some time used economic analysis to evaluate projects or programs where costs are easily ascertained and outputs are commodities such as electric power, irrigation water, and lumber, which are easily priced. In addition, engineers, who had within their profession evolved the subject of "engineering economics," were becoming increasingly concerned with the cost implications of alternative ways to achieve a desired engineering result. Some of this work was being reflected in highway studies and over-all transportation planning. Thus, work in water resources and transportation provided a source of both concepts and experts in applying economic analysis to government policy questions.

On the academic front, welfare economists had increased their interest in questions of nonmarket decision-making and public choice. Equally important, economists outside of the government were realizing and writing about the way their work related to analytical procedures used in government. Thus, for example, in 1958, Roland McKean, then a Rand employee with experience in the evaluation of military alternatives, and Otto Eckstein, then a recent Ph. D. in economics from Harvard, published books evaluating cost-benefit analysis undertaken by federal water resource agencies. [8] These books, particularly McKean's, contain many of the major elements of the PPB approach.

The marriage between the isolated analyst and the high-level decision-maker took place after President Kennedy appointed Robert S. McNamara as Secretary of Defense in 1961. McNamara himself had been involved in quantitative studies during World War II and had had considerable experience in quantitative management approaches at the Ford Motor Company. Charles Hitch, appointed Assistant Secretary of Defense (Comptroller) under McNamara, brought new ways of thinking about defense problems and a group of Rand alumni to try to apply the methods to department-wide problems. [9] Even from inside the Pentagon, it was difficult to tell which of the changes came from the new approaches brought from Rand and which from the force of the Secretary's own approach to problems. What systems analysis would have been in Defense without McNamara and what McNamara would have done without systems analysis are, and will continue to be, unknowable for the reason that many approaches are common to both the man and the system. These approaches include explicit consideration of alternatives, identification of assumptions, quantification of results, and insistence on an analytical base for recommended decisions.

We will probably never know whether President Johnson believed that systems analysis caused McNamara's success and therefore was capable of making all cabinet officers as precise, explicit, and clear-thinking as McNamara or whether the President used other reasoning. In any case, he decided to apply the system to all civilian agencies of the government. On August 25, 1965, President Johnson told the press that he had asked each of his cabinet officers "to immediately begin to introduce a very new and a very revolutionary system of planning and programming and budgeting throughout the vast Federal Government, so that through the tools of modern management the full promise of a finer life can be brought to every American at the lowest possible cost. "[10] Thus, the McNamara management revolution became the law of the land. New PPB offices were established in each cabinet department and in many subordinate bureaus and offices. Manuals were written, program memoranda and program and financial plans produced, analytical studies undertaken, staff members hired and trained in the new system, and Congressional hearings held on its implications. Predictably, all of this activity stimulated interest in academic circles, in state and local governments within the United States, and in governments outside of the United States.

The President's messages on the new system have implied that it will work near miracles. According to the President, it will provide experts to "define the goals of their department," "permit us to find the most effective and the least costly alternative to achieving American goals, "help . . . find new ways to do jobs faster, to do jobs better, and to do jobs less expensively," "insure a much sounder judgment," "make our decision-making process as up-to-date, I think, as our space-exploring program," and "enable us to fulfill the needs of all the American people with a minimum amount of waste."

This book examines the PPB approach giving rise to these high hopes. Part I expounds the PPB approach in a nontechnical fashion; hopefully, it will be found useful for those seeking to learn or teach the elements of the PPB approach. Part II deals with problems inherent in trying to apply the approach to the real world of American government. It suggests that the American political system does not operate in quite the fashion that most PPB advocates seem to presume. The final part evaluates the PPB approach on the basis of its potential as discussed in Part I and its problems as discussed in Part II.

The book is the outgrowth of a combination of academic research and practical experience in government planning and budgeting. A portion of the research was undertaken in connection with earlier (unpublished) manuscripts on the criteria actually used by congressional committees in deciding on water resource projects and on a methodology for applying cost-benefit analysis to federal housing programs. The research continued in the form of a doctoral dissertation, The Role of Economic Analysis in the Political Process: An Appraisal of the Planning-Programming-Budgeting System, which focused primarily upon whether the political system in the United States would permit national and program goals to be specified in the manner assumed necessary for PPB analysis. Permission from the George Washington University to adapt some of that material for portions of this book (particularly Part II) is gratefully acknowledged.

I have been fortunate to have been exposed to governmental decision-making problems in a variety of stimulating environments covering a wide variety of public policy matters. However, as a result of that experience, I cannot claim complete objectivity on matters of either government organization or program issues. A strong preference for a broad perspective at the departmental and Presidential level led me to employment in both the Office of the Secretary of Defense and the Bureau of the Budget, where my centralizing views were no doubt reinforced. My conclusion, which I share with most American economists, that the United States systematically overinvests in multipurpose water projects led to a research role with a Washington trade association of electric utilities. Greater familiarity with federal public works spending confirmed my initial impression of overinvestment and gave rise to one of the issues considered in this book. The persistent flow of projects justified by "economic analysis" which economists were criticizing as "economically unjustified" suggested that there might be a wide and perhaps insurmountable gap between what economic analysis would do in theory and what it would do under political combat conditions. Parts II and III of this volume are principally devoted to the question of how large such a gap may be and whether it is insurmountable. Finally, my entire Washington experience led to the conclusion that no governmental action ever comes about as quickly or as completely as expected by those who order it. For this reason, I have tried to avoid criticisms based upon a proposition that failures and problems in the first two years of PPB necessarily imply that the system cannot work in the long run.

The Bureau of the Budget library staff have been extremely helpful in providing access to their complete PPB collection and in exchanging bibliographical leads with me. Many federal and state agency publication and public information offices have generously filled my mailbox during preparation of this book. My reflections on PPB have benefited from comments by Donald W. Helm of the Food and Drug Administration, Donald A. Zimmerman and Donald D. Kummerfeld of the Budget Bureau, and, particularly, Robert Rafuse, Jr., of The Brookings Institution, who commented on an earlier draft of this book. Many other individuals have helped to sharpen my thinking on particular problems. More than the customary absolution from blame for author's mistakes is required; some of these men do not agree with some of my evaluations of the PPB approach.

My special thanks are due my former employer, Arthur Barnett, Managing Director of the National Association of Electric Companies; my current employer, William M. Jamieson of the Battelle Memorial Institute; and my wife for encouraging me to publish these reflections on PPB. Miss Carolyn Aldridge and Mrs. Joan Giles have translated my barely legible copy into something approaching a finished work.

NOTES TO PREFACE

1. "The Politics of Innovation and the Revolution in Government Management," Congressional Record (daily edition), April 25, 1967, p. S5832 (Speech before the Washington Chapter of Sigma Delta Chi, April 19, 1967).

2. U.S. Congress, Senate, Committee on Government Operations, Subcommittee on National Security and International Operations, "Planning-Programming-Budgeting, Initial Memorandum," Ninetieth Congress, 1st Session, 1967, p. 2.

3. Martin S. Feldstein, "Economic Analysis, Operational Research, and the National Health Service," Oxford Economic Papers, XV (March, 1963), 19-31.

4. Expenditures (excluding loans) are expected to be $169.9 billion in fiscal 1968 compared to $81.2 billion in fiscal 1958. U.S. Bureau of the Budget, The Budget in Brief (Washington, D.C.: Government Printing Office, 1968), p. 71.

5. This is the case even when those expenditures are reduced by the amounts of federal grants-in-aid included in them. For example, receipts of state and local governments (excluding grants-in-aid from the federal government) are estimated to have increased from $33.1 billion in 1956 to $73.1 billion in 1966. Donald A. King and Martin Lefkowitz, "The Finances of State and Local Governments," Survey of Current Business, October, 1967, p. 26.

6. U.S. Congress, Joint Economic Committee, Hearings, Fiscal Policy Issues of the Coming Decade, Eighty-ninth Congress, 1st Session, 1965, p. 66. Henry S. Rowen, while a member of the Budget Bureau staff, made a similar comment in a talk delivered to the 1965 Budget Bureau summer seminar on systems analysis and program evaluation (Bureau of the Budget, processed).

7. See Rand's pioneering report, "Selection and Use of Strategic Air Bases," Rand Report R-266 (1954, reprinted in 1963). Bruce L. R. Smith provides a good history of analysis at Rand in The RAND Corporation: A Case Study of a Nonprofit Advisory Organization (Cambridge: Harvard University Press, 1966).

8. Otto Eckstein, Water Resource Development: The Economics of Project Evaluation (Cambridge: Harvard University Press, 1958) and Roland McKean, Efficiency in Government Through Systems Analysis, With Emphasis on Water Resource Development (New York: Wiley, 1958).

9. See Charles J. Hitch and Roland N. McKean, The Economics of Defense in the Nuclear Age (Cambridge: Harvard University Press, 1960).

10. Weekly Compilation of Presidential Documents, August 30, 1965, p. 143.

Harold A. Hovey

CONTENTS

LIST OF FIGURES

PART I

THE PPB APPROACH

CHAPTER **1** THE NEED TO ANALYZE AND
PINPOINT RESPONSIBILITY
FOR CHANGE

THE NEED TO ANALYZE

The underlying assumption that things are not all they
could be is essential to program analysis in any context,
business or governmental; no analytical system, no matter
how elaborate and conceptually neat, is of any value if
analysis is not required at all. The PPB approach to governmental decisions presumes, therefore, that analysis is
needed. He who looks at policies and programs expecting
to find them perfect will generally confirm his own expectations; on the other hand, he who begins with doubt and
questioning will look longer, harder, and in more places to
find room for improvement.

The need for analysis in government is particularly
important due to the differences between government and
business. As a former director of the Bureau of the Budget
put it,

> . . . government programs rarely have an
> automatic regulator that tells us when an activ-
> ity has ceased to be productive or could be
> made more efficient, or should be displaced
> by another activity. In private business,
> society relies upon profits and competition
> to furnish the needed incentives and discipline
> and to provide a feedback on the quality of
> decisions. The system is imperfect, but
> basically sound in the private sector--it is
> virtually nonexistent in the government sector.
> In government, we must find another tool for

3

making the choices which resource scarcity
forces upon us.[1]

Even profits have limits as signaling devices. The fact
that profits may be dropping signals the need for change but
does not indicate whether more or less should be spent on
such functions as research, plant protection, and public
relations in order to improve profits. In dealing with these
specialized functions, the business manager may be little
better off than a President of the United States seeking to
determine the contributions made to national welfare by the
U.S. Information Agency, the National Science Foundation,
and the Defense Department. Nonetheless, the business
manager at least has a signal that something is wrong, even
though falling profits may not signal precisely what is wrong.
Whereas private enterprise providing advice to farmers
would quickly go bankrupt in an urban county, a Department
of Agriculture county agent could function indefinitely in an
urban environment.

Good analysis of government activities is needed for the
additional reasons suggested in the Preface--growth of
governmental activity, end of the balanced budget, growing
complexity, and new technology requiring longer lead-times
between decision and result.

The need to analyze government programs extends far
beyond the programs themselves. Because the PPB approach
directs attention toward what is being accomplished and away
from what is being done with what program inputs, implementation of the approach involves analysis of the premises
underlying government programs. Some of these premises
involve private conduct which, to many people, lies beyond
the "jurisdiction" of governments.

For example, the relationship between mother and child
is traditionally considered a private relationship, yet it is
significantly influenced by government. Programs such as
Head Start have the effect of decreasing a child's contacts
with natural parents and increasing contacts with Head Start
teachers, whereas the program of aid to families with dependent children is designed to permit the mother of small
children to stay at home with those children. Any serious
evaluation of these programs involves considering implicitly

or explicitly the value of having children raised by natural parents under circumstances in which the educational level, style of life, or moral standards of the parents may not be identical to those of a majority of the society or its leaders.

This basic argument for a wide scope of analysis proceeds not from direct philosophical principles about the role of government but from the substance of present governmental activity. It is hard to dispute the claim that the program of aid to families with dependent children is government influence (of some amount--what amount not being key to the argument) in the direction of keeping children and their natural mothers together. It is also hard to dispute the fact that the tax deduction for child care expenses and the Head Start program tend to keep mothers and natural children apart. The premise of the PPB approach is not necessarily that government should be concerned with the mother-child relationship, but that, given the fact that government does affect that relationship, understanding of the "value" of the relationship (we have as yet been unable to find a standard for such evaluation) is important in evaluating programs.

ANALYSIS ALONE IS NO SOLUTION

A drive to analyze and question is, by itself, no guarantee of improvement. Scholars and citizens have been analyzing government programs for centuries, frequently without noticeable result even though using techniques comparable to the PPB approach. Good analysis and bad programs can coexist indefinitely. For analysis to result in change, it must (a) be communicated to responsible decision-makers, (b) be accepted as valid and relevant by those decision-makers, and (c) be implemented by them. In government, these are not automatic processes.

In fact, in government, it is frequently difficult to identify who is responsible for a policy or program. One of the reasons why analysis alone is insufficient to improve any situation in government is the diffusion of, and thus loss of responsibility for, program change. It is not surprising to find civil servants who believe that the nation could not

survive without the program they help administer; what is
surprising to some is the many government employees who
are convinced that their program or activity suffers from
major shortcomings. However, such discontent with programs frequently does not lead to program changes. Instead,
individuals who sense the need for change (or their superiors)
may feel that the matter is decided and therefore not open to
change--or the action required to improve the situation may
be beyond the institutional scope of the organization (under
state rather than federal control or under the control of
another agency, for example) and therefore must be regarded
as unchangeable. The lexicon of organizational inertia is
well known: "That's a policy set by Congress"; "That was
decided years ago"; "That's what's in the Manual"; and
"That's what the law requires" are typical phrases that
excuse inaction even in the case of obvious failings of
existing governmental programs.

Of course, no organization can operate if all of its
policies are being questioned by all of its employees all
of the time. Some balance must be struck between the need
for certainty and the need for change, and between the need
for obedience and routine and the need for questioning and
challenges. The problem is to strike this balance at a point
that permits the organization to improve its effectiveness and
respond to change. To achieve this requires both institutional
recognition of the need to analyze and assignments of responsibility for the analysis and for the implementation of changes.

PROBLEMS IN ASSIGNING RESPONSIBILITY

Answering the question "Who's in charge here?" is a
problem in any organization. It is a more serious one in
U.S. Government than in most private organizations. In
the United States, we are committed to diffusion of power;
to preserve some measure of individual liberty, we have
limited the power of our governments vis-à-vis the people.
We have carved out separate spheres of activity for local,
state, and federal governments. Within these levels of
government, we have generally divided power among judicial,
legislative, and executive branches. We then frequently

split the legislative power equally between two legislative
bodies. We have also evolved many quasi-governmental
institutions such as government corporations, independent
governors of our banking system, and numerous advisory
boards and commissions with varying powers. This plural-
ism has clear advantages, but it makes responsibility more
difficult to determine. Yet that responsibility must be
identified for analysis to succeed.

The mechanics of governmental inertia are as easy to
understand as they are difficult to correct. Subordinates
recommend budgets and actions not wholly on the basis of
their views of what the government should do but on the basis
of (a) their perception of what their superiors expect and will
approve, (b) agency policy, (c) Presidential and executive
branch policy as reflected in past decisions, and (d) congressional policy reflected in committee reports and legislation,
no matter how long ago enacted. Superiors rely not only on
their subordinates' recommendations but also on their
understanding of the agency's policy and the desires of the
President, Congress, and the department head. The department head recommends policies and budgets to the President
based upon his subordinates' recommendations which, clearly,
he cannot personally review in detail. Where changes are
made, they are likely to be marginal, such as reducing many
budgets by a uniform percentage rather than clear-cut decisions to establish, reorient, or abolish certain activities or
policies. The President and the Congress approve the result,
making changes only marginally to allow for loose and tight
budgetary situations. These approvals reinforce the subordinates' views of appropriate bureaucratic behavior and permit
the cycle of mutual reinforcement of existing programs to
continue. Each participant in the process relies upon precedent and the recommendations of the other participants. The
result is that no participant in the process squarely faces
the questions "Is this program or policy a good idea? Would
I approve it if I were President?"*

---

* At this point, a word of praise must be offered for the
government employee who does address such questions.
Unfortunately, such evaluations--when they are made at all--
tend to be made to neighbors and spouses, thus failing to
influence policy.

The preceding description of a budgetary process has
intentionally been overdrawn to emphasize that critical
analysis is not an inherent part of the governmental process.
The layman's notion that government programs and policies
tend to be self-perpetuating is not necessarily wrong. In
fact, recent scholarly work examining budgeting processes
in the United States tends to confirm the belief that the process may cause incremental changes in policies and budgets
but does not usually produce significant or rapid changes in
on-going programs. [2]

AN EXAMPLE OF DIFFUSED RESPONSIBILITY

The analysis of water resource projects in the U.S.
Federal Government provides a good example of the difficulties in fixing responsibility for program change and of
the tendency for program justifications to become circular--
all participants holding someone else responsible and no one
assuming responsibility.

The water resource projects of the Army Engineers, the
Bureau of Reclamation, and the Soil Conservation Service
are justified to the public and the Congress by cost-benefit
analysis--if benefits exceed costs, the project is considered
worth undertaking. Whether benefits exceed costs depends
upon the ground rules used to calculate benefits and costs.
These rules specify interest rates, amortization periods,
and the like. Many economists have argued that some should
be changed. The purpose of this section is to consider
whether any governmental institution--Congress, the water
resource agencies, individual project engineering offices,
etc.--is in a position to consider such changes, assuming
they are worth-while.

From the perspective of individual government engineers
who design and evaluate projects, these ground rules are
guidance from "higher up" and are not subject to question.
Reviewing authorities must use the same rules for all projects in order to avoid legitimate criticisms from anxious
members of Congress that the ground rules were being
stretched to favor a particular project or tightened to

eliminate others. Thus, if change is to take place, it must
be a general change applicable to all projects. Engineers
working in particular projects are thereby excused from
responsibility for current rules. Under this circumstance,
it is possible for both the designing and reviewing engineers
to recommend projects that, individually, they might consider to be unjustified.

Of course, general ground rules can be changed by
authorities higher than those who deal with individual projects. The problem is to identify the responsible authority.
Neither the Soil Conservation Service, the Bureau of Reclamation, nor the Corps of Engineers can unilaterally alter
the guidelines applicable to the others; each agency controls
only its own ground rules. But a single agency making its
ground rules more strict would be encouraging local interests to seek to have their projects constructed by one of the
other agencies. A single agency making its project-approval
guidelines less strict would initiate competition among
agencies which could reasonably be expected to lead to
progressively lower standards on the part of all agencies.[3]
The solution to the competition problem is to require all
of the potential competitors to agree on a uniform policy or,
should they fail to agree, to force one upon them. Exactly
this action has been taken in the water resource field in the
United States.[4] Guidelines are established by inter-agency
agreement--by a committee. What a committee has done is
difficult to undo. A requirement for agreement gives every
member a veto. Equally important, the responsibility for
change rests with all the members of the committee and
thus effectively with none of them. It is easy for a policy
of government to become "locked in concrete" in this way
through inter-agency agreement, past practice, and the
like. When this happens, program officials can and do
recommend programs and budgets without necessarily
analyzing the policy and assumptions upon which they are
based.

"Who's in charge here?" is not a problem confined to
relations among executive agencies. In testifying before
congressional committees in justification of water projects,
engineers frequently refer to the ground rules as congressional ones. Obviously, if a policy is set by Congress, an
employee need not worry about its correctness. The placing

of responsibility on Congress is not confined to lower-level officials in the water resource agencies. Elmer Staats, while Deputy Director of the Bureau of the Budget, told a congressional committee:

> The projects we have submitted to the Congress since 1962, when these new standards were adopted by President Kennedy, have taken into account recreation and fish and wildlife as separate benefits. To the extent the Congress has approved those, Congress has adopted this policy.[5]

A senior Interior Department official stated in testimony before another committee:

> I am sure that somehow other standards will develop, if a general law isn't passed, that Congress by approving projects as it did last year, as the Congress did in 1962, will gradually set out guidelines that the executive agencies will follow.[6]

This shifting of some of the responsibility for a policy onto the shoulders of the legislative branch, by no means unique to the water resources field, does not cloud responsibility for change so long as the legislative branch understands that it is being relied upon as the source of guidance. In fact, in many fields the assumption of some executive officials that a policy belongs to the Congress may be matched by an assumption of many members of Congress that the same policy belongs to the executive branch. For example, in reporting the public works authorization bill to the Senate in 1965, the Senate Public Works Committee chairman, Senator McNamara, assured his colleagues:

> The committee believes that each project is economically justified, having passed the formula for authorization imposed by the Corps.[7]

The ranking minority member of the same committee told his Senate colleagues that the recommended projects "met the requirements of the Corps of Engineers."[8] When Senator Proxmire sought to act on the premise that Congress controlled the guidelines, his position was contradicted by senators who in effect were arguing that he had taken his case to the wrong court. Proxmire in 1965 (and on many other occasions) criticized the ground rules for water resource projects, cited numerous economists who have also criticized those rules, and proposed an amendment that would have substantially cut the number of projects authorized. Senator McNamara responded by arguing, "Everything the Senator said should be considered and was considered by the agencies, especially by the Army Corps of Engineers."[9] Senator Ellender (chairman of the Appropriations Committee Subcommittee which handles public works appropriations) assured Senator Proxmire that the Corps of Engineers would have another opportunity to study the projects before appropriations to be certain that the cost-benefit ratio was good.[10]

Thus, to a considerable degree, it is possible for a substantial and influential contingent of the Congress to rely upon the expertise of qualified engineers, for qualified engineers to rely upon guidance from their superiors, and for the superiors to rely upon guidance from the Congress. To the extent that such circular situations exist, responsibility may be so shared that, even if there are no political obstacles to change, no single group or individual feels he has the right to act on the basis of analysis of the program. Under such a circumstance, improvements in the quality and quantity of analysis will not necessarily lead to program change.*

----

* Diffused responsibility is, of course, not the sole problem in the water resource field and many significant political groups see major advantages in the current procedures.
The legal situation in water resources may be of academic interest to some. The President's budget is his own, for reasons discussed later in this chapter. He may, therefore, use any ground rules he chooses in deciding what to include in it and may, should he desire, present one set of ground rules in the justification material submitted to Congress and use another set for his own review. Short of limiting the President in developing his budget recommendations, Congress may require any ground rules it chooses before submission of a project to it or before construction. Currently (1968), the President uses for his review the same studies that are later presented to Congress. These are based partly on ground rules set by Congress in legislation and partly on rules adopted by the executive branch.

ASSIGNING RESPONSIBILITY THROUGH PPB

"The buck stops here" is a phrase made famous when President Truman used it to describe the role of the President. In the legal and political sense, it is perfectly accurate. The President clearly is responsible to the electorate for the actions of executive agencies. Even if total program responsibility were not constitutionally inherent in the Presidential office, a statutory basis for it also exists. The Budget and Accounting Act of 1921[11] requires that the President's budget set forth estimated expenditures and appropriations necessary in his judgment for the support of the government.

In the U.S. Government, as in any large organization, private or public, it is impossible for the head of the organization to decide all questions that arise in the organization's operation. If all the bucks that are passed in government did stop on the President's desk, he would never be able to see his desk top. The President bears responsibility for the outcome of policies but must delegate authority to make many of the decisions to lower-level officials. The fundamental problem in any organization in which the chief must delegate is to make sure that (a) the authority to make decisions follows responsibility for their outcome, (b) those given authority are also given responsibility for failures in use of that authority, and (c) everyone operates from the perspective of the chief.

An analytical system alone will neither fix responsibility nor ensure that subordinates see things from the chief's perspective. For this reason, PPB ties the analytical efforts directly into the budgeting procedure through the device of the Program Memorandum, a document intended to indicate the analytical base for, and alternatives to, the programs recommended by each agency. This arrangement links analytical responsibility and budget responsibility. If an agency head is to be responsible for his budget request, he is also responsible for the analysis that goes with it.

Merely tying program responsibility to analytical responsibility is not enough. Program responsibility itself must be clear. PPB in the U.S. Government recognizes this by explicitly establishing agency head responsibilities. The

Budget Bureau Bulletin on PPB (No. 68-2 of July, 1967)
clearly states, "Responsibility for the development and use
of Planning-Programming-Budgeting systems rests with the
head of each agency." President Johnson was equally
explicit in holding his agency heads directly and personally
responsible for program recommendations. He stated in
a memorandum on PPB to the heads of departments and
agencies in November, 1966:

> Most important, this effort requires your
> personal interest and participation. Objec-
> tives will not be questioned unless you make
> it clear you want them questioned. Existing
> programs will not be evaluated critically
> unless you insist upon it. Alternatives will
> not be presented unless you demand them.
> The hard choices will not be made well unless
> you make them, and do so on the basis of
> critiques and analyses prepared by your own
> staffs. Getting these things done is up to you.[12]

Budget Bureau PPB (Bulletin 68-2) guidance also
encourages department and agency chiefs to center comparable program review responsibilities in their subordinates:

> Since planning, programming and budgeting
> are all essential elements of management, it
> is necessary that line managers at appropriate
> levels participate in the system. Management
> responsibility should be so fixed that the agency
> head receives the recommendations of his
> principal managers on all major program
> issues. It may be desirable to provide the
> principal managers with small analytic staffs
> to insure their meaningful participation in
> Special Studies and other analytic work.
> Similar arrangements for obtaining the views
> of other echelons may be made, consistent
> with the agency's assignment of responsibility.[13]

Thus, the Bureau's guidance strongly encourages placing
responsibility for recommending program change on those
who report directly to heads of major departments and
agencies. It leaves in the hands of agency heads the balancing

of the need to question in order to improve programs with the
need to accept without question in order to administer programs. This responsibility extends both to the quality of
recommendations on matters subject to Presidential decision
and to the quality of decisions made by the agency head on
matters he alone can decide.

SUMMARY

The basic presumption underlying the PPB approach is
that a need for analysis exists because not all current
government programs are perfect. The gap between what
is and what should and could be (a concept we have not yet
sought to define) measures both the need for analysis and
the potential contribution analysis could make if implemented.
To ensure that analysis does take place and can be implemented, someone must be held responsible for program and
budget recommendations. PPB in the U.S. Government
involves clear assignments of responsibility to cabinet
officers and their immediate subordinates. It also ties the
planning and programming cycle to the analytical results in
an attempt to ensure that the analysis is related to recommended budgetary actions.

NOTES TO CHAPTER 1

1. Charles Schultze in U.S. Congress, Senate, Committee on Government Operations, Subcommittee on International Operations, Hearings, "Planning-Programming-
Budgeting," Ninetieth Congress, 1st Session, 1967, Part I,
p. 21. It is rarely noted that government does get some
performance signals--public criticism, press review, and
scholarly comments--which are not usually available to
profit-making business.

2. See, for example, Richard Fenno, The Power of
the Purse: Appropriations Politics in the Congress (Boston:

Little, Brown and Company, 1966); Aaron Wildavsky, The
Politics of the Budgetary Process (Boston: Little, Brown and
Company, 1964); and Otto A. Davis, M. A. H. Dempster,
and Aaron Wildavsky, "A Theory of the Budgetary Process,"
American Political Science Review, LX (September, 1966),
323-41.

3. Exactly these problems have arisen in public-works
programs in the United States. See Arthur Maass, Muddy
Waters: The Army Engineers and the Nation's Rivers
(Cambridge: Harvard University Press, 1951).

4. The "Green Book," U.S. Federal Inter-Agency River
Basin Committee, Subcommittee on Benefits and Costs,
Proposed Practices for Economic Analysis of River Basin
Projects (Washington: Government Printing Office, 1950,
with a 1958 revision) served this purpose in the 1950's. In
the 1960's, government agencies have been using Senate
Document 97, U.S. President's Water Resources Council,
Policies, Standards, and Procedures in the Formulation,
Evaluation, and Review of Plans for Use and Development of
Water and Related Land Resources (Washington: Government
Printing Office, 1962), Eighty-seventh Congress, 2nd
Session, even though it was initially approved for use on
a "temporary" basis.

5. U.S. Congress, House of Representatives, Committee on Interior and Insular Affairs, Recreation Allocation
Policy, Hearings, Eighty-eighth Congress, 1st Session
(Washington: Government Printing Office, 1964). Emphasis
added.

6. Testimony of Kenneth Holum, U.S. Congress,
Senate, Committee on Interior and Insular Affairs, Water
Project Recreation Act, Hearings, Eighty-ninth Congress,
1st Session (1965). Emphasis added.

7. Congressional Record (daily edition), July 27, 1965,
p. 17688. Emphasis added.

8. Ibid., pp. 17688-89.

9. Ibid., p. 17696. Emphasis added.

10. Ibid., p. 17697. Emphasis added.

11. 31 USC 11. The judicial and legislative branches are not subject to the budget reviews discussed here.

12. Weekly Compilation of Presidential Documents, January 30, 1967.

13. U.S. Bureau of the Budget, Bulletin 68-2 (July 18, 1967, processed).

CHAPTER **2** IDENTIFYING GOALS,
CONSIDERING ALTERNATIVES,
AND DEVELOPING A MODEL

GOALS

The cornerstone of economic analysis of government
programs is the identification of program or agency goals.
Until it is decided what effect a program is supposed to have,
no amount of information about the effect it does have will
be of any value.

The Planning-Programming-Budgeting System (PPBS)
is an approach to mission-oriented, purposive goal-oriented
management. The logical sequence of establishing programs
is conceived to be (1) deciding what needs to be done, (2) considering alternative ways to do it, (3) establishing the costs
of alternatives, and (4) selecting the best alternative. For
most of us, this logic is faultless as a description of "rational"
thought, though it may not be an accurate reflection of the way
most of us make decisions in fact.[1] If the purpose of a program cannot be identified clearly, alternatives to achieve
that purpose cannot be formulated. Likewise, performance
cannot be measured unless a standard for measurement
exists.

Thus, former Budget Director Charles Schultze told a
congressional committee in 1967 that the first step in PPB
was "a careful specification and analysis of basic program
objectives in each major area of governmental activity."
He continued:

The key to this part of the operation is forcing
federal agencies to back away from the particular
program they are carrying on at the moment and

17

to look at their objectives. What are they really
trying to accomplish? The objective of our inter-
city highway program, for example, is <u>not</u> to
build highways. Highways are useful only as
they serve a higher objective, namely transporting people and goods effectively and efficiently
and safely. Once this is accepted as an objective,
it then becomes possible to analyze aviation,
railroads and highways to determine the most
effective network of transportation. But so
long as we think of the ultimate objective of
the highway program as simply laying concrete,
this comparison of different transportation systems is impossible.[2]

In the statement to cabinet members and agency heads
in which he introduced the PPB system, President Johnson
said that the system would make it possible to

(1) Identify our national goals with precision and
    on a continuing basis.

(2) Choose among those goals the ones that are
    most urgent . . ."[3]

He told the press the same day:

Under this new system each Cabinet and agency
head will set up a very special staff of experts
who, using the most modern methods of program
analysis, will define the goals of their department for the coming year. Once these goals
are established, this system will permit us to
find the most effective and the least costly
alternative to achieving American goals.[4]

The Bureau of the Budget's first bulletin on PPB argued
that under then-existing practices "objectives of agency programs and activities have too often not been specified with
enough clarity and concreteness."[5] The bulletin required
the agencies to develop "program categories" which would
group agency programs in relation to the broad objectives
they serve. Such groupings could obviously be made only
after the relevant objectives had been determined. The

planning-programming-budgeting process is, according to
the bulletin, concerned with developing "a translation of
concretely specified agency objectives into combinations of
agency activities and operations designed to reach such objectives in each of the stated time periods."

The Bureau's February, 1966, supplement to the basic
PPB guidance was equally insistent on the importance of
defining objectives. [6] According to this guidance, the "Program Memorandum" to be prepared by each agency for each
major program was to "specify national needs in the area
covered by the memorandum . . . /and/ define the agency's
objectives with respect to those needs in precise and concrete
terms." Broad general discussions of objectives or problems
were inadequate. The supplement commented:

> The Memoranda should be as specific and as
> quantitative as possible. Broad, general state-
> ments of national needs, such as the "develop-
> ment of a safe and efficient civil aviation system"
> or the "elimination of poverty," though adequate
> for some purposes, cannot form a basis for
> analysis. The adequacy of specific programs
> cannot be assessed unless their goals are stated
> precisely--quantitatively wherever possible--
> and the time span for their accomplishment is
> specified.

This emphasis on determining the objectives was continued
in the Bureau's 1967 guidance for the Program Memorandum
which stated:

> In addition to showing what choices have been
> made, the Program Memoranda should make
> clear why particular choices have been made,
> by identifying agency objectives in a measurable
> way, and comparing alternative programs in
> terms of their costs and their achievement of
> the objectives. [7]

This stress on determining objectives as the first step
in analysis is not unique to the U.S. Government's PPB
approach. The New York State PPB manual states, "The
planning-programming-budgeting system is a concept for

the comprehensive goal-directed management of government"
and directs New York agencies to "devise long range goal
statements to guide the preparation of comprehensive State
policies in major functional areas."[8]

A draft instruction on PPB for local government prepared
under the auspices of the State-Local Finances Project at
George Washington University indicates that the system is
designed to "spell out more concretely the objectives of
governmental programs." It requires agency and department
heads to "identify, within the agency's sphere of interest,
major governmental objectives, /and/ criteria for evaluating
performance in relation to these objectives . . . ."[9] The
State-Local Finances Project also issued a pamphlet entitled
"What is PPB?" in which it advised state and local officials
that systematic analysis of alternatives is the crux of PPBS.
The first step in that analysis was said to be "identification
of governmental objectives."[10] In the introduction to a recent
book on cost-effectiveness analysis, Edward S. Quade commented:

> One of the first and most important tasks of the
> analyst is to attempt to discover what objectives
> the decision-maker is, or should be, trying to
> attain through this policy, and how to measure
> the extent to which they are, in fact, attained.[11]

In short, establishing the objectives of governmental
activity is crucial to the success of the PPB approach because:

(1) Objectives provide the basis for determining
what programs and activities are related to
what others. This is necessary information
for the structuring of the program budget.

(2) Objectives provide the basis for determining
whether a program is achieving anything
worth-while.

(3) Objectives provide a basis for developing criteria of performance which permit accomplishments to be quantified. The effectiveness in
cost-effectiveness analysis, for example, is
effectiveness in reaching an objective.

ALTERNATIVES

The best alternative clearly cannot be selected if it is not even considered; the alternatives must all be known.

This need is particularly significant in government, because the normal processes of planning and budgeting tend to obscure alternatives rather than highlight them for explicit consideration by the decision-maker. A government bureau is assigned a specific program, not a set of objectives. Its budget and personnel are developed around that program, not around a perception of a problem which may be met by that program and other programs. For example, the Bureau of Public Roads was established and is administered to manage a road-building program. Its normal processes of decision-making do not focus upon whether or not roads should be replaced by mass transit. Instead, they seek to make the most out of whatever dollars the federal government can make available for road construction.

The basic documents establishing PPB in the U.S. Government emphasize the importance of identifying alternatives. The President's August, 1965, statement to cabinet members and agency heads stated that the new system would enable government decision-makers to "search for alternative means of reaching . . . goals most effectively at the least cost."[12] Budget Bureau Bulletin 68-2 requires that the agency's Program Memoranda "should make clear why particular choices have been made, by identifying agency objectives in a measurable way, and comparing alternative programs in terms of their costs and their achievement of the objectives." Gene H. Fisher identified various characteristics of "cost-utility" analysis in a volume on program budgeting prepared by staff members of the Rand Corporation. He argued:

A most fundamental characteristic is the systematic examination and comparison of alternative courses of action that might be taken to achieve specified objectives for some future time period. Not only is it important to systematically examine all of the relevant alternatives that can be identified

initially, but also to design additional ones if those
examined are found wanting.[13]

Examination of alternatives is as important for "little"
decisions as for "big" ones. In fact, in proper analysis,
each of the little decisions is made within each alternative
before big decisions about which alternative to select are
made. Analysts usually call this "suboptimization." It
simply means that each component of a system and each
system should be designed in the best possible fashion to
achieve a given objective before the system is compared
with other systems to achieve the same objective. Suppose,
for example, one were seeking to ensure the availability
of military supplies at some remote location in the event
of a brush-fire war. If the problem were specified clearly
(for example, the objective of the system is to ensure
availability of 10,000 tons of a specified type of military
supplies at specified locations within 10 days after the
initiation of hostilities), a variety of programs or systems
could be considered. These could include pre-positioning
of supplies on land, partial or complete pre-positioning in
freighters, airlift, sealift, etc. The concept of suboptimizing
reminds us that it is insufficient merely to compare these
systems with existing equipment and existing operational
concepts. Instead, the analyst must proceed to consider
alternatives within each alternative. He must answer the
question "What is the most effective way to achieve the
objective if I had to use freight vessels only?" and ask
comparable questions about the design of each alternative
in relation to the basic objective. Only after he has perfected
each alternative can the comparison among them be made.

DEVELOPING A MODEL

All governmental decisions involve explicit or implicit
concepts of the impact of a potential program or policy. We
spend money for teachers because we believe that the combination of teachers, classrooms, and books will educate
our children. We pour concrete on our land on the assumption that it will permit us to reach our destinations more
quickly and safely. We provide food stamps to our needy

in the expectation that their standard of living will improve
or that crop surpluses will be reduced.   In each case, there
is an expected relationship between the resources we are
using and the valued result.

To analyze any program, or even to adopt it intelligently,
requires a model, which describes the relationship between
what we put into the activity (inputs) and what we expect
to get out of it (outputs).   Good models explain what exact
relationships are, not just that a relationship exists.   They
tell us how much more education we get (of course, education
hasn't been defined, so the statement is inherently vague)
for how much more in teachers' salaries.   To require that
the model be made explicit is one of the greatest potential
contributions of systematic analysis to government.   An
explicit model can be studied, criticized, evaluated, and
improved.

Too often decisions are made without explicit models.
The result can never be better than if the model is explicit;
it can frequently be worse.   For example, a school principal
reports to his superintendent and his school board, "My
school needs painting."   Such a statement may well cause
the educational system to spend for painting money that
could otherwise have been used for instructional materials
or teachers' salaries.   Whether money can better be spent
on more painting rather than more books depends on the
usefulness of the painting relative to the usefulness of the
books.   Behind a principal's simple remark "My school
needs painting" could lie several different models of the
relationship between education and paint.   For example,

(1) The current paint is dirty and flaking; if
    uncorrected, this situation will create an
    atmosphere of dirt and disorderliness
    which will cause student performance to
    worsen.

(2) The current paint is dirty and flaking; if
    uncorrected, this situation will create an
    atmosphere of dirt and disorderliness
    which will cause teacher performance to
    worsen.

(3) The current paint is flaking; if uncorrected, this situation will cause cracking and structural deterioration which would cause higher costs later in order to keep the school operating.

(4) The current paint is in good condition, but a change of colors every two years is necessary for good teacher and student performance.

(5) The current paint is in good condition, but it is "sound practice" to repaint on a two-year cycle.

As this example shows, being explicit about the model can change the environment for a decision substantially and thus can change that decision itself. In the example above, four models of the relationship between painting and education were given. The fifth statement is, of course, not a model. It is included to show one of the values of forcing explicitness about one's model. "Sound practice" of repainting on two-year cycles may have been established in a day when paints would deteriorate in that period. However, once the practice was established, the reasoning behind it could be forgotten, so that decision-makers (the school board members in the example) who knew the fallacy of the model through their own experience with paint would never have the opportunity to apply that experience because of the way in which the decision was put to them.

In this example, the school board may well view the painting request differently depending upon the model that underlies it. If it is presented with the reasons for the principal's painting recommendation, the board will be in a position to challenge the recommendation if it appears to be outside of the principal's "expertise." For example, model 3 above is based upon technical conclusions on the deterioration of structures. The school board might review more carefully a decision based on that model than one based on a model relating to student performance, a field in which the principal is presumably more knowledgeable than the board.

For this reason and for reasons which can readily be
inferred from the example given in Chapter 8, the PPB
approach increases the political decision-maker's role.
In most political systems, "specialists" (agency heads,
experienced staff members, etc.) provide for decision-
makers' recommendations that are an assortment of technical
determinations which the specialist is best equipped to
give, other technical determinations, and value judgments.
Because he is unable to sort out these three elements and
how important each is to the recommendation, the political
decision-maker is hard put to make significant changes.
The PPB approach can force the "specialist" to signal when
he is making technical judgments out of his field and, more
important, when he is making value judgments, which
elected representatives of the people are in a better position
to make. PPB may shift power among political decision-
makers (e. g., by giving the President information which
he does not make available to Congress), but it seems
unlikely indeed to erode the power of political decision-
makers as a group, as contrasted to "experts" and "specialists" as a group.

A general description of models has been provided by
Charles Hitch and Roland McKean:

Models are abstract representations of reality
which help us to perceive significant relations
in the real world, to manipulate them, and
thereby predict others. They may take any
of numerous forms. Some are small-scale
physical representations of reality, like model
aircraft in a wind tunnel. Many are simply
representations on paper--like mathematical
models. Or, finally, they may be simple
sets of relationships that are sketched out
in the mind and not formally put down on
paper. In no case are models photographic
reproductions of reality; if they were, they
would be so complicated that they would be
of no use to us. They have to abstract from
a great deal of the real world--focusing upon
what is relevant for the problem at hand,
ignoring what is irrelevant. Whether or not
one model is better than another depends

not on its complexity, or its appearance of
reality, but solely on whether it gives better
predictions (and thereby helps us to make
better decisions). In systems analysis models
of one type or another are required to trace
the relations between inputs and outputs,
resources and objectives, for each of the
systems to be compared, so that we can
predict the relevant consequences of choosing
any system.[14]

As Hitch and McKean emphasize, models relate inputs
to outputs. Stated another way, inputs can be considered
as costs and usually, but not always, can be expressed in
dollars. Outputs are valued consequences. They are valued
either for themselves or because they contribute to something else that is valued. These outputs can be considered
as increments of benefit, as increments of effectiveness,
or as increments of utility. When inputs are considered
in relation to outputs, therefore, we can speak of cost-
effectiveness, cost-utility, or cost-benefit analysis.

No matter what the outputs are called, a decision can
be no better than the model relied upon to relate inputs to
outputs. Although we have governmental policies for
practically everything, we know little about some of the key
input-output relationships involved. Some of these key
relationships, which PPB may force to be considered more
explicitly, are shown below:

How much, if any, of this output	. . .	can an increment of this input produce?
More corn and beans		Irrigation water
More farm income		Price supports
Less crop loss		Weather forecasting
Faster travel		Interstate highways
Safer travel		Speed limits
Better deterrence of attack		Fallout shelters
Reduced death from cancer		Research
Better mathematical knowledge		Teacher salaries
More self-sufficiency		Social workers
More home-ownership		Mortgage insurance
Better health		Sewage treatment works

Reduced fire loss	Fire stations
Reduced crime	Foot patrolmen
Less time lost from labor disputes	Federal mediators

Systematic analysis focuses attention on questions such as those above by requiring that specific increments of inputs be related to specific increases in the outputs. This creates an incentive to develop explicit models that relate effectiveness to inputs and thus to cost. Naturally, the construction of models itself is not a contribution of the PPB approach, nor is it unique to that approach. However, bringing explicit models into governmental decision-making promises to improve the decisions made if for no other reason than the way in which it will affect the use of "judgment" and "intuition."

The relationships within a model reflect determinations of, or assumptions about, the way in which inputs affect outputs. Such determinations are the subject of scientific inquiry and frequently can be verified by scientific procedures. When models and the resulting policy conclusions are clearly separated, political dialogue can center on those issues which can best be resolved by political decisions. For example, political debate over whether increases in irrigation water will increase the yield of corn from Midwestern fields is both unnecessary and undesirable. Agronomists, botanists, and biochemists can study the relationships involved and ought to be able to agree on an answer (or to disagree within a fairly narrow range). Presumably, there is a "true" relationship to be discovered by experimentation and reasoning on the basis of knowledge of plant growth phenomena. A political decision that "more water wouldn't cause more corn" could be made, but, assuming that the scientific conclusion indicated that increased irrigation water could increase corn growth, such a political decision would be "wrong."

On the other hand, working on the basis of an uncontroverted model of the relationships between water and corn growth, a political decision-maker could well decide not to provide for a program of irrigation. He could decide that the added corn was not worth the cost of providing the additional water (more on that later). He could reason

that the water would be paid for by the taxpayer but the
benefits would go to the corn grower, in which case he
might decide against irrigation because he thought the corn
farmers were already well enough off. The advantage of
an explicit model is that it isolates the political decision or
the value judgment from the technical decision on the relationships involved in the model. A decision based upon the
assumption that one group should or should not benefit at
the expense of another is always a political one; it involves
a value judgment in a circumstance where there is no
scientific way to identify a correct answer or to call another
answer "wrong." On the other hand, a decision based upon
a false model is "wrong," even in the most rigorous scientific sense.

The PPB approach separates the model from the
question of the valuation of outputs. In that sense, it may
shift some decisions now made politically into the hands
of the "experts." On the other hand, it will make clear
those areas in which the "experts" have little or nothing
to say and thereby permit political decisions in those areas.

OPEN AND EXPLICIT ANALYSIS

The PPB approach has as one of its primary values
the emphasis on clear and explicit identification of what is
being sought by what methods. To return to the example
of the school that "needs paint," the PPB approach should
raise debate above the level of one party saying that the
school needs paint while the other says, "I disagree." If
the person recommending painting is forced to adopt a model,
debate can and probably will then occur on a somewhat more
useful and higher informational level. Argument may then
take place along the following lines:

(1) Disagreement with the objective: I agree
    that painting will enhance the education of
    our children, but I don't believe that that
    education should be enhanced.

(2) Disagreement with a finding of fact: I do not
    agree that the existing paint is dirty and
    flaking.

(3) Disagreement with the model: I agree that
    the paint is dirty, but I believe that that has
    nothing to do with what the children learn.

(4) Introduction of an alternative: I agree that
    the paint is dirty and that dirty paint affects
    learning, but I believe that (given my model)
    greater improvement in learning can be
    obtained by spending the money for an edu-
    cational television.

(5) Evaluation that the added output is not "worth"
    the added input: I don't think the gain in
    learning from new paint is worth the cost
    of the paint job.

Of these five bases for argument, the first and fifth
cannot themselves be "solved" or "decided" by analysis.
Men differ in their assessment of personal and governmental objectives and in their evaluation of various results
of government. This is what politics is all about. Until
cost-benefit analysis has reached the point where costs and
benefits are measured in the same dollar dimension, such
controversy will always be with us. However, it is important to realize that 2, 3, and to some extent 4 in the list
above are circumstances where the "expert" can provide
authoritative information to the political decision-maker.

The key to PPB is to get out in the open what is guess-
work, what is alleged to be fact, what is the model, and
what are the assumptions. Among PPB practitioners,
Alain Enthoven most frequently emphasizes this scientific
component of systems analysis and PPB. In late 1967,
he told a Senate subcommittee that the concept of "open
and explicit analysis" was the single most important idea
he wished to communicate to the subcommittee. He continued:

An analysis is "open and explicit" if it is
presented in such a way that the objectives

and alternatives are clearly defined, and all
of the assumptions, factors, calculations, and
judgments are laid bare so that all interested
parties can see exactly how the conclusions
were derived, how information they provided
was used, and how the various assumptions
influenced the results. We do not achieve
this in every case, but this is the objective,
and important issues are almost always
approached this way /in the Pentagon/.

In other words, systems analysis is a
method of interrogation and debate suited to
complex, quantitative issues. Systems
analysis is a set of ground rules for con-
structive debate; it gives the participants
useful guidelines for proceeding to clarify
and resolve disagreements. It requires the
participants to make their methods of calculation and their assumptions explicit so
that they can be double-checked: it helps
to identify uncertainties, makes these uncertainties explicit, and aids in evaluating their
importance: and it identifies and isolates
issues.[15]

These same criteria for evaluation of whether systems
analysis has been appropriately accomplished are reflected
in I. Heymont, "Guide for Reviewers of Studies containing
Cost-Effectiveness Analysis," published by the Research
Analysis Corporation.[16] In this document, the reviewer
is told to look for, among other things, an explanation of
the model being used and an explicit statement of criteria
used to judge effectiveness and select alternatives.

SUMMARY

This chapter has considered three important components
of the PPB approach. Identifying the objectives is an essential first step in the process of analysis and program budgeting. Objectives form the basis for the grouping of programs

in the program budget and for the measurement of effectiveness in the analytical process. Investigating alternatives is essential because even the best alternative cannot be selected unless it has been considered. Developing a model is essential because it relates the resources used (inputs) to the valued outcome (outputs). Finally, analysis must be open and explicit to permit political debate to center on truly political issues and to provide enough information to permit scientific analysis and replication of the nonpolitical portions of analysis.

NOTES TO CHAPTER 2

1. The alternative decision-making process is that of accepting and continuing current actions and thoughts until strong reasons exist for change. It can also be argued that we do not, in fact, consistently seek out the best alternative, but stop when we find a satisfactory approach. The questions involved raise a host of questions of psychology and philosophy. For discussions of these issues in a context reasonably related to government see, for example, Charles E. Lindblom, The Intelligence of Democracy: Decision Making Through Mutual Adjustment (New York: The Free Press, 1965), and various articles by Lindblom cited in that book, and Herbert A. Simon, Administrative Behavior (2nd ed.; New York: The Free Press, 1957), and Models of Man (New York: Wiley, 1957).

2. U.S. Congress, Senate, Committee on Government Operations, Subcommittee on National Security and International Operations, Hearings, "Planning-Programming-Budgeting," Ninetieth Congress, 1st Session, 1967, Part I, p. 20.

3. Weekly Compilation of Presidential Documents, August 25, 1965.

4. Ibid.

5. U.S. Bureau of the Budget, Bulletin No. 66-3 (October 12, 1965).

6. U.S. Bureau of the Budget, Supplement to Bulletin No. 66-3 (February 21, 1966).

7. U.S. Bureau of the Budget, Bulletin 68-2 (July 18, 1967, processed).

8. State of New York, Executive Department, Guidelines for Integrated Planning, Programming, Budgeting (Albany, 1967).

9. "Planning, Programming, Budgeting for City, State, County, Objectives," State-Local Finances Project, PPB Note 3, January, 1967.

10. "What is PPB?" State-Local Finances Project, January, 1967.

11. Thomas A. Goldman (ed.), Cost-Effectiveness Analysis: New Approaches in Decision-Making (New York: Frederick A. Praeger, 1967), p. 4.

12. Weekly Compilation of Presidential Documents, op. cit.

13. David Novick (ed.), Program Budgeting: Program Analysis and the Federal Budget (Washington, D.C.: Government Printing Office, 1965), pp. 37-38. This volume is now available from the Harvard University Press.

14. The Economics of Defense in the Nuclear Age (New York: Atheneum, 1965), p. 119. This Rand Corporation Study was originally published by the Harvard University Press.

15. U.S. Congress, Senate, Committee on Government Operations, Subcommittee on National Security and International Operations, op. cit., Part II, p. 73.

16. RAC Study 63.2 (McLean, Va.: Research Analysis Corp., 1965).

CHAPTER **3** ANALYZING COST

SCARCITY AND OPPORTUNITY COST

Almost nothing is free. This simple four-word proposition is the cornerstone of both PPB and economics. Economics is sometimes called the study of the allocation of scarce resources; PPB reminds everyone that the process of government also involves to a significant degree the allocation of scarce resources.

Even in the context of personal day-to-day decisions, practically nothing is free. A decision to devote time to reading this book was a decision not to devote time to sleeping, chatting with one's office colleagues, or working on something else. Even if the time used to read it is unpaid time, it has a cost. The cost is measured by what was foregone. Thus, the price of reading is the loss of enjoyment from watching television, and the price of watching television is the loss of time from reading or some other pursuit. Even if there were no prices in our world, everything would have a cost as long as not everything could be done at once. The cost of time used for anything is simply the value of the best alternative use of the same time. Economists call this concept "opportunity costs," implying correctly that the cost of an action is the loss of the opportunity to do something else.[1]

Time is not the world's only scarce resource. The space occupied by the moosehead could have held a painting or a movie screen. The space occupied by the offices of the National Aeronautics and Space Administration could be occupied by the staff for an expanded federal rat control program. Likewise, automobiles, desks and paper, airplanes, and even missiles can all be used for a variety of

activities. However, so long as the supply is limited,
use for one purpose prevents use in another. Broadly
speaking, PPB concerns itself with questions of resource
analysis, that is, questions of choices among alternative
uses of scarce resources. [2]

Price is the usual common denominator of most forms
of opportunity cost because most resources can be given
dollar values in a business or government environment.
Time reflects itself in appropriations for salaries and
expenses of government employees. Space costs are
reflected in rental or construction payments. Desks,
automobiles, and missiles are all purchased or manufactured at a price. On a higher level of generality, the
opportunity cost of expanding one program is frequently
simply a cutback or decreased expansion of another program. For most of the discussions in this book, it is
assumed that prices measure opportunity costs.

The PPB approach seeks to remind decision-makers
that behind price there lurks opportunity cost. The fact
that "the price of a pad of paper is 10 cents" should not be
permitted to obscure the fact that the price of the pad may
have been the same as that for two pencils. Likewise, the
fact that a defensive missile system "costs" $10 billion
reflects an underlying reality that the taxpayer is being
asked to forego $10 billion worth of private consumption or
$10 billion in civilian government programs as the "price"
of going ahead with the missile system.

Not all the opportunity costs of governmental actions
are readily translatable into dollars. A decision to use a
river for a scenic park forecloses the use of the falling
water for generating power or for low-flow augmentation
to prevent pollution. A decision to build a government
building on a plot of land forecloses the use of that land as
scenic open space. Even decisions that can readily be
expressed in dollars and cents in the long term cannot be
so treated in the short run. In the long run, an army
division can be built from scratch if money for training,
pay, and equipment is available. Thus, in the long run,
a decision to commit a division to Korea has the opportunity cost of whatever it costs to establish and deploy a
division. In the short run, however, the number of divisions

is fixed, and better protection in one place can only be
"bought" with weaker protection of another.

The fact that it is possible to identify opportunity costs
of government decisions does not imply that all government
decisions are based upon a full awareness of these costs.
Government is considerably more complex in its thought
process than an individual. Most government costs do not
become readily translated into costs for the individual
decision-maker; this is a problem of most large organizations whether private or public. When a private individual
uses a piece of paper--for which he must pay and ultimately
purchase replacements--he is aware that the price of using
the paper is other purchases. Purchasing an additional
pad of paper per year may mean giving up only one ice
cream cone or ten cigarettes, but it does mean giving up
something. The individual user is well aware of both the
price of the item and the alternative purchases which he
could make. At the office, however, the situation changes.
To the individual employee of a government agency, the
source of paper is his secretary, his secretary's source
is the supply room, and the supply room's source is the
General Services Administration. To the individual
employee, paper costs nothing. If he uses twice as much
one year as another, there are no penalties; if he uses only
half as much, there are no rewards. Thus, even considering
something as simple and inexpensive as a piece of paper,
the signals given to an individual employee by his environment
are not the same as those seen by the President or Congress
in reviewing consumption of paper in the government.

To some degree, at least, we all behave like the
"economic man" who permeates economic reasoning. If
either one of two things can do the job equally well, we will
tend to take the cheaper. The more expensive something
becomes, the more careful we are to minimize its use where
we can. This perfectly natural reaction in our personal
decisions produces the most satisfaction that can be obtained
from any particular level of economic assets and income.
Equally important, it produces maximum attainable satisfaction from society's point of view, so long as certain
conditions are met. [3]

These concepts also make sense in governmental decision-making. It is cheaper for the government to use railroads, trucks, and aircraft to carry the mail than to use missile delivery systems or revive the pony express. When a decision is made to abandon pony express or avoid starting "missile mail," all benefit, because government is not wasting resources.

Problems arise, however, when the cost signals given to a government administrator are not the same as those seen by his superiors or by the public as a whole. The paper example is a simple one, but one which typifies many more important governmental decisions. From the President's standpoint, paper costs money; from the employee's standpoint, it appears to be free. Other examples involve more money but are comparable issues in cost analysis. The Defense Department, one study indicated, found itself in the position of receiving nuclear weapon warheads "free" from the Atomic Energy Commission. That is, the Commission manufactured the warheads out of its own budget; if more warheads were required, it did not mean that other items in the Defense budget had to be sacrificed to pay for them. The result was an allocation of resources that was clearly nonoptimal from the standpoint of society at large, even though the Defense Department decision-makers acted intelligently to minimize those costs that fell on them. [4]

FULL SYSTEM COST

All cost analysts insist that "full system costs" should be counted. From the standpoint of the nation as a whole, and presumably from the perspective of a President of the United States, full system costs means much more than costs that are apparent to a decision-maker in a private enterprise or federal agency. Full system costs include cash outlays plus "free" inputs from other government agencies, from state and local government, and from private citizens, and opportunity costs associated with the use of existing assets that could have been put to other uses.

Direct Governmental Outlays

Direct outlays are the most visible government costs.
In procuring a weapon for the Defense Department, they
are the payments that must be made to contractors for
producing the weapon, for transporting it, for spare parts,
for training and technical assistance in its use, for pay
and allowances of military personnel to man the weapon,
for logistical facilities to support it, etc. While there are
some major problems in determining what governmental
outlays go with what weapons system or project, identifying
direct outlays is relatively easy. It is easy because cash
must come from the Treasury. The Treasury will not pay
unless certain procedures--which include developing a budget
and getting Congress and the President to approve it--have
been followed. Thus, cash outlays of government must be
budgeted somewhere. When they are budgeted, they are
hard to overlook.

Costs over Time

One way direct governmental outlays can be overlooked
is when they arise in the future. An expenditure may be
required by some earlier action but be totally ignored until
it surfaces in the form of a budget request. A decision to
procure an additional Polaris submarine carries an implication for direct government outlays, namely the cost of
the submarine. It also carries with it a decision to purchase
the man-hours and equipment necessary to deploy that
submarine and keep it manned and on station. The PPB
approach requires that attention be focused on both current
and future costs.

In introducing the Planning-Programming-Budgeting
System into the federal government, President Johnson
said that the system would "enable us to . . . inform our-
selves not merely on next year's costs, but on the second,
and third, and subsequent year's costs of our programs."[5]
One of the failings of the then existing budgeting system
pointed out in the Budget Bureau's original directive on
PPB was that "in a number of cases the future year costs

of present decisions have not been laid out systematically enough."[6] The need for full system costs reflecting more than a single budget year were recognized in the Pentagon with the development of the concept of a five-year program and financial plan, a concept incorporated in the guidance given federal agencies for their PPB systems.

The insistence on considering full costs over time extends to full government programs, not merely to particular weapons systems or civilian activities that support program goals. Henry S. Rowen, in a paper written while he was an Assistant Director of the Bureau of the Budget, reflected this in his comments on the current budgeting system:

> One important defect of our present Budget system is its limitations (sic) to one year. A Programming System, on the other hand, should lay out programs for several years ahead. Our program decisions have important future consequences, sometimes not obvious, which definitely ought to be considered before decisions are taken. Having for example, a Five-Year Program forces on us such a look ahead.[7]

The importance of looking at future costs of present decisions had been recognized by the U.S. Congress before any formal planning-programming-budgeting system was installed by the executive branch. Public Law 801 of the Eighty-fourth Congress[8] requires that any executive recommendation for, or even report on, legislation entailing an estimated annual expenditure of over $1 million

> shall contain a statement, . . . for each of the first five fiscal years during which each such additional or expanded function . . . is to be in effect, disclosing the following information:
>
> (a) the estimated maximum additional--
>
> > (i) man-years of civilian employment, by general categories of positions,

    (ii) expenditures for personal services,
        and

    (iii) expenditures for all purposes other
        than personal services,

which are attributable to such function.

The Senate Post Office and Civil Service Committee, which reported the bill, described it and its purposes in the following terms:

> The purpose of this measure is to assure that congressional committees are fully advised concerning the personnel requirements and costs of major legislative proposals. Not only is each committee entitled to complete knowledge of the payroll increases and other costs involved in each major piece of legislation it considers, but such information would enable Congress to consider such proposals in their proper perspective from the beginning. [9]

As a practical matter, political decision-makers do not, normally, leave a government construction project unfinished. For that reason, the PPB approach stresses the importance of focusing on the full capital costs involved regardless of the year in which funds will actually be expended. Maintenance costs should also be considered at the time the decision is made to undertake a project.

Inputs from Other Government Agencies

The costs of a government activity do not all occur within the agency administering the activity; sometimes agencies may impose major costs on each other. Delivery by mail of a free government pamphlet is not free, even though the agency benefiting from the service does not buy stamps. In the interstate highway program, it is necessary to build highways with sufficient clearance over rivers to permit river navigation to take place. Such

navigation clearances are quite expensive for the state
highway departments and the Bureau of Public Roads to
provide.[10] These costs are imposed by the Army Corps
of Engineers in its role as protector of inland navigation.
The costs are paid by highway agencies and ultimately by
those who buy gasoline. The reverse situation is equally
relevant. If the highway planners could jam all navigable
waterways with slightly elevated strips of concrete, then
they would be imposing burdens on navigation, and on the
navigation-promoting agencies such as the Corps of Engineers, without having to consider those costs in their road-
building budget.

Inputs from Other Levels of Government

Costs to the economy as a whole are not diminished
when a different level of government pays them. Thus,
when a state government decides to spend funds for a program which is 90 per cent cost-shared by the federal
government, the costs to the state agency represent only
10 per cent of the total cost impact of the action being
considered. The reverse situation may also be important
in a cost-sharing program. The federal agency, in measuring how much program result it is getting for its expenditures, may (but in the PPB approach should not) ignore
the costs paid by cooperating state and local agencies.

Private Costs

Government can make its citizens pay for public benefits
without proceeding through the process of appropriation
and expenditure justification. Some of the costs, what
economists call "externalities," are those which government, like a business firm, may impose on its neighbors
without creating a legal obligation to pay them. Pollution
is an example. Other categories of these costs are those
which involve substituting a private loss in order to cut
the "cost" of a public service. For example, a state
liquor store can cut its costs by reducing the number of
its outlets, thereby forcing buyers (where state stores

are monopolies) to drive farther to the store. Such an
economy move may merely involve translating government
costs into private costs for gasoline and oil (plus time).
Many of the political difficulties in urban renewal programs
can be traced to the fact that in the early years of the
program urban renewal officials failed to recognize that
the cost of land purchase and clearing did not measure the
full costs of slum land. While owners were being reimbursed for the value of the land, tenants were forced to
move with little or no reimbursement. Government was
creating these private costs without paying them or recognizing them in the total calculations of cost of urban renewal.[11]

Behind many public and administrative issues lie fairly
simple questions of the perspective from which various
participants may be perceiving costs. Systematic analysis
of costs using the approach described above can describe
the full cost picture. From that point, it can be argued
by rational men that some costs should be ignored and some
should not.[12] However, for rational discussion to proceed,
costs must be clearly identified.

An Example

A hypothetical program of federal grants-in-aid to
major cities to eliminate at least one half of the level of
rat infestation (measured as estimated number of living
rats) provides an example of the impact of considering full
costs. Assuming that the program was a 50 per cent grant
program embodying a variety of approaches (e.g., poison-
ing, increased sanitation efforts by the city, enactment of
ordinances requiring more strict sanitary procedures by
private citizens and business, more frequent building
inspection, etc.), the level of full costs and of apparent
cost would be substantially different.

Apparent federal costs would be the annual appropriation to the federal rat control agency for (a) operating
expenses and administration and (b) grants to the participating cities. The full costs of the decision to initiate the
program would involve much more, including:

...the nonbudgeted costs of office space in
existing federal buildings

...the added review and administrative costs
in coordinating and controlling agencies
such as the Public Health Service and
Bureau of the Budget

...some portion of the future expenditures
required to keep the impact of some programs (for example, more frequent garbage pickup) from being lost by reversion
to the earlier status quo--with a corre-
sponding increase in the rat population

...the 50 per cent of expenditures borne by
state and local governments

...the added costs to private individuals and
businesses for tighter garbage cans, etc.

Thus, in the example, the federal budget (and the costs
most apparent to federal decision-makers without PPB)
would clearly understate the costs of the program. In this
circumstance, the question "What would Congress have to
appropriate to eliminate half of the rats in our nation's
cities?" is by no means the same question as "What would
it cost to eliminate half of the rats in our nation's cities?"
One basic element in PPB is to make sure that the first
question is not substituted for the second, at least not
without some thought being given to the second.

SUMMARY

Cost analysis is a key element of the economic approach
to government decision-making. Nothing is ever free,
because the use of each resource has a cost measured by
the lost opportunity to use the resource for something else.
In measuring costs, it is necessary to look beyond the budget
of a particular agency for a particular year to find full system costs, including costs over time, costs imposed on

other agencies and levels of government, and costs imposed
on individuals.

NOTES TO CHAPTER 3

1. For an ingenuous attempt to apply this approach to
resource allocation in the Soviet Union, see Leonid V.
Kantorovich, The Best Use of Economic Resources (Cambridge: Harvard University Press, 1965).

2. The fact that it is scarce resources (which may or
may not be quickly and easily measured in dollars) being
allocated is emphasized by use of "resource analysis" as
an operating term. The difference is important where
many resources do not have dollar costs apparent to the
decision-maker. See, for example, G. H. Fisher, "What
is Resource Analysis?" Rand Corporation Paper, P-2688
(1963).

3. These conditions are discussed in Chapter 10.
Thinking economically about government is possible without
becoming an economist, but those who seek precise discussions of the welfare implications of the price system
would be well advised to consult a good economic text
(e.g., Paul Samuelson, Principles of Economics (New
York: McGraw-Hill, various editions), followed by a more
elaborate discussion of price theory. Robert Dorfman,
The Price System (New York: Prentice-Hall, 1964), provides a good introduction and citations to more advanced
literature.

4. See Malcolm W. Hoag, "The Relevance of Costs,"
Ch. 6 in E. S. Quade (ed.), Analysis for Military Decisions
(Chicago: Rand McNally, 1964).

5. Weekly Compilation of Presidential Documents,
August 30, 1965.

6. U.S. Bureau of the Budget, Bulletin 66-3 (October 12,
1965).

7. U.S. Bureau of the Budget, "Improving Decision Making in Government" (processed August, 1965). The address is reprinted in U.S. Senate, Committee on Government Operations, Subcommittee on Executive Reorganization, Hearings, Federal Role in Urban Affairs, Eighty-ninth Congress, 2nd Session (1966), pp. 859-68.

8. Act of July 25, 1957, 70 Stat. 652.

9. U.S. Senate, Committee on Post Office and Civil Service, Report No. 2534 (to accompany H.R. 10368), July 12, 1956. As Representative Bennett pointed out on the floor of the House of Representatives on June 1, 1966, this law "has been complied with only on a limited scale." Congressional Record (daily edition), June 1, 1966, p. 11353.

10. This situation is discussed in U.S. Congress, House, Documents 54 and 72, Final Report of the Highway Cost Allocation Study, Eighty-seventh Congress, 1st Session (1961), pp. 92-93.

11. Cost analysis involves many interesting issues too complex for treatment here. For discussions of interest rates and opportunity costs of capital, cost analysis models, joint products, and salvage value, as well as other issues, see the more detailed discussions cited in the Bibliography.

12. For a perceptive discussion of this point, see Roland McKean's "Costs and Benefits from Different Viewpoints," in Howard Schaller (ed.), Public Expenditure Decisions in the Urban Community (Washington, D.C.: Johns Hopkins Press, 1963).

CHAPTER EVALUATING RETURNS
IN RELATION TO COST

Preceding chapters have stressed the need to analyze,
the measurement of cost, and the establishment of objectives
and measurement of output received from a program's inputs. None have even purported to explain how to determine
whether a program or activity is worth-while. Yet, in the
opening of this book, it was contended that helping decision-
makers to evaluate programs was one of the key features
of the PPB approach. This chapter begins the discussion
of "worth-whileness" with the approaches of cost-utility
and cost-effectiveness analysis. What is generally called
"cost-benefit analysis" will be discussed in the following
chapters.

COST-EFFECTIVENESS

Cost-effectiveness is no more than a model in which
the inputs have been priced but the outputs have not.[1] As
an example, suppose that the federal government has under
consideration a program of cancer-care clinics (of specified
size and location with specified equipment, staffing patterns,
and operating procedures) to reduce deaths from cancer.
If health authorities had the capacity to produce a model
of the relationship between cancer-care clinics and cancer
deaths, it would take the following form:

Number of Clinics	Annual Number of Deaths Prevented[2]
1	100
5	450

Number of Clinics	Annual Number of Deaths Prevented
10	890
100	6,000
200	10,000

This model may be converted to a cost-effectiveness statement by pricing the clinics. Assuming that the clinics each cost $1 million per year for operation, maintenance, and rental or amortization of equipment and facilities, the preceding table becomes the following one:

Cost (Millions of Dollars)	Effectiveness (Deaths Prevented in an Average Year)
1	100
5	450
10	890
100	6,000
200	10,000

Costs, as discussed in the preceding chapter, are generally more complicated than in the example shown. However, the example correctly reflects the fact that in many nonmilitary programs the greatest difficulties lie in constructing the model, not in developing cost-effectiveness relationships once the model has been developed.

The value of cost-utility analysis can best be understood by contrasting analysis in government to analysis by a super-market customer. In a supermarket, a consumer is given the option of buying essentially unlimited quantities of any goods at a fixed price per unit. Soap is so much per box, apples so much each, potatoes so much per pound. The consumer decides whether a head of lettuce is "worth" a quarter. Because the satisfaction from a head of lettuce is not hard for a housewife to understand, she has little difficulty comprehending the utility side of a cost-utility relationship. Likewise, cost is easy to comprehend--even in opportunity-costs terms--for what housewife doesn't have many alternative uses of money (opportunity) which

she will forego (opportunity costs) when she, for example,
spends the quarter for lettuce?

The government decision is more difficult because the
measures of government output are frequently not analogous
to ultimate objects of consumption like soap and potatoes.
Many government budget choices are offered in dollar terms
(e.g., spend $50 million more on cancer research this
year), in percentage terms (e.g., a 10 per cent increase in
Strategic Air Command readiness), in terms of a subordinate's judgment of "adequacy" (e.g., to provide an adequate
level of weed control on Bureau of Land Management land),
"necessity" (e.g., to meet necessary expenses for the
operation of the Coast Guard), "need" (e.g., the program
will provide 20 per cent of the new low-income housing
needed over the next five years), or "demand" (e.g., the
program will relieve some of the backlog of loan applications
that have not been filled for lack of funds). Because these
various measures of additional budgetary effort do not
describe the expansion of ultimate outputs which could be
compared, the balancing of satisfactions is more difficult
in government budgetary decisions than in personal consumption decisions.

This situation tends to make it difficult to choose
government expenditures with knowledge comparable to
that utilized in making consumer expenditures. One suspects
that the phenomena is more serious on the down side than
on the up side. The consumer can clearly see the consequences of dropping her order from seven apples to six,
but what would be the consequences of failing to provide
an "adequate" level of weed control on public lands or
failing to meet the "necessary" expenses of the Coast
Guard? Problems of this type are handled in the PPB
approach by seeking explicitness on the outputs associated
with particular costs. In colloquial terms, the approach
seeks to tell a decision-maker precisely, "This is what
you can have, and this is what you will have to pay for it."
As Charles Hitch has put it,

> Our aim is to help the decision maker. What
> help does he need in making a decision--in
> choosing among alternatives? He needs to
> know the consequences of his choices--positive

consequences, in achieving his objectives, and
negative consequences or "costs" in a broad
sense. [3]

In many cases, this comparison of cost and utility will
be prevented by lack of an adequate model. For example,
even assuming that there was general agreement on the
objective of education, there is no accepted model of how
much increased expenditures for audio-visual material
affect achievement of that objective. Even when there is
such a model, it may differ significantly from the situation
confronting the supermarket buyer. The supermarket
buyer can always (or practically always) buy additional
quantities of the same commodity for about the same price.
If the first head of lettuce costs a quarter, then the twen-
tieth head and the two hundredth head will also be about
twenty-five cents each. In government programs, incremental cost-return relationships are not always the same.
The first 2 per cent increase in educational attainment
(measured by some standard test) may be available for a
$25-per-pupil expenditure on audio-visual materials, but
it may take as many as $125 worth of such materials to
produce another 2 per cent increase. After the 4 per cent
increase, additional materials might clutter the classroom
but have no returns in educational output.

As this example indicates, the incremental costs and
outputs of government programs may vary significantly
depending upon where one is on the curve of cost and effectiveness. For that reason, the PPB approach demands
concentration on incremental costs and utility. When facts
of these incremental gains and costs are known, the basis
for rational decisions about program level is present. For
example, if a fire protection system was offered to a city
on such a basis, the selection would probably look something like this:

Alternative	Annual Cost	Average Annual Property Loss	Loss of Life
O	$ 0	$2,000,000	5
A	100,000	1,000,000	3
B	500,000	500,000	1

| C | 1,000,000 | 250,000 | $3/4^*$ |
| D | 1,800,000 | 150,000 | 1/2 |

It will be remembered from the preceding chapter that this
set of estimates reflects a model of the relationship between
fire protection expenditures and the damage caused by fire.
It is a simple model in that it ignores functions of fire
departments, such as rescue work, that are not directly
related to fire fighting. It also treats uncertainty by developing average annual values, even though to decision-makers
such a treatment might be unsatisfactory, particularly if
the life or property that a decision-maker saves by greater
expenditures might be his own. Assuming that the political
jurisdiction was recently incorporated and was, therefore,
considering fire protection for the first time, the PPB
approach would immediately suggest that these alternatives
most conveniently can be analyzed incrementally. Thus,
from the information in the preceding table, an incremental
table can be constructed as follows:

Incremental Change from Alternative __ to Alternative __	Cost Change	Added Property Loss Prevented	Added Loss of Life Prevented
O to A	+$100,000	$1,000,000	2
A to B	+ 400,000	500,000	2
B to C	+ 500,000	250,000	1/4
C to D	+ 800,000	100,000	1/4

When increments of gain and cost are considered, it is
frequently possible to reach conclusions reasonably rapidly.
The movement from O to A looks like a good one by almost
any criteria. Assuming that taxes can be raised to pay for
it (and that the tax funds couldn't be used more productively
in some other way), the movement from Alternative A to B
seems capable of saving the residents more than its costs,
even if loss of life is not considered. On the other hand,
one needs to value life relatively highly to recommend
Alternative C. However, a level of protection between B
and C might appear attractive. To most observers, the
point of politically, as well as economically, diminishing

---

* Three lives every four years.

returns would have been passed well before consideration
of the high level of protection suggested by Alternative D.

The value of looking at various levels of gains and costs
is clearly indicated from the example. It is a fair inference
that most people would not choose to adopt Alternative D,
which by comparison with Alternative C bought $100,000
in loss prevented and the saving of a life every four years
for a price of $1 million a year.[*] In short, D would probably
not appear worth-while if all of the increments were considered.

Suppose, on the other hand, Alternative D were presented
as a program without a discussion of alternatives. The
potential fire chief, fire equipment salesman, or fire protection consultant devises a fire protection plan for Our Town.
This plan offers decreased property losses of $1,900,000
and the potential to save 4-1/2 lives every year, all for a
price of $1,800,000, which the consultant correctly can
point out is less than the property loss prevented alone.
This is Alternative D which, if presented on this basis,
might be adopted. The moral is clear: Make sure enough
alternatives are considered, and look at increments of gain
and cost. The moral applies whether some of the elements
of gain can be measured in dollars (such as fire loss prevented) or whether they must all be measured in some other
dimension such as missiles on target, lives saved, drop-
outs prevented, or whatever.

The concept of suboptimization needs to be repeated in
connection with the example. Fire protection alternatives
in the example were all presumed to provide the greatest
protection for life and property for the given dollar value.
The fire protection results shown for Alternative D should

---

[*] To adopt Alternative D would imply that saving a life
every four years is worth $700,000 per year or a total of
$2.8 million per life saved. Even if one valued human life
at that much, the town would be better advised to expend
its $2.8 million for (a) highway patrol, (b) police protec-
tion, (c) inoculation programs, and (d) a new hospital, all
of which would probably result in saving lives at a much
lower cost than $2.8 million each.

conceptually be the protection from the best of all alternatives to provide as much fire protection as $100,000 would
buy.

So long as costs are expressed in one dimension (dollars)
and utility or effectiveness in another, value judgments will
be required to decide whether additional increments of cost
and utility make sense. Who is to say that the value of a
free outdoor concert is five dollars, five hundred, or five
thousand? Except in the special case of cost-benefit analysis,
the PPB approach does not purport to make these value judg-
ments--it simply focuses attention on them so that proper
political authorities can make them intelligently, at least as
intelligently as the woman in the supermarket.

ECONOMY

Although political value judgments are required to
determine what level of cost and utility is appropriate,
under special analytical circumstances the analyst using the
PPB approach can still have considerable useful advice
to offer a political decision-maker. First is the case where
effectiveness is "given," that is, already decided upon. In
this circumstance, it may be possible to develop a series
of alternatives to the existing way of doing things, each one
of which produces the same output and one of which may
produce the same output at less cost. This special circum-
stance--the economists' definition of economy--is one case
in which analysis can produce actual "savings" in government
activity. In the fire protection example, suppose that the
city decided upon protection by less than the optimal method
(i.e., it did not suboptimize). In such a circumstance, an
analyst could advise the political decision-makers, "I can
show you a way to get exactly the same protection you get
now and spend less money getting it." Such a result can be
identified (assuming it exists) by the PPB approach:

(1) Specify the objectives--decrease the damage
    caused by fire.

(2) Establish criteria of effectiveness (loss of
    property and life).

(3) For economy considerations, take the present
    effectiveness as the target.

(4) Consider alternatives and their costs to
    achieve the same objective.

(5) Recommend the alternative that uses the
    least resources to achieve the objective.

The "savings" from finding a better way can be used in
any way in which the resources ($) could have been used in
the first place. They can be kept in the same program to
increase the level of service, they can be used for other
government programs, or they may be returned to the taxpayer in reduced taxes.

EFFICIENCY

The reverse twin of economy is efficiency--getting the
most out of what you spend. Instead of holding effectiveness
or utility constant and examining the costs of various alternatives, efficiency considerations involve holding cost
constant and examining the outputs of various alternatives.

The usefulness of holding costs constant and then looking
at effectiveness of different alternatives does not end when
the types of effectiveness are varied. Just as it is possible
for the consumer to consider the usefulness of 10 cents worth
of bubble gum, candy, or popcorn, so can a government
decision-maker face questions of choice by determining what
his money will buy if spent on various alternatives. For
example, $2 billion might buy a 4 per cent reduction in the
personal income tax, a complete three-year program to
eradicate hard-core unemployment in city slums, or a
comprehensive hospital or school construction program.
In this application, cost-effectiveness analysis provides
information analogous to that provided by consumer research
organizations. In such research, equally costly alternatives

do not produce different quantities of the same output (the pure efficiency situation), but produce different quantities of different outputs.

SUMMARY

This chapter introduced the concepts of evaluating returns in relation to costs through cost-effectiveness or cost-utility analysis. Such analysis tells the decision-maker what he gets (in terms of increments of achieving an objective) and what he gives up (costs) to get it. In special cases cost-effectiveness analysis may tell the decision-maker which is a preferred program. If the decision-maker has decided on both a cost ceiling and the output he values, one alternative can be shown to be preferable to others. Likewise, if the decision-maker has decided upon the outputs he wants and is concerned only with minimizing costs, the least-cost alternative will be the best alternative. In technical language, the first situation is called efficiency (maximizing return from fixed inputs) and the later economy (minimizing inputs for a fixed return). In analysis of relationships of costs and effectiveness, it is essential to look at increments of each.

NOTES TO CHAPTER 4

1. The tremendous complexity of existing cost-effectiveness studies frequently obscures this simple concept. The complexities arise from such factors as (a) alternative assumptions about the model itself, (b) treatment of risk and uncertainty, (c) sensitivity analysis to determine how responsive the conclusions are to changed assumptions, (d) discussion of the extent to which the model used reflects the complexities of the real world situation, and (e) difficulties of being precise about cost.

2. The decreasing returns per clinic reflect an assumption that the most opportune locations (large cities) are selected first, and each succeeding clinic, even though involving the same equipment and staff, can serve fewer of the specialized cases because there are fewer such cases in the city it serves. Whether, in fact, this would be the case for any particular clinic program is of no importance to the present discussion. In connection with this example, it should be noted that when the PPB approach flounders for lack of a model it may be successful in pointing out the need for a model and getting started in making one. On the issue covered by the example, the chief of PPB in the Department of Health, Education and Welfare recently told the Joint Economic Committee that "estimates of improvement in health attributable to medical care are almost nonexistent." (See U.S. Congress, Joint Economic Committee, Subcommittee on Economy in Government, Hearings, "The Planning-Programming-Budgeting System: Progress and Potentials," Ninetieth Congress, 1st Session, 1967, p. 7.

3. "Decision-Making in Large Organizations," delivered at a Royal Society Nuffield Lecture, London, October 25, 1966, reprinted in U.S. Senate, Committee on Government Operations, Subcommittee on National Security and International Operations, "Planning-Programming-Budgeting, Selected Comment," Ninetieth Congress, 1st Session, 1967, pp. 10-17.

CHAPTER **5** RELATING BENEFITS
TO COSTS

Information on a program's effectiveness and cost does
not automatically determine whether it should be undertaken
even if it is the least costly program to achieve a particular
objective. Given the fact that the most effective way to provide water to a given arid area is to build a dam, should the
dam be built? Given the fact that an increase in educational
expenditures of 25 per cent would increase achievement test
scores by 10 per cent, is the added performance worth the
cost? These questions, and others like them, form the core
of the hard decisions facing government administrators, the
Congress, and the public. Cost-effectiveness and cost-utility
determinations do not answer them, nor does the technical
expertise of safety engineering, military strategy, education,
or civil engineering.

WHAT IS COST-BENEFIT ANALYSIS?

Ultimately the questions boil down to determining the
value of the output. How much are irrigation water and
better achievement test scores worth? Because it does seek
to answer such questions as these, cost-benefit analysis is
inherently a more powerful aid to decision-making than is
cost-effectiveness analysis. It is also harder to perform.

Cost-benefit analysis, like cost-effectiveness analysis,
involves attaching to models values or prices that reflect
the impact of program inputs on valued outputs. In cost-
effectiveness, the input side is translated into dollars, while
the output side is left in non-dollar units (deaths prevented,
children educated, families housed, etc.). In cost-benefit

analysis, both the inputs and the outputs are given dollar
valuations. Because both inputs and outputs are measured
in the same dimension, cost-benefit analysis by its nature
is a system for recommending program decisions. It does
not necessarily eliminate the political value judgments
necessary to translate cost-effectiveness studies into decisions. Instead, it incorporates those value judgments into
the analytical criteria, thereby making the result a single
simple answer. The end result of cost-benefit analysis
is a determination that the benefits are (a) greater than,
(b) equal to, or (c) less than the costs. The first outcome
argues that the program should be undertaken, the third
that it should not, and the second is ambiguous (and highly
unlikely).

Among PPB practitioners, there are wide differences
of opinion concerning the immediate practicability of cost-
benefit analysis. These differences, however, should
not be permitted to obscure the basic consensus that the
more known about the "values" of benefits the better, even
where the "values" involved may be values inferred from
decisions or expressed by political groups rather than
values that might be attached in a free market to government outputs.

EVALUATING BENEFITS IS UNAVOIDABLE

It is easy to argue that value questions are unanswer-
able, that no one can evaluate a human life, attach a price
tag to something as vital as water, put dollar signs on
military capabilities, or estimate the worth of a price-
less investment in education. Yet, whether we do it con-
sciously or not, the interaction of individuals and social
institutions puts price tags on these valuable outputs every
day. In setting standards for highway design, a state
highway department decides that additional lane width,
which it is guessed might cut highway deaths by ten over
the life of the road, is (or is not) worth the additional
$500,000 in construction and right-of-way acquisition
costs. Logical inference: Saving a life is (or is not)

worth $50,000 of highway funds.* When government builds
a dam to provide one hundred million gallons of irrigation
water annually for an annual cost including the amortized
investment of $10 million per year, the logical inference
is that water is worth $100 per thousand gallons.

All decisions society makes (remembering that a decision to change nothing is itself a decision) give rise to
inferences of the monetary value associated with a given
output. If a decision-maker does not know the implicit
valuations he is making, he is uninformed. If he is not
prepared to accept the logical inference from his decision,
he is deciding irrationally. A highway planner who believes
that a human life should be valued at more than $50,000
but refuses to invest $50,000 to save one, is acting contrary
to his own assumptions of value.

Thus, the frequently heard argument about whether
cost-benefit analysis is possible is probably nonsense.
Mankind has from his first days on the planet--as the
Jackson Subcommittee staff suggested by its suggestion
that analysis began with Eve's decision in the Garden of
Eden--weighed potential gains against costs. Frequently,
but not always, such decisions have been made in monetary
units. In government budgeting and resource allocation
decisions, one dimension is always dollars, so it can be
expected that inferences about benefits can always be made
in dollars. Thus, the question is not whether benefits will
be accorded a dollar value, but whether the process of
deciding how much government outputs are worth can be
conducted more openly, explicitly, and scientifically than
it is today. The PPB approach forces explicitness about
both the models that underlie a recommendation and the
value which the recommending party places upon the output.
Cost-benefit analysis has always been with us, yet the
practitioners of PPB are normally referring to a process

---

* This conclusion holds even if the intent in saving money
on the widening was to use it for additional new roads to
replace old unsafe ones. In that circumstance, assuming
that the cost per life saved was less for new road building
than improving road quality, society in setting the highway
budget implicitly valued life at less than $50,000.

somewhat more sophisticated than that described above.
One can always infer that a decision-maker valued an output
or a product at at least as much as what he was willing to
pay for it. True cost-benefit analysis, however, goes
beyond the inference of values from program decisions
and moves to evaluating the output of governmental programs
as an input to program decisions.

STRATEGIES FOR MEASURING BENEFITS

Attaching values to governmental outputs is easy enough.
We can say that the outcome of a policy of reducing race
discrimination in the labor force is worth $5.00 for every
Negro hired who would not otherwise have been hired. We
can also say that the value of the program is $500 per person
hired or $5,000. Again, the question is not whether or not
values may be attached to these program outputs, but how
reasonable the values may seem to all the decision-makers
involved. Equally important, to be measured as a benefit in
a replicable cost-benefit analysis a commodity or service
must carry approximately the same benefit regardless of the
analyst or decision-maker evaluating the program.

The need for "objective" benefit measurements gives
rise to standard strategies for measuring benefits. The
simplest of these is to determine the market price of the
good that government is making and selling. Government
does provide goods and services that are, or could be,
sold in the open market. For example, the benefit from the
Government Printing Office to particular agencies for
which it does printing can readily be measured as what
it would cost those agencies to have their printing done
outside by the lowest bidder. The benefit when the General
Services Administration provides office space and cleaning
services can be measured by what it would cost agencies
to obtain the same thing from private contractors. Less
mundane examples are available. The benefits from governmental output of electric power and of water, to mention
two examples, are readily comparable to the prices charged
for those commodities in regulated markets.

Many goods produced by government, however, are not also produced by private suppliers. Frequently, the reason for governmental activity is that private suppliers do not provide the good or service desired, or provide it in such a way that government intervention to change the existing arrangement is desirable. Thus, while useful, finding the exact market price for the outputs of governmental programs is a limited methodology. It is totally inapplicable in such situations as education and defense.

Government Contributions to Production

Some governmental activity contributes to intermediate stages of production of goods ultimately sold to consumers. For example, irrigation water is provided not as an end in itself but as part of the process of producing crops. These crops from irrigated farms will, of course, ultimately be sold for a price. Under such circumstances, it is possible to measure the contribution the irrigation water makes to the production process. If cotton sells at $100 a bale and if an added gallon of irrigation water will result in an added one-half bale of cotton without further effort by the farmer, then clearly the irrigation water is worth $50 to the farmer. This $50 value reflects the extent to which the irrigation water can increase the gross income of the farmer. At any price lower than $50, the water will be more valuable to the farmer than its cost to him. It, therefore, can legitimately be valued as a benefit, or potential benefit, of up to $50 to the farmer. *

A surprising number of governmental activities are in one way or another tied to the ultimate production process. In recent years, economists have increasingly realized that productivity increases in the United States and other developed nations have not been based solely on increased investment in machinery and capital equipment; investments in human

---

* If the commodity or service can be provided by an alternative method (e.g., private wells), it is generally agreed that the benefit is the lesser of the contribution to production or the alternative cost.

capital enhance productive capabilities just as do investments
in machinery. The more technically sophisticated Americans
become, the more efficiently they can work. Given this fact,
education contributes to production much as a new machine,
or new combinations of machines, contributes to production.
Education, like machinery, involves heavy investments in
the early stages followed by a stream of benefits running
through the life of the machine or the individual being educated.[1]

It is possible to calculate the benefits of education in
roughly the same way that benefits are calculated for irrigation water or labor-saving machines. If it is assumed
that the market prices paid for labor in our society are
roughly indicative of the value society places on that labor,
then an income of $10,000 a year implies that the individual
is providing benefits to society of at least $10,000 a year.
If such is the case, it is possible to compare the productivity
(as measured by wages) of workers with and without education
and, if the inference can properly be made, to decide that
education's value to the individual in higher wages is also a
value to society. Thus, studies have inferred that the
difference in income between persons, say, with or without
a college education reflects both a benefit to the educated
individual and a benefit to society from his greater productivity.[2]

A more practical example of measuring returns from
education are recent attempts to measure the benefits of
government manpower-training programs. Generally
speaking, they seek to compare the employment expectations of an individual without training with expectations for
a comparable individual with training. The difference
reflects the benefits to society from the training.[3]

Conceptually, a benefit is a cost averted, and a cost is
a benefit foregone. The following table shows examples
of federal governmental activities which, to one degree or
another, have significant enough contributions to production that some of their benefits can be measured in terms
of the value they add to ultimate marketable products or
in terms of the costs they avert in the process of production.

Program or Activity	Output
Public-works agencies	Water, electric power, navigation channels, and flood control
Post Office	Movement of mail and goods
Interior Department	
Bureau of Commercial Fisheries	Facilitating commercial fishing
Bureau of Mines	Utilizing minerals
Geological Survey	Mapping and geological surveys
Bureau of Land Management	Minerals, grazing rights, etc., on public lands
Department of Agriculture	Facilitating production of farm products
Department of Commerce	Information for business use on everything from markets to weather
Maritime Administration	Transportation
Departments of Health, Education and Welfare and Labor Department	Manpower programs, and development of human productive resources through health and education programs
Department of Transportation	Transportation
Tennessee Valley Authority	Transportation, power, and water

The considerable argument over whether the PPB approach can quantify noneconomic benefits of government programs should not be allowed to obscure the fact that "economic" benefits are the rationale of many programs and activities. When this is the case, the PPB approach seeks to determine whether the economic objectives of the program are being achieved and whether the achievements relate reasonably to the economic costs of the program.

Government Contributions to Consumers

Not all government programs are related to production. Many programs provide, directly or indirectly, goods or services for ultimate consumption rather than for use in further production by business. For example, most of the functions of the Department of Housing and Urban Affairs concern the construction of dwelling units which ultimately provide shelter for consumers rather than offices or factories for business. The valuation of an item ultimately used for consumption is, as mentioned previously, simply a determination of the market price of that item (plus consumer's surplus) if a market price is available. Frequently, however, no such price is available. A variety of techniques have been suggested to determine the value or benefit of an item not sold on an organized market. These techniques are adequately summarized in the literature on cost-benefit analysis and will not be repeated in detail here. [4]

The concept underlying these techniques is that a governmental product or service is worth to an individual no more than he would be willing to pay for it. The value of a park, for example, is the lowest fee that would deter him from entering the park. If he would go to Yellowstone Park for any admission fee less than $2 but would decide the park was too expensive at $2.01, then for that individual the day in Yellowstone is worth $2. Determining how much people will pay for things when they are not asked to pay for them at all requires considerable ingenuity. Most of us don't really know what price increase would cause us to stop buying something and would not make such decisions until faced by real prices rather than a survey questionnaire. Nonetheless, it is possible to make reasonable inferences about consumer desire for goods and services so that benefits can be attributed to specific government outputs such as housing and parks.

THE POTENTIAL OF COST-BENEFIT ANALYSIS

Conceptually, the cost-benefit ratio is the best signal any analyst can provide to the political decision-maker. A cost-benefit ratio serves him in the same way that a profitability determination serves the private decision-maker. A cost-benefit ratio of greater than one-to-one says to a decision-maker, in effect, if you do this project or this program, the benefits to society as a whole will exceed the cost to society as a whole, and, therefore, society as a whole will be better off as a result of your decision. Such a clear and unambiguous piece of advice is certainly nothing to be scoffed at, even though achievement of it may be a long way off for many programs. If cost-benefit ratios could be applied to all governmental programs, we would reach the millennium where rational, sensible analysis controls decisions in the political process or provides sufficiently strong signals so that decision-makers would have to have very good political reasons to override what is shown by the data.

The potential beauty of the cost-benefit ratio is perhaps best illustrated in connection with multiple-purpose dams and reservoirs. The problem begins with several assets available for potential utilization: Land that, for lack of water, is not being used to produce useful crops; water that, without a dam, is flowing to the sea without releasing its resources of power; and money, a scarce resource, but one potentially available if its use can be justified. An engineer with a dream appears. The engineer says,

> Dam this canyon, put in generators to provide power for our mills and our homes, use the water backed up in a beautiful reservoir for boating and recreation, and further use it to irrigate our fields so that land will be green where now it is brown. Use the capacity of the reservoir to prevent the floods that have threatened our homes and our crops. Make the water above the reservoir available for navigation so that the products of our industry may move more cheaply. Finally, use the water in the reservoir for our plants and for

our municipal water supplies, and, when
pollution threatens downstream, release some
of the pure waters from the reservoir to dilute
the polluted ones and make them clean again.

All these dreams can be offered as justification for
many dams, yet, obviously, not all streams should be
dammed all of the time by dams of maximum height. How
can the choice be made? The answer currently used in
water resource agencies is reasonably simple. One seeks
to treat the governmental project as though it had to survive
in a simulated market place. The market place is simulated
because, for a variety of public-policy reasons, not all of
the outputs of the dam might be sold even though they could
command a price if a decision were made to sell them.
For example, access to the public's reservoirs is not
normally sold at as high a price as could be obtained for
it if the government chose to maximize profits from recreation operations. Nonetheless, it is legitimate to say that
the benefit from the reservoir is what people would be
willing to pay for using it, not necessarily what they in
fact will pay. Given this basic concept in cost-benefit
analysis, it is easy to see how a determination could be
made as to whether a dam in a particular location would be
worth-while.

The value of the electric power produced by the dam
would be the price individual electric power companies or
municipal power departments would be willing to pay for
it. The flood-control benefits of a dam can readily be
measured by the damage that would have occurred had the
dam not been built. The value of irrigation water is, at
maximum, the increase in the value of crops sold, which
results from utilization of the irrigation water to supplement water resources already available. The benefits from
municipal and industrial water supply are what the municipal
and industrial users would be willing to pay for it. For
existing users of such supplies, this means the lowest
price at which they could provide the additional water that
they need by wells, by trucking, or by smaller dams. For
potential new users of water supply, such as industries
moving into a region, the price may be the price to which
water supplies would have to drop in order to entice the
industry to move into the region. This price might well be

lower than the prevailing price in that region before a dam was built. The value of low-flow augmentation is somewhat more difficult to calculate. It is the reverse of the cost of pollution. If pollution has a measurable cost to the downstream users, then abating that pollution through low-flow augmentation has a benefit equal to pollution's cost in the watershed. Recreation benefits are essentially reflected by the willingness to pay of those who would use the facilities. Navigation benefits are readily reflected, but difficult to calculate, in the savings to existing transporters of goods and supplies by being able to ship to the navigation facilities involved plus the value to potential new users. All benefits can be stated on an annual basis or expressed in the form of a rate of return. If they are expressed as annual benefits, they may be compared to annual costs.

Turning to the cost side, the major cost component of a dam is construction cost. Construction and land-acquisition costs can be spread over a series of years (amortization) with interest (reflecting the opportunity cost of the money used for the dam) to indicate annual capital costs. To this, operating and maintenance charges can be added to derive an annual cost. *

The preceding discussion has considered benefits and costs without delving into the question of who gets the benefits and who pays the costs. Obviously, for most government programs, these two will be quite different groups. The benefits from the irrigation water, to the extent they are not recouped by user charges, will accrue to the farmer; the benefits from power, recreation, and navigation to the users. The benefits normally accrue to persons and businesses in the region where the project is being built. The costs, on the other hand, are spread over taxpayers as a whole.

Differences between who benefits and who pays are even more striking in certain other government programs

---

* This description is intentionally oversimplified; for greater detail, see the comprehensive studies of cost-benefit analysis of water resource projects cited in the notes to Chapter 12.

that have as their major impact the transfer of resources
from one group in society to another. Public housing and
welfare programs are examples. To reflect these differences, cost-benefit analysis can proceed in two dimensions.
The first considers economic efficiency from the standpoint
of society as a whole and measures benefits to whomsoever
they may accrue. The second, the one in which political
factors are more important, considers the geographical
distribution of benefits and burdens of particular programs
and projects and considers the types or classes of people
who receive the benefits and what they must do to receive
those benefits. If both the distributional aspects and the
allocative efficiency aspects are considered, it is possible
for cost-benefit analysis to indicate the full richness of
policy considerations that may go into the design of many
types of government programs and policies. It is for this
reason that cost-benefit analysis has so much potential to
assist the political decision-maker. Also, for the same
reason, cost-benefit analysis is more difficult to perform
than cost-effectiveness analysis.

SUMMARY

      Cost-benefit analysis differs from cost-effectiveness
analysis in that cost-benefit analysis gives dollar values
to both inputs and outputs. Such a method puts value judgments into the ground rules for analysis rather than forcing
the decision-maker to consider them in connection with
every program or project. It is most valuable where the
output of a government program is sold at market prices
or is an element entering into the production process. If
it is, then the measure of benefit (limited by alternative
costs of producing the same good or service) is the value
of production it causes to be added or the costs of production it saves. If the government good or service is designed
for consumption, its benefit is what persons would be willing
to pay for it.

      This formulation does not exhaust the alternatives for
cost-benefit analysis. Many government decision-makers
will value governmental outputs regardless of a person's

willingness to pay for them. Also, decision-makers will be concerned with the distribution of benefits and costs, perhaps more than with the absolute magnitudes of benefit and cost. These factors reduce the usefulness of cost-benefit analysis but to some extent can be handled by its techniques.

The chapter has sought to give the reader some idea of the methodology of cost-benefit analysis. However, it has not sought to develop rigorous proof of the benefit-measuring methodologies nor to consider the expanding discussion of the merits of various cost-benefit approaches. Readers concerned by these important questions will find many suggestions in the Bibliography.

NOTES TO CHAPTER 5

1. For a full discussion of this parallel, see Gary Becker, Human Capital: A Theoretical and Empirical Analysis (New York: Columbia University Press, 1964).

2. Examples of what can be accomplished with this approach are Frederick Harbison and Charles A. Myers, Education, Manpower and Economic Growth: Strategies of Human Resource Development (New York: McGraw-Hill, 1964); Selma Mushkin, Economics of Higher Education (Washington, D.C.: U.S. Office of Education, 1962), and Theodore W. Schultz, The Economic Value of Education (New York: Columbia University Press, 1963).

3. A sample of this approach is David A. Page, "Retraining Under the Manpower Development Act: A Benefit-Cost Analysis," Public Policy, Vol. 13 (Cambridge: Harvard University Press, 1964). Also Brookings Reprint 86 (Washington, D.C.: Brookings Institution, 1964).

4. See, for example, A. R. Prest and Ralph Turvey, "Benefit-Cost Analysis: A Survey," Economic Journal, LXXV (December, 1965), 683-735.

CHAPTER **6** PLANNING, PROGRAMMING,
BUDGETING, AND
ADMINISTRATIVE CONTROL

THE ROLE OF PLANNING

Planning has long been an activity of government and
private business organizations. It can provide a sense of
direction to an organization by informing employees of the
organization's goals and the general types of policies which
the organization intends to pursue to accomplish those
achievements. Planning is an integral part of goal-oriented
management; so long as goals are incapable of achievement
in the current year, planning will be required to inform
management of the potential to attain its goals and the
resources that must be committed to attain them. Planning
can serve all of these functions, yet historically in government it has failed to serve many of them. To understand
why, it is essential to know the uses of planning information
in government. In PPB terms, the objectives of planning
must be identified before criteria of accomplishment are
specified.

To some extent, planning is used on a contingency
basis. That is, plans may be drawn to determine what a
governmental activity will do if a particular event occurs.
For example, a contingency plan may be constructed for
civil defense authorities in the event of an enemy attack
on the United States. Such plans are the vehicle for deciding
and communicating how an agency will react when a stipulated
event takes place. They are most necessary when action
must be taken shortly after the event (e.g., reaction to an
enemy attack). These plans have the least influence on the
types of resource allocation with which PPB concerns
itself.

The plans having the most resource-allocation impact are those which specify the activities an agency intends to pursue over some future period. Such plans vary in content and detail. In general, their common elements consist of a forecast of the environment in which the agency will be operating, a statement of the objectives the agency intends to pursue, and a discussion of how the agency intends to go about pursuing those objectives and, in all probability, resources required to achieve the objectives.[1]

The plan has many important implications for budgetary decisions. Perhaps the most important of these in a military context and in some civilian contexts is the effect it has on the advance procurement of long lead-time items. If an airport is to be used in 1975, a certain amount of preconstruction planning must take place as early as 1970. A site must be acquired, preliminary drawings made, and production begun on complicated electronics equipment. Only by planning what will be used in the future can a decision-maker know what needs to be done now. Thus, the first major function of the plan is to signal the current budgetary decisions that must be made in order to realize future programs.

A second function of planning in government is to give an agency some idea of its future requirements for existing assets and for assets that can be acquired. For example, how large is the new building for the Federal Aviation Administration (FAA) to be? Obviously, it should not be exactly the right size to accommodate the FAA's current staff. Whether the building should be smaller or larger than that required to accommodate the current staff depends on whether or not the FAA will grow in the next twenty, thirty, or forty years, and if so, how much. An agency long-range plan can provide this information.

Planning is also important in consideration of the utilization of existing resources. If an agency has equipment no longer needed because the function it performed is no longer necessary, should it retire the equipment or should it keep it for future agency programs? The answer to this question depends on what the agency plans. To the extent that it can properly forecast its own needs, it will not waste storage funds on equipment it should have retired, nor will it retire equipment it should have kept.

Important program decisions depend upon the level of effort an agency plans to undertake. A good example is available in space programs and in other programs involving large-scale equipment procurement. In the space program, there is a requirement for launch vehicles. These vehicles are essentially missiles that take the "pay load" of capsules or satellites into the appropriate point in space. To a large extent, the launch vehicle used for one mission can be used for another; and, to a significant degree, for various types of missions, some launch vehicles are better and/or less expensive than others. How can the National Aeronautics and Space Administration exercise its choices among launch vehicles? How does it decide whether it is better to design and procure a new launch vehicle for a specific type of mission or to use existing vehicles with modifications? In these circumstances and in the procurement of military hardware, there is usually a degree of planned utilization where it is preferable to design equipment for one specific job. This occurs if planned utilization is sufficient to amortize the high costs of research, development, and production start-up for the item considered. Thus, for NASA to develop a special booster for certain types of communications satellites might make great sense if it planned to use such a booster 1,000 times but might seem foolish indeed if it only planned to use the booster ten times and could modify a more expensive booster-type configuration for use in the communications mission. Modifying expensive heavy boosters for the communications mission might be foolish when a less expensive vehicle could be designed for the specific mission and amortized over 1,000 flights. If the launch vehicle designers are given an erroneous impression of the number of planned launches, their choices will probably be wasteful.

Perhaps the easiest way to convey the importance of planning and the costs of poor planning is to cite the author's own experience in the planning of the military assistance program. During the late 1950's and early 1960's, the U.S. program of providing military hardware and services to our military allies was operating on a level of approximately $2 billion per year. During that period, military assistance was being planned on the basis of five-year projections of resource requirements and the weapons those resources would buy. The financial guidelines for making these plans

were substantially in excess of the resources later made
available during the period for which the plans were made.
As a result:

(1) Frequently items were held in inventory
to meet future military assistance program
requirements when in fact the items were
(for lack of funds) never refurbished and
used for military assistance and therefore
should have been disposed of at an earlier
time.

(2) Foreign governments were led to expect
more help than they got. The resulting
disappointments frequently had significant
foreign-policy repercussions.

(3) Decisions were made to re-equip military
forces over a fairly short period with
equipment of a new type. As resource
requirements exceeded the funds available,
the resulting replacement program caused
undesirable mixes of different equipment
with attendant maintenance and servicing
difficulties and extra costs.

(4) The hard choices about priorities were
made at the last minute to meet a budget
ceiling rather than in the context of long-
range plans. This meant that the long-
range plans themselves could not fulfill
one of their fundamental purposes--to
enable the administering agency to determine the future implications of current
hard choices.

This situation is not atypical in government planning
activities with no tie to realistic budget problems. The
PPB approach adopted within the federal government is
an attempt to avoid precisely such problems.

Planning also permits programs to be evaluated in
terms of where they lead. A decision-maker may be
offered a program to construct A or to do B. If that

program is part of an integrated whole, designed and planned
to be expanded in the future, it is desirable to know that fact
when the initial decision is made.

The potential contribution of planning to good management was not being realized in the Defense Department when
Secretary McNamara took over in 1961.[2] Extensive plans
were being made by each of the U.S. military departments,
the Army, the Navy, and the Air Force. These departments
planned on the basis of needs as they saw them. These needs
were substantially in excess of the resources President
Kennedy and President Johnson would have been prepared
to make available to the Defense Department. They also
exceeded what President Eisenhower was willing to commit
to defense. The disparities were enormous (plans were as
much as 50 per cent above the amounts made available by
the decision-makers), and these disparities were magnified.
There are certain continuing costs in military activities--
particularly the operation and maintenance of existing
equipment and the training, pay, and allowances of existing
personnel--and when these factors are taken as constant
costs, a 50 per cent spread between plans and reality meant
that in key procurement decisions, the disparity between
probable budgets and plans was nearly as great as the
probable budgets themselves.

Naturally, in such a context, erroneous recommendations were made. Recommendations were made for more
weapons systems of more specialized types which it was
assumed could be amortized because of the large number
called for by the plans. When procurement decisions were
faced in a realistic budgetary context, the result was
normally a stretch-out or a smaller buy than intended.
These resulted in sufficiently high costs for individual
weapons (such as the B-58) that it is highly unlikely that
production would have been authorized if funds available
for purchase had been accurately predicted. The problems
of planning without realistic assumptions about resource
requirements were magnified by the fact that, so long as
there was no need to relate what one wanted to do to the
resources available to do it, there was no incentive for each
military department to review the programs of the others.
In a planning context, the Army could have its divisions,
the Navy could have its carriers, and the Air Force could

have its manned bombers. The manned bombers did not
come at the expense of the carriers or at the expense of
the divisions, and increases in divisions did not cause
decreases in carriers or manned bombers. Under this
circumstance, the Joint Chiefs of Staff, by default, let key
posture decisions be made in the Office of the Secretary of
Defense. There, hard budgetary choices with tremendous
strategic implications were made at the last minute with
very little justification that could be understood by the
military planners and with dissatisfaction all the way around.

The PPB approach deals with the problems of unrealistic
planning in two major requirements: First, planning must
be conducted by officials responsible for the programs
ultimately to be carried out rather than by a specialized
staff of planners whose "plans" need not be considered or
reviewed by line managers; and second, planning must be
tied to budgeting.

THE BRIDGE BETWEEN PLANNING AND BUDGETING

The McNamara-Hitch solution to disparities between
planning and budgeting was to tie the two together in the form
of programming. A Five-Year Force Structure and Financial
Program, now called the Five Year Defense Program, was
used to make this bridge. This basic programming document,
and the management system which accompanied it, have
been described and evaluated in such a wide variety of books
and articles that extensive discussion here would serve no
useful purpose. [3]

Fundamentally, the Defense programming system was
characterized by:

   ...a plan, approved by the Secretary of Defense
      and changed only with his approval

   ...a budget, consisting of the first year of the
      five-year financial program

...realism, because the plan was tied to the
budget and both had been considered by the
Secretary of Defense

...orientation toward program choices, because
the categories were established to reflect
programs (e.g., strategic forces) rather
than inputs (military pay).

This system permitted decision-makers to relate desires
for added military capacity to what that capacity would cost.
The bridge between planning and budgeting certainly did not
solve all the problems of planning or budgeting in the
Defense Department. On the other hand, it did seem to
use the Joint Chiefs of Staff and military judgment more
often in the final decisions of what would be bought with the
current year's budget. It also provided an opportunity for
civilian authorities, such as the Secretary of Defense and
the President, to convey to military planners, at a time when
it would be of some use to them, some idea of probable
resource limitations.

So long as programming reasonably relates the budgets
expected to be available to the plans for use of resources,
it is unlikely that serious overestimates of resource requirements will occur. It is unlikely, therefore, that long lead-
time items will be bought when the final product will not be
procured or that procurement decisions will be made on the
basis of long production runs that will never materialize.

The guidance for planning-programming-budgeting in
the federal civilian agencies originally followed the defense
programming system closely. The Budget Bureau's October,
1965, Bulletin 66-3 provided that each agency was to have a
"Multi-year Program and Financial Plan." This plan was
originally to be comparable to the Defense Department's
Five-Year Force Structure and Financial Program in that
it was to reflect the agency head's hard decisions about
future actions. In the words of the Bulletin, the Multi-
year Program and Financial Plan was to "show the program
levels which the agency head thinks will be appropriate
over the entire period covered by the multi-year plan."
Under the Bulletin's guidance, agency heads were asked to
maintain McNamara-like control over forward planning:

The Program and Financial Plan, as approved
or modified by the agency head in conformity
with guidance received from the Bureau of the
Budget and the President . . . will form the
basis for the agency's budget requests. Therefore, it should not be changed except in accordance with a procedure approved by the agency
head.

For the civilian agencies, the U.S. Budget Bureau soon
retreated from this concept of the five-year programming
process. Bulletin 68-2 of July, 1967, provided new guidance
on a number of PPB subjects including the program and
financial plan. According to that Bulletin, "This projection,
therefore, is not designed to predict comprehensively future
budget totals for agencies or for major programs." The
Bulletin reinforced the point by indicating that the document

. . . is to show the implications of current
decisions and will not necessarily reflect
accurate estimates of agency budget totals
for the years beyond the budget year, because
it omits new programs not yet recommended
and fails to reflect program level changes,
including the termination of some existing
programs, decisions on which are not part
of the current budget cycle.

The rationale for this change was provided by Budget
Director Charles Schultze in testimony before a congressional committee:

When the chips are down, no President, no
Cabinet officer or Budget Director--or Congress for that matter--is really willing to
commit himself in advance to decisions in
1967 about the specific level of Federal programs in 1970 or 1972 . . . . And there is
no use pretending that we need make these
decisions before we have to--indeed, making
such decisions prematurely would be harmful.[4]

When considered in this fashion, the program can no longer
serve to keep planning realistic by bridging the gap between

planning and budgeting. Schultze told the same committee,
"As you might expect, the sum total of all the forward plans
of all federal agencies tends to exceed, by far, any reasonable
projection of available resources."[5] Thus, whether forward
programming of full costs is now a part of the PPB approach
depends upon whether Defense Department or civilian agency
practice controls the definition of "PPB approach."

PROGRAM BUDGETING

Whether the time horizon is one year or five, the PPB
approach insists on a concept frequently called "program
budgeting." The essence of program (or performance)
budgeting is that it seeks to relate costs to outputs, turning
attention toward what the program is about and away from
detailed breakdowns of input categories such as "pay" and
"supplies." The concept of program or performance budgeting is by no means a new one. Standard definitions of
the concept published in the 1950's sound very much like
what PPB practitioners are discussing today. For example:

> At a broad definitional level, performance
> budgeting can be most appropriately associated
> with a budget classification that emphasized
> the things which government does, rather than
> the things which government buys. Perform-
> ance budgeting shifts the emphasis from the
> means of accomplishment to the accomplish-
> ment itself. The kind of classification re-
> quired must therefore be very different from
> one based on objects of expenditure classified
> according to type. The object classification
> shows what government purchases but not
> why; accordingly, it does not show the nature
> of governmental programs or accomplish-
> ments under those programs. [6]

A widely used government finance textbook presents a
similar discussion:

In the last two decades, substantial interest
has developed in the performance approach to
budget organization, whereby emphasis is
placed upon the objectives to be accomplished,
rather than upon the items purchased, as such.
The budget is carried on; and in turn, each
program is broken down on the basis of the
performance of the agencies involved in its
accomplishment, in such a manner as to
facilitate measure of performance and ascer-
tainment of cost. Information about objects
acquired is presented in terms of their use
in accomplishing particular programs, not
with respect to the objects themselves, per
se. Thus, for example, at the municipal
level, the portion of the budget relating to
expenditure on streets is organized in terms
of miles of streets to be paved, to be repaired,
etc., rather than in terms of tons of gravel
and barrels of cement purchased, number of
men hired, etc., as such; data on these items
are presented in terms of their use in the
paving of a certain mileage of streets, etc.[7]

The report of the first Hoover Commission is an interesting and early precursor of the Planning-Programming-
Budgeting System. The Commission's recommendations on
budgeting are partially summarized in the Concluding Report
as follows:

In our report on budgeting and accounting we
suppose far-reaching changes in these areas.
In order to produce a budget plan which will
be a more understandable and useful instru-
ment, both to the President and to Congress,
we recommend that the budget document be
completely recast along the lines of work
programs and functions. Such a document
which we designate as a "performance budget"
would analyze the work of Government departments and agencies according to their major
functions, activities, or projects. It would
thus concentrate attention on the work to be
done or service to be rendered rather than

> on things to be acquired such as personal
> services, contractual services, supplies,
> materials, and equipment. A performance
> budget, moreover, would facilitate congres-
> sional and executive control by clearly show-
> ing the scope and magnitude of each Federal
> activity. It could also show the relationships
> between the volume of work to be done and
> the cost of the work, a measurement which
> cannot be made under the present system. [8]

This material is nearly identical in scope and approach
to the current justifications of program budgeting in the
PPB context.

In October, 1949, the Senate Committee on Expenditures in the Executive Departments (the predecessor of
the Senate Government Operations Committee) published
a document compiling the responses of federal departments
to the Hoover Commission reports. This document included
comments from the Bureau of the Budget on the general
performance budgeting recommendation as follows:

> The Bureau has for some time believed that
> the goal of a performance budget is desirable,
> and has already developed plans for achieving
> it. These plans require changes which are
> complex and affect most executive agencies
> and the Appropriations Committees. We hope
> that the 1951 budget will make a major stride
> toward a performance basis, and that con-
> tinuing action will be taken over a period of
> several years to accomplish the objective
> completely. [9]

The Senate Committee's compilation of steps taken by
agencies to comply with the Hoover Commission recommendations also included a comprehensive statement by the
Bureau of the Budget which indicated that compliance with
the performance budgeting recommendation was proceeding,
with neither a requirement for new legislation nor simul-
taneous requirements for change in appropriation titles.
This statement, presumably a press release, noted:

The President announced, in a message to
Congress on June 20 /1949/, that he had
instructed the Director of the Bureau of the
Budget to work out a system for preparing
budget estimates on a performance basis . . . .

The change which will be most noticed
in the 1951 budget . . . is the addition of
textual statements on program and performance . . . . The new budget will present
two plans: The financial plan, in tables and
figures, and the program plan, in narrative
style.

. . .

Where more than half of the appropriations in the past have not been accompanied
by any breakdown showing how the dollars
would be related to programs, it is anticipated that the new budget will break down
over 90 percent of the appropriations to
show the programs, projects, or activities
to be carried on and the dollars to be devoted
to each . . . .[10]

Performance budgeting was a key element in the 1949
controversy over the proper organization of the Department
of Defense. Out of the controversy came a section in the
National Security Act Amendments of 1949 providing for
performance budgeting in the Department of Defense and
authorizing the Secretary of Defense to reorganize budget
structures in order to implement the concept. The key
portion of the section stated:

The budget estimates of the Department of
Defense shall be prepared, presented, and
justified, where practicable, and authorized
programs shall be administered . . . so as
to account for, and report, the cost of performance of readily identifiable functional
programs and activities.[11]

In response to a request from the Senate Government
Operations Committee, the Defense Department in the

fall of 1959 (pre-McNamara) presented a summary of how
it had implemented this section. These departmental
comments described the new appropriation titles that had
been adopted and noted that "great progress" had been
made toward meeting the requirement of a budget relating
cost of performance to "readily identifiable functional
programs."[12]

The second Hoover Commission's task force on budgeting
and accounting reviewed the recommendation of the first
commission for "performance budgeting" and agreed that
the basic concept was sound. It recommended, however,
that the conceptual difference between the review of proposed
new programs and that of performance of previously authorized activities be emphasized by renaming the performance
budgeting concept "program budgeting."[13] The task force
concluded that the installation of performance budgeting in
the federal agencies had met with "varying degrees of
success."[14]

The PPB approach continues the emphasis on the development of meaningful program categories. Budget Bureau
Bulletin 68-2 requires the establishment of program categories that facilitate "analytic comparisons of the costs
and effectiveness of alternative programs." Actual program
categories for most government agencies are shown in an
attachment to the Bulletin. For illustration, the listings
within the education category are shown below:

(1) Development of basic skills and attitudes

(2) Development of vocational and occupational
skills

(3) Development of advanced academic and
professional skills

(4) Individual and community development

(5) General research

(6) General support

In the federal implementation of PPB, the program category
serves to provide a basis for the fundamental analytic
document--the Program Memorandum--as well as a framework for the program budget. By utilizing a variety of
coding schemes, it is possible to provide program information in program category terms and at the same time
not lose the identity of the group being benefited, the type
of financing, the agency administering the program, and a
host of other information. The Department of Health,
Education and Welfare has perfected an elaborate system
to record (and thus analyze) such information for its programs.[15]

The difference between what one is getting and the
categories in which one is getting it is an important one.
It is a useful improvement in budget information to know
that one is getting $100 million for improved teaching of
retarded children, rather than to know that one is getting
$100 million in salaries and wages and travel and trans-
portation for employees of the Office of Education. However,
the conjunction of an expenditure number with an objective
"improving the teaching of retarded children" does itself
not provide information on whether the activity is worth
the expenditure. For that reason, as noted in the discussion
of goal determination in Chapter 2, the PPB approach
demands that goals be sufficiently specific so that units of
accomplishment can be identified. Naturally, as the retarded
children example illustrates, selecting quantifiable measures
of valued outputs is no easy task.

Even if PPB cannot insist without exception on precise
output indicators, it can insist on the value of a search for
them. The premise of this approach is simple. Any decision-
maker who spends $100 million for education of retarded
children is using $100 million that could have been used for
private consumption (through lowered taxes) or for other
education programs, additional defense, etc. Under such
circumstances, he should be forced to think in some detail
about exactly what he believes the $100 million is buying,
so that higher decision-makers can consider what his $100
million will buy in relation to what other officials think that
$100 million would buy if spent on their program activities.

The ideal program budget provides indicators of ultimate output rather than intermediate products such as classes conducted, persons trained, or hospitals built. In ideal form, it would consist of association of a dollar estimate with an ultimate output. Thus: "The recommended budget includes $5 million to provide outdoor recreational experiences (an average of 7 hours per person) to 150,000 disadvantaged Americans who would not otherwise receive them" or "The budget recommendation is expected to save 100 lives per year which otherwise would be lost to scarlet fever." The PPB approach means striving for just such measures of program performance.

ADMINISTRATIVE CONTROL

The Planning-Programming-Budgeting System has had its origins in attempts to improve the way in which resource-allocation decisions are made in a budgeting context. The basic focus has been upon the process of making forward plans and programs and establishing budgets related to those plans and programs. The problems considered have been related to questions of how much to spend on what, and which programs to cut back (in a budgetary sense) and which to expand. These questions, while important, are by no means the only administrative problems of a government such as that of the United States.

Every day, administrators make resource-allocation decisions. A boss decides how to use the time of his staff. A resource manager decides who gets to occupy a building for a time period. Another administrator decides who gets a grant or a contract. These decisions are all considered administrative ones, but they obviously will ultimately control how well any budgetary amount is used to achieve its purpose. Basically, the outputs in the program structure, the benefits in cost-benefit analysis, and the effectiveness in cost-effectiveness analysis are merely predictions of the outcomes if certain sums are spent for certain purposes.

What a PPB approach must provide is some check to make sure that the predicted effectiveness does materialize if the recommended budget is made available. Also, the system needs a way of checking on its own prediction of effectiveness. Finally, administrators need all the ways available to ensure that their subordinates act in accordance with the basic purposes of the organization they serve. If benefits can be predicted and if effectiveness can be planned and designed into highways and weapons systems, it would follow that these could be measured after construction was completed and the program was in operation. If so, what better measure of employees' and agencies' performance could be found?

Thus, in the January, 1967, budget message, President Johnson suggested that the Planning-Programming-Budgeting System would assist in "evaluating actual performance" as well as perform the other functions indicated in previous chapters. In one sense, it is desirable to apply a system to actual performance as rapidly as possible, but, in another sense, that is not receiving first priority in government implementation of PPB. The reason is simple: One of the basic arguments for PPB has been that government objectives have not been clear. If objectives are not clear, it is difficult logically to fault an administrator for failing to act in conformity with them. Until measurements of output are developed for program planning, it would be difficult to hold administrators to them in program administration.

As might be expected, because programming has been in effect there for several years, application of the PPB approach to management problems is proceeding most rapidly in the Defense Department. The Department is seeking to provide management systems to implement President Johnson's Memorandum to Heads of Departments and Agencies on Financial Management, which stated:

> I want every manager to think of this part of
> the total Government in terms of everything
> he owns, everything he owes and the full cost
> of doing every job in relation to the products
> resulting from these costs. I want him to
> think of minimal costs and cost reduction as
> profit. And I want him to think in terms of
> his profits as a result of how he uses all the
> resources entrusted to him. . . . [16]

Consistent with this guidance, the Department of Defense has undertaken an extensive effort, called Project Prime, to improve resource management. The essence of this effort is to (a) relate more closely programming, budgeting, and accounting, (b) make managers more aware of the costs that they cause, and (c) hold them accountable for those costs in relation to performance and for performance in relation to plans and promises. The problems the Project seeks to cure are multiple. First, costs are not often signaled directly and unambiguously to actual managers. As Defense Comptroller Robert Anthony put it:

> We plan in careful detail by total costs, and by missions, as we should, but our field managers focus on only the 20% of the costs for which they are funded, and they have no way of relating these costs to results achieved. [17]

Merging the programming system with budgeting and accounting is a continuing problem in the U.S. Government. A Defense Department booklet issued in 1966 described the situation as follows:

> If programming is conducted within a mission structure, budgeting within an appropriation structure, and accounting and management within an organization structure--with no firm interrelationship among them--there is, at best, only an indirect way of actually tracking performance against plans. [18]

Project Prime is seeking to make managers aware of and responsible for more elements of cost by altering the budgeting system and by developing prices for goods and services (such as the time of military personnel) that often appear as "free" goods to particular activity managers.

SUMMARY

Planning plays an important role in the operation of any large organization. It can give the organization a sense

of direction, permit intelligent evaluation of the use of
fixed resources, allow procurement of long lead-time
items and commencement of long lead-time activities,
and permit intelligent decisions about choice of machinery,
weapons systems, and other items whose value depends
upon planned use. Planning permits decision-makers to
see the direction in which their decisions are leading them
and thereby to become more aware of the future consequences
of present decisions.

In government, planning may fall short of these objectives, because there is a tendency for planning to proceed
to "blue sky" assumptions about resources unless it is
firmly tied to resource implications at every stage of the
planning process. Programming can provide the bridge
between planning and budgeting to the benefit of both. The
long-range program becomes the vehicle for development
of the budget proposal, which is essentially the resource
implications of the first year of the longer-range program.

Under the PPB approach, both the budget and the program
need to be organized on the basis of program categories
reflecting valued outputs of government programs. When
organized in that fashion, they permit decision-makers to
consider all costs in relation to the purposes being pursued
by government. Further, PPB seeks measures of output
that can be directly related to increments of input. If these
can be discovered, they also permit the results of the PPB
approach to be used as an administrative tool, but this
application is just beginning.

NOTES TO CHAPTER 6

1. For detail on the planning function, see books such
as George A. Steiner, Managerial Long-Range Planning
(New York: McGraw-Hill, 1963); Harold Koontz and Cyril
O'Donnell, Principles of Management (2nd ed.; New York:
McGraw-Hill, 1959); and David W. Ewing, Long-Range
Planning for Management (Revised ed.; New York: Harper
and Row, 1964).

2. A good discussion of the problems is found in
Chapter II of Charles Hitch, Decision-Making for Defense
(Berkeley: University of California Press, 1965). My
comments, based on personal experience in the Office of
the Secretary of Defense, reflect the same conclusions
as Hitch's. This convergence, to use a bit of bureaucratic
jargon, shows that when the tribe is snafued, it's hard to
hide it from either the indians or the chief.

3. The Bibliography provides details. For those
unfamiliar with the Defense Department, Hitch's Decision-
Making for Defense is a good first exposure.

4. U.S. Congress, Senate, Committee on Government
Operations, Subcommittee on National Security and Inter-
national Operations, Hearings, "Planning-Programming-
Budgeting," op. cit., Part I, p. 22.

5. Ibid., p. 23.

6. Jesse Burkhead, Government Budgeting (New York:
Wiley, 1956), p. 133, and bibliography, p. 157.

7. John F. Duc, Government Finance: An Economic
Analysis (3rd ed.; Homewood, Ill.: Richard D. Irwin,
1963), p. 62.

8. U.S. Commission on Organization of the Executive
Branch of the Government, Concluding Report (Washington,
D.C.: Government Printing Office, 1949), pp. 14-15.

9. U.S. Congress, Senate, Committee on Expenditures
in the Executive Departments, Progress on Hoover Commission Recommendations, Report No. 1158, Eighty-first
Congress, 1st Session, 1949, p. 142. Most agencies indicated that they had implemented or were in the process of
implementing the performance budgeting recommendations.

10. Ibid., pp. 177-78.

11. Act of August 10, 1949, Public Law 216, Eighty-
first Congress, 63 Stat. 578, Sec. 403(a).

12. As quoted in U.S. Congress, Senate, Committee on Government Operations, Financial Management in the Federal Government, S. Document No. 11, Eighty-seventh Congress, 1st Session, 1961, p. 170.

13. This is the title of one of the "bibles" of PPBS-- David Novick (ed.), Program Budgeting (Cambridge, Mass.: Harvard University Press, 1965).

14. U.S. Commission on Organization of the Executive Branch of the Government, Task Force Report on Budget and Accounting (June, 1955), p. 27.

15. See its manual, "Planning-Programming-Budgeting: Guidance for Program and Financial Plan," (Office of the Assistant Secretary for Program Coordination, April, 1967).

16. Weekly Compilation of Presidential Documents, May 24, 1966.

17. "Strengthening Defense Management" (Speech delivered before the 1966 Naval Supply Conference in Harrisburg, Pennsylvania, May 4, 1966).

18. U.S. Office of the Secretary of Defense, A Primer on Project Prime (Washington, D.C.: Department of Defense, November, 1966).

CHAPTER **7** THE POTENTIAL OF THE PPB
APPROACH: AN EXAMPLE

The purpose of this chapter is to demonstrate the
potential of the PPB approach to improve government decisions. The example chosen--the provision of fire protec-
tion--is a relatively mundane government function, but
it provides a chance both to demonstrate an idealized model
of PPB and to provide a basis for the discussion, in Part II
of this book, of the difficulties in applying the PPB approach.
Naturally, the data used are fictitious, but comparable data
are, or could be, made available (at a price) to government
officials who make or recommend decisions about fire
protection. An entire chapter is devoted to this example
to show the usefulness and problems of PPB in a way abstract descriptions can never fully achieve.

THE SITUATION

The Gotham fire department was established in 1850,
when a group of civic-minded citizens realized that neighbor
help was no longer a satisfactory way to put out fires in
a growing city. The department established a fire station
in the center of town, purchased a horse-drawn hand pumper,
ladders, and other equipment. As Gotham grew and the
fire budget permitted, additional firehouses were constructed
to keep pace with population growth. Improvements in fire
equipment are continuously brought to the attention of the
Gotham department by salesmen for the equipment companies.
The city's firemen are in relatively frequent contact with
fire-protection officials in other cities, so that they have
a general familiarity with what are considered to be appropriate fire-fighting doctrine, training, and equipment.

The Gotham fire chief, who has in thirty years risen in the ranks from a private to chief, is intimately familiar with the department and its "needs." The budget he presents annually to the mayor and members of the city council looks something like this:

Operating Budget	Last Year	This Year
Pay of firemen: increase due to pay increase enacted by council last month and due to addition of nine men to man the C station which will be completed during the year	$2,000,000	$2,100,000
Contribution to retirement fund: reflects mandatory increase under state law	155,000	167,000
Maintenance of equipment	40,000	43,000
Operation of equipment (gas, oil, etc.)	33,000	33,000
Utilities for firehouses	25,000	26,000
Maintenance of firehouses	10,000	5,000
Purchases of training manuals, office supplies, etc.	12,000	13,000
Pay of nonuniformed personnel	20,000	20,000
Expenses of state training program for firemen	15,000	14,000
Expenses for fire chiefs' convention	2,000	2,000
Total Operating	$2,312,000	$2,423,000

Capital Budget	Last Year	This Year
Complete construction of C station	$ 150,000*	$ 50,000*
Purchase new hook and ladder type HT67B	--	90,000
Purchase new Model GA75E pumper (minus trade-in)	--	75,000
Purchase equipment for C station	10,000	100,000
Renovate main fire station	--	75,000
Construct D station north side		15,000**

* Not part of budget request; paid for out of proceeds from bonds issued previously.

** First year of a four-year project proposed to be funded from bond issue.

The mayor's budget review process consists of receiving submissions like these from each of the city's department directors. The requests are added together and the total compared to the revenues the tax or finance director estimates will be available from existing taxes and state and federal grants-in-aid programs. If revenue appears adequate to cover the requests, they are approved as long as they are "reasonable" (where "reasonable" means "bears a close resemblance to the prior year budget except for differences which can readily be explained"). If the total requests add to more than the revenues available, something must be cut. Through cabinet meetings, private discussions, and staff work by a budget office, the mayor seeks to get each department head to identify lesser priority items in his budget. If the department managers cooperate, the budgets are then reduced in areas they consider to be of lesser priority. If they don't cooperate, there is a good chance that they will be asked to absorb a cut of a fixed percentage, say 2 per cent, as best they can. Alternatively, the mayor, after deciding that his department managers

feel strongly about their budgets, may decide that a tax
increase is necessary.

The city council's review of the budget is likely to focus
on those items that are most readily changed and that do not
require great expertise to consider. These include firemen's
pay, the increased purchases of training manuals, and
specialized programs such as the fire chiefs' convention
expenses. All of these are highlighted by the manner in
which the budget is presented. Ultimately, the budget is
approved and implemented roughly along the lines submitted
by the fire chief, who will use the funds to put out fires and
prepare a comparable budget for the following year.

WHAT'S WRONG?

From the perspective of the PPB approach, this typical
budgeting process suffers from many serious deficiencies.
These are noted in the initial Budget Bureau Bulletin 66-3,
which established PPB in the federal government. The
Budget Bureau's citations of problems in that Bulletin are
presented below by subheadings.

"Program Review for Decision-Making
Has Frequently Been Concentrated
Within Too Short a Period"

In the fire department example, it is not clear that
any of the decision-makers (the fire chief, the mayor, and
the city council) would have done anything differently if
more than a short budget-review period had been available.
However, had other conditions and motivations been condu-
cive to analysis, they would have found themselves forced
to a relatively quick decision by their own budgetary process,
which does not raise major questions of operation except
in an annual budget review.

"Objectives of Agency Programs and Activities
Have Too Often Not Been Specified with
Enough Clarity and Concreteness"

Nowhere in the preceding description of budget review
did any party find it necessary to specify the objectives
of the proposed expenditures. "What's the problem in that?"
it can be argued, "Everyone but a simpleton knows that
fire departments exist to put out fires." Yet analysis of
the actual operations of a city fire department might well
indicate that not all of its budgets are used to fight fires.
The department, for example, may exist to prevent fires,
not just to extinguish them, and to rescue cats from tall
trees. There is no way of knowing in the process described
above whether the chief's objectives are what the council
and mayor might assume they are. The "operation of
equipment" budget could, for example, reflect costs for
(a) travel to open fire hydrants for children to play in the
water, (b) operation of equipment in parades to enhance
civic pride, and (c) the rescue, special service, fire-
protection and fire-extinguishing functions described above.
Not having known what the objectives of the budget were,
the mayor and council were in no position to review the
value of proposed fire department expenditures in relation
to other programs of the city.

"Accomplishments Have Not Always
Been Specified Concretely"

No participant in the Gotham situation could answer
the question "Is this budget adequate to achieve the objectives of the fire department?" because no objectives had
been specified in even the most general terms (e.g., provide fire-extinguishing services). Even if objectives were
available, no criteria relating fire performance to cost
were available for judging the performance of the fire chief
in doing what he said he would do with his budget. No one
in the process asked the fire chief to specify the added
protection (measured in response time or damage limita-
tion) to be afforded by the recommended new fire station.

"Alternatives Have Been Insufficiently Presented for Consideration of Top Management"

In the Gotham situation described, no alternatives were considered. The only changes considered were incremental changes to a budget that was itself an incremental change to a budget approved the prior year, which was itself an incremental change to a budget . . . , etc.

"In a Number of Cases the Future-Year Costs of Present Decisions Have Not Been Laid Out Systematically Enough"

In the situation described, future-year costs of present decisions are not specified at all. The result is that many of the costs in the annual budget are truly uncontrollable or controllable only in a legal sense, not in a practical political one. For example, the budget provides for the pay and retirement of firemen to man the C station being completed during the year. It is politically unrealistic to expect a mayor and council (much less a fire chief) to pay to have a fire station built and then refuse either to man it or to put equipment in it. Thus, the new hook-and-ladder truck and equipment in the capital budget and the firemen's pay in the operating budget are uncontrollable costs, for they were really decided upon when the council approved construction of C station. Were the costs considered in connection with the decision to build C station? Probably not. The sample budget suggests that a D station is to be constructed without full knowledge of the total system's costs associated with it.

"Formalized Planning and Systems Analysis Have Had Too Little Effect on Budget Decisions"

To make the example more vivid, the situation has been drawn to exclude all systems analysis and formalized planning. In actual fire departments, some planning for future equipment replacement and for additional stations

undoubtedly does take place. In addition, the very roughest
form of systems analysis probably is reflected in planning
the location of new stations. (We won't have any coverage
of the north side unless we build a new station; it takes 15
minutes to reach it from downtown.) However, unless
analysis is communicated to the mayor and council in their
review of the budget, it will be the priorities determined
by the fire chief, not those of elected officials, which will
control the systems analysis and planning.

MAKING IMPROVEMENTS

Defining the Objectives

The first prerequisite to the program budget, planning
and programming, and systems analysis is the identification of the objectives. The basic analytical problem is to
answer the question "What are fire departments for?" The
research methodology is simple. It involves seeking to
infer objectives from what the fire department is actually
doing (it is rescuing cats from trees, therefore, one of its
objectives must be saving pets; it puts out fires, so one of
its objectives must be putting out fires), from what fire
officials say they are trying to accomplish, and from what
civic leaders and decision-makers believe the fire department is set up to do. *

Such an exploration might indicate the following sets
of objectives and subobjectives for a city fire department:

(1) Minimize fire damage to persons and property

_____

* Working with the federal government is easier in this
respect, because Presidential and congressional statements
on policy are available in comprehensively indexed written
form as are reams of materials about what agencies are
trying to do and doing. At the local level, this information
is not so readily obtained.

(a) Prevent fires

(b) Where fires occur, minimize damage to persons and property

(2) Reduce death and sickness (mortality and morbidity) from accident and disease by providing first-aid services and rapid transportation to care centers by a rescue squad

(3) Provide incidental services to the city and its citizens made possible by specialized equipment and capabilities

(a) Opening fire hydrants for children's play

(b) Assisting in clean-up drives

(c) Providing ladder capabilities for rescue of animals and people

(d) Participating in parades

(e) Providing a source of high-pressure water for riot control

Identifying these objectives makes it possible for the city to consider alternatives to achieve these objectives and to develop the program budget.

Restructuring the Budget

The program budget is not a substitute for program analysis but can, by its very nature, offer inducements to general analysis by political decision-makers. Retaining the annual-cost concepts of the sample budget, the fire department budget could be restructured along these lines:

TO MINIMIZE FIRE DAMAGE TO
PERSONS AND PROPERTY

    Preventing fires
        Inspection for compliance
        with fire regulations
        Education campaigns
        Program of free fire inspec-
        tions for homeowners and
        businesses requesting it

    When fires occur, minimize
      damage
        Reporting system (fire alarm
        maintenance, switchboard,
        etc.)
        Fire fighting (here would
        appear detail on firemen's
        pay, retirement, etc., and
        equipment except for activ-
        ities appearing elsewhere)
        Education on what to do if a
        fire starts

TO REDUCE DEATH AND SICKNESS
FROM ACCIDENT AND DISEASE

    Provide first-aid services and
    rapid transportation to care
    centers by a rescue squad

TO PROVIDE INCIDENTAL SERVICES

    (showing only out-of-pocket incre-
    mental costs for these functions)

    Such a presentation of a fire department budget invites
meaningful questions and analysis from political decision-
makers.[1] The earlier budget format encouraged decision-
makers to look at such questions as "Why do you want to
send firemen for state training instead of training them
here?" and "Why is the utility bill going up?" The program

budget obscures these questions (which is, of course, something of a loss, for occasionally utility bills will get out of line) in order to bring to the surface the types of questions suggested by the sample budget: "Would we have to spend less on putting fires out if we spent more on prevention?" "Why is there no increase in our rescue service--our population is growing, isn't it?" These problem- and program-oriented questions may or may not in themselves bring forth meaningful analysis of functions and performance. What they will do is focus attention in the right place and encourage decision-makers to determine whether they are getting returns roughly proportionate to what they are paying.

Specifying Criteria of Accomplishment

Performance has not been measured by the program budget; that budget has only served to relate costs to the objectives of the fire department's programs. Accomplishment of the major objective of the fire department--minimizing fire damage to persons and property--can readily be measured in dollar terms. Because damage estimates are part of fire routine in many cities, it is not difficult to keep data on fire losses, or at least reported fire losses. An obvious criteria of accomplishment for a fire department is to minimize the property losses, deaths, and injuries from fire. Ideally, this would permit objectives to be stated quite specifically: "The objective for 196_ is to hold fire property damage in the city to not more than $500,000; minor injuries to not more than three; and loss of life to none." Formulation of such a precise objective would permit exact costs to be measured and would readily enable the city council to monitor the fire department's success during the year.

The attempt to formulate such a precise objective immediately raises two analytical problems. The first is whether any fire department or city council would ever settle for less than perfection (preventing all losses) as an objective. This political difficulty with the PPBS will be considered in Part II. Assuming that such an objective could be set, where should it be set? How much loss of

life and property is tolerable to a city council will depend
in part on how much it will cost to achieve increments of
life saving and property-damage reduction. That relationship can be understood only when increments of inputs
(firemen, trucks, alarm systems) are related to reductions
in fire losses. To develop such a relationship requires
a model for each alternative way to reduce fire losses.

Identifying Alternatives

There are many ways to spend $2 million annually to
minimize fire damage. Some of these alternatives might
not appear in the short run because the city has committed
itself to its existing system of firehouses and equipment.
Taking the long view, a wider range of alternative systems
of protection is available to the city. For the purposes of
practical analysis, one can take the existing situation as
indicating the general "ball park" for analysis and consider
either one of two questions:

(1) Given the assets currently available to the
fire department, plus a little over $2 million
a year indefinitely, what combination of
actions will produce the least fire damage
to persons and property?

(2) What combination of actions will provide
the current fire protection levels at least
cost?

Assuming that the current system is relatively efficient,
the answer to one question will not differ markedly from
the answer to the other, so either may be used in a practical analytical circumstance. If analysis were free, which
it clearly is not, decision-makers would be best served by
an analysis that provided the least-cost alternative for
every level of protection imaginable (a fully suboptimized
system). For purposes of illustration, such an analysis
is described later in this chapter.

In this example, the first question will be considered.
(PPB technicians will recognize this as an efficiency problem

of maximizing output from fixed inputs.) A nearly infinite
number of differing combinations of specialized and general
equipment, firehouse locations, shift plans, use of ancillary
personnel, fire prevention and education, etc., are possible.
In practical terms, the alternatives must be held to a
reasonable number, with changes in the mix among them
made in cases where the alternatives are not mutually
exclusive. Five alternative plans are shown below.

ALTERNATIVE A.   The existing system perpetuated. The
                 major elements of the system are a
                 few fire boxes downtown, minor pro-
                 tection and code enforcement activities,
                 geographically spaced firehouses with
                 regular fire-fighting units, shift manning,
                 certain specialized units deployed from
                 downtown.

ALTERNATIVE B.   A quick-response system, which sacri-
                 fices ability to fight a medium-sized
                 fire well underway in order to build
                 capability to combat fires while they
                 are small. The system is based on
                 the fact that all big fires that are hard
                 to put out begin as small fires that could
                 be easily extinguished. The standard
                 fire unit would have an inexpensive van
                 equipped with metal ladders, two men
                 constantly on duty, fire extinguishers,
                 and small bore hose. These cheaper
                 units would be deployed in garage-like
                 structures. The cheaper equipment
                 and reduced number of men per truck
                 would permit more stations and, there-
                 fore, cut the time lag between a fire
                 report and arrival of the first truck at
                 the fire. Where quick response fails,
                 back-up capacity would be available
                 from the existing heavier equipment
                 and specialized equipment downtown.
                 An education campaign would be con-
                 ducted to encourage (a) automatic
                 alarms in buildings, (b) quick calls
                 to the department for even the smallest

fires, and (c) learning the fire department's phone number. Because the
cost of responding to alarms (including
false ones) is much smaller, it may
also be possible to use more street
alarms.

ALTERNATIVE C.   A slower response system, which
                  sacrifices existing response capability
                  somewhat in order to provide a greater
                  capability to bring large specialized
                  equipment to bear. Instead, for example,
                  of striving for five-minute response to
                  at least 90 per cent of the population
                  with one truck and fifteen minutes for
                  additional equipment, strive for a
                  seven-minute response with the first
                  truck and additional trucks. Such a
                  system would rely on fewer, but larger
                  and better-equipped, firehouses.

ALTERNATIVE D.   A prevention-oriented system in which,
                  say, 20 per cent instead of 10 per cent
                  of the department's budget was devoted
                  to education and inspection rather than
                  direct fire fighting.

ALTERNATIVE E.   A cadre-reserve system, in which
                  full-time firemen would be utilized
                  to move equipment to the fire, while
                  additional firemen hired on part-time
                  or stand-by basis report on the call
                  of a dispatcher from their homes
                  directly to the scene of the fire.

Obviously, other alternatives could have been chosen.
Though the Gotham fire chief may not have made explicit
decisions about these alternatives in his budgeting process,
he does make such choices implicitly or let others make
them for him. He chooses Alternative A when he simply
expands his existing system to accommodate additional
population and changes in the characteristics of property
being protected. He moves toward Alternative B when he
chooses more smaller trucks and firehouses in preference

to fewer but larger trucks and firehouses. He moves toward
Alternative C when he makes decisions that are the reverse
of Alternative B. He moves toward Alternative D when
deciding to devote more of his budget to prevention. He
decides against any version of Alternative E when he continues
a rotated-shift system using only full-time firemen. The
question is not whether he will make the decisions. He will.
The question is whether he will consider all relevant alternatives in making those decisions.

Developing Models

To choose intelligently among these alternatives, the
fire department must have some idea of how each of them
would contribute to the objective of minimizing property
and personal loss from fire.[*] This can only be accomplished by building models that relate inputs of men and
equipment to outputs of damage prevention. Such models
must be based upon an understanding of the underlying
phenomena (fire and its causes) and upon an understanding
of the interaction of the various fire prevention and control
programs and those phenomena. Frequently, scientific
evidence is insufficient to permit models to be constructed

---

[*] By this point in the fire discussion, alert readers
will have thought of numerous problems in the procedure.
They are reminded that the discussion is intended to show
only the potential of the approach. Whether the potential
can be realized in a governmental context is the question
addressed in Part II. Also, this chapter is not designed
to demonstrate expertise in fire protection. Someone more
familiar with fire protection than the author could design
more attractive alternatives and produce a better discussion
of the model. Also, it should be added to the caveats,
elaborate analysis, even if undertaken for a group of cities,
has its costs. On the other hand, it should be recognized
that engineers design factory complexes and in the process
make decisions about the relative mix of fire fighters,
specialized equipment alarms, hoses, sprinklers, etc.,
which involve many of the same considerations being discussed here.

with great confidence. However, in many fields, the absence
of models is as indicative of a lack of demand for them as
a lack of ability to construct them if demanded. The model
shown below, which relates response time to damage,
shows what can be done. It is similar to an analysis of
arrest percentages in relation to response time recently
conducted for the President's Crime Commission.[2]

The phenomenon of fire differs in its impact and actions
(spread, speed, etc.) in various types of structures under
various weather conditions. Ignoring the very sophisticated
(but available) techniques for handling variations in operating
conditions and structure types within a category of structures,
it should be possible to relate response time to damage for
"average" conditions and structures. For example, in
single-family detached dwellings, a key variable affecting
the damage done by fire will be the speed with which it is
detected. A second key variable will be the speed with
which the fire department can respond to the call giving
the information about the fire. Dealing only with average
fires and average detection times, there is presumably
general agreement that the faster a fire department can
respond, the less property damage and personal damage
will occur. The question is how much less. A study might
indicate that the relationship is roughly that shown in
Figure 1. Of course, property damage will not be a function
of response time alone.[*] It will also depend upon the quality
of response made--the versatility and quantity of equipment,
the training of the firemen, and the water pressure and
chemical agents available. All of these inputs can be
translated into dollar costs. Fire losses also depend upon
actions taken to prevent fires, as well as on action to put
them out once they have started. Thus, a model of the
relation between prevention activity and loss prevented
is also needed in order to compare these two approaches.

----

[*] Even to the extent that property damage is a function
of response time, the relationship may differ from area to
area within a city depending upon (a) the value of property
being protected, (b) the potential for spreading, and (c) the
degree to which particular types of buildings and contents
(which differ in the need for quick response) are found in
the area. These complicate analysis but do not alter any
basic principles.

FIGURE 1

DAMAGE IN RELATION TO RESPONSE TIME
AVERAGE SINGLE-FAMILY DETACHED DWELLINGS

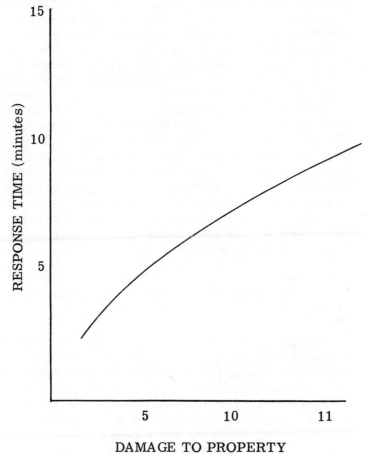

DAMAGE TO PROPERTY
($ thousand)

If such models can be constructed with reasonable certainty, it will be possible to construct a "best" alternative for fire protection for every level of effectiveness (loss prevented). The problem--which is comparable to that of an airlift-sealift study conducted for the Defense Department (described in Chapter 8)--is to find the combination of inputs that most economically results in the desired level of output. Using a linear programming method, this can be accomplished by what amounts to a number of successive substitutions. Given a starting point (any of the assumed alternatives), the question is asked: May costs be cut without reducing effectiveness if, say, additional protection effort is substituted for an increment of the fire prevention program? Desirable substitutions of this type are made until no more substitutions can be found which result in reduced costs for a given level of effectiveness. If such calculations were made for each level of potentially desirable fire department activity, the city decision-makers can be presented with a wide choice of potential levels of fire department activity. They will be able to consider these choices with full knowledge of the costs associated with each, assuming that the model and the costs associated with each input have been calculated reasonably accurately.

Can Decision-Makers Get By Without Models?

Inventing alternatives and developing a model in the manner just discussed is unquestionably difficult. It can be, and is, argued that the work is unnecessary, that expert judgment can provide the proper recommendation in circumstances such as this. The contention is demonstrably false. Behind every expert judgment about the appropriate level of a public service there lies a model. The PPB approach does not create the need for a model; it just brings models out into the open where they can be reviewed. The following dialogue is designed to reveal the hidden model.

COUNCIL MEMBER: I assume that in preparing this budget you have based your recommendations on careful consideration of the marginal efficiency of using personnel and funds in fire prevention as against using them in fire fighting.

FIRE CHIEF: I have done nothing of the sort. My budget is based upon my training in fire protection and my thirty years in the department. I know the city's fire protection needs and have recommended this budget to meet those needs within the funds available to me.

COUNCIL MEMBER: Do you have firemen assigned permanently to fire prevention?

FIRE CHIEF: Yes, out of the 300 firemen we have two permanently assigned to going around to schools and civic clubs to make talks on fire hazards. They also make inspections when requested. We supplement that with off-duty firemen who volunteer for it.

COUNCIL MEMBER: Have you thought about assigning two more men to fire prevention duties?

FIRE CHIEF: Yes, but my budget isn't big enough.

COUNCIL MEMBER: Why don't you request an increase in your budget for that purpose?

FIRE CHIEF: I think it would be turned down, or someone would approve the idea but tell me I had to pay for it out of my normal budgetary amount.

COUNCIL MEMBER: If you could show that the two new men could significantly reduce the number of fires, I don't think you would have trouble getting money for them. Let's assume you're right, though. Why don't you take two firemen off station duty and put them on fire prevention work?

FIRE CHIEF: That would reduce our fire-fighting capabilities.

COUNCIL MEMBER: So what?

FIRE CHIEF: So we would have greater losses from fires, that's what. Certainly you don't want that.

COUNCIL MEMBER: Why would you want two more fire prevention men if you could get the money?

FIRE CHIEF: Because I think they would help us prevent fires.

COUNCIL MEMBER: That is, they would help reduce fire losses in the city, right?

FIRE CHIEF: Right.

COUNCIL MEMBER: So, taking any two men in the department, if you assign them to fire fighting, they will cut fire losses, and if you assign them to prevention, they will cut fire losses. Put another way, you could take the two men now on prevention and put them on fire fighting, thereby letting more losses happen for lack of prevention efforts but avoiding some losses because you have better fire-fighting effort. Or, the other way around, you could put two more men on prevention, thereby preventing more fires (and thus fire losses) but increasing some losses because your fire-fighting ability isn't as good.

FIRE CHIEF: I guess that's right, though I've never really thought about it that way.

COUNCIL MEMBER: It seems to me that you have to think about it that way, otherwise how can you justify assigning two men to fire prevention instead of only one, or three?

FIRE CHIEF: No one but you has ever asked me to justify how I divide my men among prevention and fire fighting.

COUNCIL MEMBER: If two men will prevent fire losses whether assigned to prevention or fighting fires, how do you decide where to put them?

FIRE CHIEF: Obviously, you put them where they are needed most.

COUNCIL MEMBER: That is, where they will make the greatest contribution to minimizing fire losses?

FIRE CHIEF: Yes.

COUNCIL MEMBER: And how do you know where that is?

The answer to the council member's final question must be either that the chief doesn't have a basis (e.g., that he can't defend his existing table of organization and will admit it) or a model comparing inputs in prevention and fighting in terms of how they affect fire losses. Thus, either the choice is purely arbitrary (one decision is as good as another) or it is based upon some sort of a model, no matter how carelessly it might have been considered. Part of the PPB approach is to encourage the recognition of implicit models and to force experts into more careful consideration of what they are spending money for in relation to what they are trying to accomplish.

Calculating Costs

Detailed discussions of cost analysis have not been a part of this discussion of fire protection alternatives. Nonetheless, for the benefit of the more technical reader, it should be pointed out that interesting questions of interest rates and opportunity costs in the use of assets (such as exist in firehouses) all enter into detailed consideration of costs.

For all readers, it should be noted that minimizing damage from fire is accomplished through more budgets than simply that of the fire department. The fire-fighting function calls upon police budget support to handle crowds and redirect traffic. Normally, fire department budgets do not include bills from the city water department for fire fighting. Also, fire prevention may take place through the development of more strict building codes (e.g., requiring more electrical outlets and heavier wiring, thereby reducing the chances of electrical fires) or more stringent requirements placed on builders (e.g., a requirement to install more hydrants in new developments).

Finally, it may be noted that decreases in fire department spending might not be matched by an expected increase in fire damage. This could occur if private avoidance and mitigation actions were taken by business (automatic sprinklers, private fire-fighting capability in large plants, increased use of fire doors and fire lanes in warehouses,

more extinguishers, and improved alarm systems). From
a national perspective, all of these costs are as relevant
to the decision as fire department costs themselves. From
this perspective, it would be false economy, for example,
to cut back fire department activity by $50,000 with the
knowledge that damage wouldn't increase significantly
because private parties would take actions costing them
$75,000 to obtain equivalent protection. Likewise, from
the national point of view, if a community values added
fire protection from a new $50,000 hook-and-ladder truck
at $30,000, it should not buy it. This is true whether it
is considering a $50,000 expenditure for a $30,000 value
OR IF IT IS CONSIDERING A $25,000 EXPENDITURE FOR
A $30,000 VALUE WITH THE REMAINDER PAID FOR BY
A FEDERAL GRANT.

Local decision-makers may not see things this way,
however. The fire chief may look at his small budget,
compare it with the tremendous resources of a corporation with a plant in his town, and decide that it wouldn't
hurt if the corporation spends a little more for its own
protection. The city council may see the obvious advantages
of using $25,000 of local money to get $30,000 of local
benefit.

Selecting the Level of Expenditure

Assuming that the models discussed above had been
developed and the inputs costed, decision-makers would
have sufficient information to permit an informed and rational judgment about the appropriate level of fire protection expenditures. That level might be well above or considerably below the level submitted in a budget based upon
tradition, habit, and incremental increases. In the case
of fire protection expenditures, where costs and many of
the benefits would be expressed in dollars, the range of
reasonable choice would be limited. In other words, given
the facts, all political decision-makers would probably
agree on approximately the same answer. In the case of
the rescue service, this might not be the case, for the
range of judgment is greater. Rescue services primarily
protect life, while fire services have a major property

protection component.   Decision-makers can be presumed
to be more interested in economic reasoning when property
is at stake than when people are at stake.

Figure 2 shows what can be produced by the PPB
approach if everything goes well.   It relates fire losses
and total fire costs to differing levels of prevention expenditures.   The greater the fire protection effort, the smaller
the fire losses, as the figure indicates.   However, as more
and more funds are used, the marginal efficiency of additional expenditures in preventing losses goes down.   According to the hypothetical estimates in Figure 2, an increase
in protection expenditures from $0.1 to $0.2 million (a
$100,000 increase) would cause a decrease in fire losses
from $1.5 million to $1.2 million (a $300,000 saving in
loss).   However, increasing fire prevention and protection
expenditures from $1.0 million to $1.5 million would only
prevent $100,000 in fire losses.   Such diminishing returns
are typical of many governmental programs as well as
private investments.   If the residents of Gotham were not
responsible for taxing themselves to pay for the fire department, they would prefer the highest level of fire protection
attainable.   As they are taxpayers as well as potential
sufferers of fire loss, their representatives in council
should be attracted by the level of fire department expenditures that makes the total cost of fire as low as possible.
Ignoring the protection of life for the moment, that criterion
would indicate a level of protection of $400,000, which would
hold fire costs (the fire department budget plus fire losses)
to about $1.3 million, the lowest possible amount.

The potency of the PPB approach does not end when
economic costs of fire protection have been related to
economic gains from prevention of monetary loss but can
also develop useful information on loss of life and personal
injury due to fire.   Considering loss of life alone for sim-
plicity, Figure 2 provides the basis for calculating the net
costs of increasing expenditures on fire protection.   From
a social point of view, it is incorrect to assume that increasing
fire expenditures from $0.4 million to $0.5 million (in order
to save lives) would cost $100,000.   Instead, the net cost
of the increase is the increase in protection costs minus
the reduction in losses caused by that increase.   In Figure 2,
that net is shown graphically by the vertical distance between

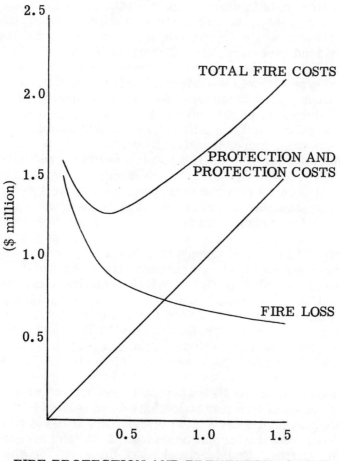

FIGURE 2

THE COSTS OF FIRE

FIRE PROTECTION AND PREVENTION COSTS
($ million)

society's lowest fire cost point ($1.3 million) and the total
fire costs. Thus, the net cost of increasing fire department
expenditures by $200,000 from $0.4 million to $0.6 million
is $100,000, not $200,000. It is this net cost which must
be considered in determining whether additional fire expenditures are desirable to help prevent loss of life. Assuming
the existence of a model that relates fire protection inputs--
and thus costs--to life saving just as another model related
those inputs to property saving, the PPB approach would
lead to the information conveyed by Figure 3.

   Figure 3 suggests that additional fire costs (expenditures
on protection plus losses) can purchase life saving when the
costs appear in the form of increased fire department expenditures. However, the costs of saving lives obviously shoots
up when nearly complete protection against death from fire
is sought. Again, the situation can best be viewed incre-
mentally--which has been done by providing a smooth, continuous curve. The incremental cost of saving the first
one-half life (one life every two years) appears to be about
$20,000. The second one-half life, if Figure 3 is correct,
could be saved for around $30,000. The third half-life
would be salvageable for about $70,000, and the figure
indicates that about $100,000 would be required for the
fourth half-life. Given this information, the Gotham city
council can increase or cut the fire department budget
with full knowledge of the impact of its actions.

   This procedure places a price on human life. So does
any other procedure that denies all the money a fire department could productively use to improve its chances to save
lives. Because every fire department in the United States
could improve its life-saving capability with more money,
every city council in the nation is putting a price on human
life by saying that we won't or can't give you more money
than your current budget. Whether putting a price on human
life is desirable is a false question. The true question is,
when decisions are taken that assume a value for human
life, is it better for decision-makers to know what they are
assuming or not? The PPB approach insists that these
determinations be brought to the surface. The main reason
why such implicit values need to be brought to the surface
is that it is more, not less, compassionate to make these
decisions explicit.

FIGURE 3

ADDED FIRE COSTS RELATED TO LIFE SAVING

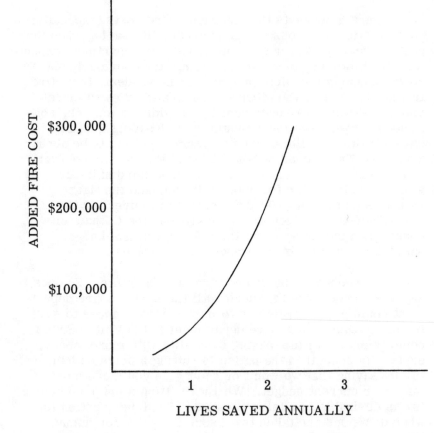

Assuming the accuracy of the underlying analytical models, even a city council could expect to improve its decisions by such explicit analysis. Suppose, for example, that the city decided on the fire protection budget that implicitly valued a human life at $70,000. Now suppose that, with analysis and models the council believed, other department heads reported budgets to the council that, at the margin, placed other values on human life as follows:

Building code (reduce chance of death from gas explosion by requiring special automatic shut-off devices)	$100,000 per life saved
Rescue squad (get patients to hospital more quickly)	$ 25,000 per life saved
Health department (innoculations for children's diseases to under-privileged children)	$ 2,000 per life saved
Street department (eliminate grade crossings)	$ 3,000 per life saved

Even ignoring the building code requirement (which calls for expenditures out of private rather than government budgets), if the council had this information, it could save twenty times as many lives by investing in health or eliminating grade crossings as by increasing fire expenditures. A compassionate decision to save lives by transferring funds to the street department cannot be made, however, unless the life saving is priced explicitly.

A Second-Best Solution

Analysis need not be complex, and analysts themselves, even the most ardent PPB advocates, will concede that the decision to undertake analysis is itself subject to analysis. There is no point in spending half a million dollars trying to save ten thousand. In general, a little analysis, no matter how quickly or cursorily performed, is probably better than none, particularly when it is likely that after

analysis the decision-maker will feel (correctly) less dog-
matic about the value of past practice than before he undertook analysis. Even if the fire chief does not perfectly
evaluate the relative efficiency of expenditures on fire
prevention versus fire fighting, an advance has probably
been made if he at least thinks about the subject. Likewise,
if council members and citizens are alert to the possibilities,
they can approach analysis on a much less sophisticated
level. To provide an example:

> Most of our citizens are covered by fire insurance.
> So as far as property damage is concerned, we
> are more interested in property insurance rates
> than with the property losses themselves.
>
> Insurance rates depend in part on how the
> fire protection available meets underwriting
> standards. The better our fire protection, the
> lower the insurance rate. I have learned from
> my insurance agent that our town could improve
> its underwriting rating one whole class just by
> buying a pumper and keeping it in operation.
> To improve our rating beyond that would involve
> making our fire department full-time and
> installing many new hydrants.
>
> On the basis of tax records, the value of
> property in our town is about $50 million. Of
> this, the land that can't burn probably accounts
> for $15 million, leaving $35 million of property
> subject to fire losses. Fire and casualty in-
> surance costs about one thousandth of the prop-
> erty insured. This means that our total in-
> surance bills are probably about $35,000 each
> year.
>
> We can buy a pumper and keep it opera-
> tional for less than $3,500 a year, assuming
> that we could amortize it over fifteen years.
> Buying it would up our rating one notch, which
> would reduce our insurance bill by 10 per cent,
> or $3,500. To take the next step, a full-time
> fire department, would cost lots more than
> $3,500 a year, but would only save $3,500 by

another improvement in our rating with the insurance companies. So, let's buy a pumper, but no more.

SUMMARY

This chapter has described the application of the PPB approach to a hypothetical situation, the Gotham City Fire Department's budget and activities. Its purpose was to show that substantial improvements in decision-making can be made by openly and explicitly analyzing alternatives, considering full costs, doing incremental analysis, and developing appropriate models. The chapter ended with an example designed to show that the PPB approach is by no means available only to deal with expensive problems and sophisticated audiences. PPB incorporates many of the elements of rational thinking long ago adopted by many who have never heard of anything called a Planning-Programming-Budgeting System.

Applied in any practical context, the PPB approach is bound to encounter data problems, constraints, and limitations on the analysis that can be made within the time and resources available. However, in evaluating the approach, it is important to consider the right question--not whether PPB can be applied to a fire department in a way that will satisfy all firemen, politicians, economists, public administration specialists, and taxpayers simultaneously, but whether incremental changes toward the type of analysis reflected in this chapter are worth their costs.

NOTES TO CHAPTER 7

1. The premise of the PPB approach is that (a) any decision-maker should consider such questions and (b) even if the fire chief or any program manager uses the approach in reaching his own recommendations, decision-making will

be improved if he also presents those recommendations in
a form useful to other decision-makers. However, it is
possible to implement the PPB approach in deciding on what
budget to recommend but use an older input-based budget
to present those recommendations for legislative approval.
This is exactly how PPB is being implemented in federal
government departments in the United States, a situation
reflected in Bulletin 68-2's requirement for crosswalks to
permit conversion of program structures into appropriation
structures.

2. Institute for Defense Analyses, "Police Operations--
The Apprehension Process" (Task Force Report to the
President's Commission on Law Enforcement and Adminis-
tration of Justice), Science and Technology, Ch. 2.

CHAPTER **8** PROGRAM ANALYSIS
IN ACTION

One of the easiest ways to consider the potentials and
limitations of the PPB approach is to examine what happens
when it is applied to actual situations. This chapter selects
some examples of successful program analysis and provides
brief descriptions of their methodology and conclusions.

The first series involves cases where the value of the
output was not translated into dollars, although the costs
were expressed in dollar terms. Using the nomenclature
discussed previously, these are examples of cost-utility or
cost-effectiveness analysis. The outputs considered are
movement of men and materiel, lives saved, bombs on target, shelter, and urban transportation. The second series
involves pricing of both inputs and outputs in dollars. These
cases are cost-benefit analyses as we have defined the term.

COST-EFFECTIVENESS ANALYSIS

Airlift and Sealift

On December 21, 1965, the Secretary of Defense (Robert
S. McNamara) sent a memorandum to the President request-
ing approval of a comprehensive program of airlift and sealift forces for the period fiscal 1967 through fiscal 1971.
This memorandum (excluding classified material) and the
material supporting the recommendations were circulated
to government agencies by the Bureau of the Budget as an
example of good program analysis.[1]

The analysis begins with a discussion of the various
concepts of rapid force deployment and varying degrees of
risk, flexibility, and "spill-over effects" associated with
choices of deployment methods. * The analysts set as the
objective "the restoration of the status quo ante following
an attack on some allied nation." This could be achieved
by any one of three strategies: (a) getting large forces to
the scene very quickly (these concepts of "large," "scene,"
and "quickly," of course, have quantitative values attached
to them in the study), (b) choosing a median route between
rapid deployment and slower deployment of larger forces,
and (c) letting the enemy get all but major population centers
and then counterattacking. The costs of the alternatives to
restore the status quo after attack were measured as:

> (a) The peacetime cost of owning the rapid
> deployment capability; (b) the peacetime cost
> of owning the combat forces; (c) the actual
> out-of-pocket costs of fighting the war; (d)
> the duration of the resultant conflict; (e) the
> casualties suffered by both the indigenous
> forces and our own; and (f) the land and its
> assets--human, material, political and
> psychological--lost during the campaign. [2]

The analysis of these alternatives was performed by a group
(presumably military) reporting to the Chairman of the Joint
Chiefs of Staff. They studied what would happen if each of
these alternatives were used in specific situations, namely
enemy invasions of Korea, Iran, and a Southeast Asian
nation. Their analysis indicated that strategy b was about
three times as expensive, and c about six times as expensive, as strategy a, the rapid-deployment strategy. These
conclusions lead to an objective for the transport capabili-
ties--namely, to provide deployment capabilities consistent
with strategy a.

Because the initial portion of the airlift study illustrates
vividly some of the limitations of cost-effectiveness analysis,

---

* These descriptions are not intended to repeat all the
nuances of analysis. Therefore, they omit such important
points as treatment of uncertainty and sensitivity analysis.

these will be emphasized here. First, the study does not
tell a decision-maker whether Iran will be attacked at all,
nor whether he should come to its aid if it is attacked, nor
whether if he does come to its aid he should seek to restore
the status quo ante instead of settling for a truce along a
different line. Second, the study presumes that U.S. response to an attack in Iran would not involve full-scale
nuclear retaliation upon the attacker (presumably the Soviet
Union). If the decision-maker plans a massive nuclear
response to a Soviet attack of this type, the airlift-sealift
study will have produced incorrect answers. Third, small
gradations of response were not considered; in the actual
analytical process only three major strategies were considered. This follows from the fact that to work out each
presumably required that a complete war be fought on the
drawing boards--a time-consuming task indeed. These
comments underline the significance of continued dialogues
between the planner or analyst and the decision-maker.

Detailed logistic requirements associated with strategy
a were not reported in the unclassified study, no doubt
because of both security and space restrictions. In their
most detailed form, these requirements were probably
expressed as lists of required deliveries (e.g., one M-47
tank delivered to Port X at mobilization day plus one). The
objective of the military airlift-sealift system could then
be considered to be to deliver the specified men and materiel
within the specified time to the specified locations. Phrased
this way, the objective is a fixed one, and the problem is
simply to find the least-cost way to produce the fixed output.
Thus, the airlift-sealift study is a search for "economy"
as defined in Chapter 4. Considered as an economy problem,
it is similar to that of a freight manager for a manufacturing
company trying to figure out how best to get his product to
market. The traffic manager's alternatives include locating
warehouses close to markets (the military equivalent of
which is pre-positioning), air transport (airlift), and slower
methods (sealift in the military case, presumably train or
truck in the civilian case). Complications are introduced
by uncertainty and the capability to buy one's own transport.
The solution to the economy problem, as formulated, included procurement of a new transport aircraft (C-5A) and
Fast Deployment Logistic Ships.

Defense Against Ballistic Missiles

Throughout the 1960's, a controversy has raged over whether the United States should deploy an antimissile missile system. Such a system would have possible usefulness in three contexts--first, in protecting U.S. offensive striking forces against an attack launched by the Soviets; second, in protecting the U.S. population against an attack from China; and third, in protecting the U.S. population against an attack from Russia. In his 1967 "posture" statement before the Senate Armed Services and Senate Appropriations Committee, Defense Secretary McNamara presented an analysis of these alternatives. [3] For present purposes, only the mission of protecting the U.S. population needs to be considered.

McNamara's basic position was that the Soviet Union feels a "requirement" for a given (fixed) level of "assured destruction capability" of the United States just as the United States feels the need for a comparable capability vis-à-vis the Soviet Union. Therefore, he argued, any deployment of antiballistic-missile missiles by the United States would be met by Soviet deployments of increased offensive capabilities to compensate exactly for, and thereby make worthless, the increased U.S. defensive deployments.

However, he presented to Congress a detailed analysis of the impact of decisions other than the one which he recommended. Stripped of its caveats and qualifications (which are important for an understanding of the ballistic missile defense question, but not for an understanding of the general cost-effectiveness approach), this analysis accepted, arguendo, the assumption that the Soviets would not change their offensive deployments to react to improved U.S. defenses. Three basic defense structures were chosen: (a) the "approved" program, which in essence was no special ballistic missile defense force, (b) "Posture A," which represented a general area defense of the continental United States and selected "point" defenses of cities, and (c) "Posture B," which was composed of the "area" defense of Posture A, plus point defense of twice the number of cities. Given the earliest operational date of Posture B (again ignoring caveats), the McNamara statement presented the following estimates, for a Soviet first strike, collected here from two separate charts.

Program	Investment Cost ($ billions)	Operating Cost ($ billions)	Effectiveness (millions of U.S. fatalities)
Approved Posture	xxx	xxx	120
Posture A	9.9	0.38	40
Posture B	19.4	0.72	30

This table is a good example of the results of a cost-effectiveness study. The output (change in fatalities) is quantified and related to different levels of dollar input.

Air Base Selection

One of the earliest Rand Corporation defense studies to receive widespread attention centered on developing the optimal base structure for use by U.S. strategic bomber forces in the 1950's and early 1960's. [4] The purpose (objective) of the bombers and the bases was clear--to maximize damage to enemy targets. For the purpose of the exercise, these targets could be identified. The questions for analysis were what mixes or choices were appropriate among (a) flying one-way missions--letting pilots go down with planes in Russia, (b) basing in the continental United States with (1) refueling at intermediate overseas bases or (2) aerial refueling and return, or (c) basing strategic aircraft overseas closer to their targets. The most difficult portion of the analysis was to develop a reasonable approximation of the factors that make for success in getting over the target. These were taken to be, inter alia, number of aircraft seeking to penetrate defenses, penetration patterns permitted by remaining fuel, attrition caused by enemy damage to flying aircraft, and attrition caused by enemy damage to bases and to aircraft on the ground. The study concluded, largely on the basis of the vulnerability of the overseas bases to enemy action, that U.S. operating bases combined with overseas bases for refueling would be preferable to overseas operating bases. That is, for a given effectiveness (bombs on target) there would be less total cost (both procurement and operating) involved in a U.S. operating base concept.

Housing for the British

The British Government has a fairly extensive (and expensive) program of direct government construction of housing units. The basic purpose of the program is simply to provide housing, which is traditionally measured in "units," of specified size with specified design features. P. A. Stone undertook to examine the best methods to provide housing among alternatives of building (1) elevator-type or (2) walk-up (garden-type) apartments in (a) existing cities, (b) existing small towns, or (c) new towns.[5] Then-current British policy was to develop new towns and to construct elevator-type dwellings in existing cities.

Cost elements considered by Stone included the basic costs of land at market prices (regardless of ownership of the land before development), the costs of developing the land and of the dwellings, the costs of utility connections, schools, maintenance expenditures, and differential living costs in different parts of England. The study concludes that the least-cost type of construction (on a per unit basis) including land and operating cost is the garden type rather than the elevator type and that building in existing small towns is preferable to building in new towns and existing larger cities.

To Save a Life

In his budget message for fiscal 1968, President Johnson listed several examples of analysis. One was a report on research in life saving. In the President's words:

> The Department of Health, Education and Wel-
> fare has completed an analysis of the relative
> cost and effectiveness of selected disease con-
> trol programs. Cost per life saved and other
> criteria of relative effectiveness were developed.

These programs are being reviewed and funding priorities are being reexamined in light of these findings. [6]

The underlying study may be viewed both as a cost-benefit study (there was an attempt to measure the value of human life by, in effect, taking the present value of estimated future earnings of someone saved as a result of a program of detection and cure) or as a cost-effectiveness study. Viewed as a cost-effectiveness study, it illustrates the cost required to save a life by utilizing various health programs--which, unlike the antiballistic-missile programs in the Defense Department study, are not mutually exclusive. To reach these conclusions, of course, the HEW analysts had to develop a "model" of how each government program would work its way into actual lives saved. In other words, they had to consider explicitly how many would die of the disease without, say, a testing program, what percentage would be tested, how much the tests would cost, what percentage of those tested would have surgery, what percentage of the surgery would be successful, and what it would cost. Given all the conclusions inherent in each of these models, the results appear as shown in the table below: [7]

Program	Cost Per Life Saved
Cervical-uterine cancer screening program	$ 3,470
Lung cancer smoking education program	6,400
Breast cancer screening program	7,663
Syphilis blood screening expansion	22,252
Tuberculosis, increase research and control	22,807
Head and neck cancer detection research	29,100

Assuming the validity of the basic data--presumably no decision-maker has better data than the Department of Health, Education and Welfare--the study shows that if the objective of governmental activity is life saving (or to the extent that it is) a program of cervical-uterine cancer screening should be undertaken before a program of head and neck cancer detection research. As is the case in all cost-effectiveness studies, the data do not reveal whether (a) none of the listed programs should be undertaken because they are too expensive or (b) all should be undertaken. Instead, they simply point to preferred alternatives to achieve a given objective. If a cervical-uterine cancer program is not being undertaken for lack of funds, expanding syphilis screening is an "inefficient" method of life saving. For every life lost to syphilis by transferring resources from the syphilis program to the cervical cancer program, an additional six lives would be gained.

The Urban Transportation Problem

A group of analysts at the Rand Corporation have recently directed their attention to a variety of nonmilitary problems. One outgrowth of this interest was a study of urban transportation alternatives. [8] The analytic portion of the study, modestly labeled "Comparative Costs, " provides a framework for conducting urban transport cost analysis. The author's own description of how they proceeded is hard to improve upon:

> The central (but not exclusive) focus of these cost analyses is the provision of services to commuters traveling between home and downtown workplaces during rush hours. The systems analyzed thus incorporate high-performance, high-volume capabilities seldom encountered or needed on other than urban radial, CBD /central business district/-oriented transportation facilities.

> The total CBD commuter trip pattern (between home and downtown) can be separated into three functional components for analysis: residential collection; line-haul service; and downtown distribution. The first pertains to the collection and distribution of travelers at the residential end of the trip. It can require an entirely separate feeder service (and a passenger transfer),

as in most rail and some express bus systems.
Other technologies though, /this is an oblique
reference to private passenger cars/ can provide continuous movement, with no transfer at
the intermediate point between residential collection and the line-haul.

The line-haul component connects the residential and downtown services. Modes are
express bus, regular bus service, mass transit
and private cars.

. . .

Downtown distribution is the movement of
passengers between the points where they get
off the line-haul system and their final destinations. They may walk, or use private automobiles, taxis, transit service, or other means.[9]

The most significant feature about this study was that
it ignored institutional lines in seeking an optimal solution
to the problem thus defined. The problem was not viewed
from the standpoint of a commuter seeking ways to get to
work, nor from the standpoint of a bus company seeking to
determine profitable routes, nor from the standpoint of a
single local government seeking to provide transport services
at least cost to itself, nor from the standpoint of the federal
budget. Instead, the study took the perspective of a government or decision-maker willing to consider all costs--
government and private--on a comparable basis. The costs
of initial equipment--buses, subway cars, and private
automobiles--were considered to be the manufacturing
costs alone, without consideration of differing excise taxes
that might be applicable to each and without consideration
that one would be purchased by a local government, one by
a private company, and one by an individual commuter.
The costs of operation were considered as the economic
costs of paying operators (with no compensation assumed
for automobile drivers, who were assumed to be indifferent
regarding riding and driving).

Taxes on gasoline and diesel fuel were left out of the
analysis. The costs of the line-haul facility (roads or
transit line) were considered in considerable detail as

were necessary terminal and/or parking facilities, regardless of who would provide or pay for them.

This led the authors to the conclusion that on the whole the automobile is not a bad way to get people to work, from an over-all social point of view.

COST-BENEFIT ANALYSIS

Dam the Grand Canyon

Throughout 1966, a debate raged in Congress and across the pages of the nation's newspapers on a proposal to build two additional power dams on the Colorado River. Proponents said that the dams were amply justified by their cost-benefit ratios and that the revenues from the power were needed to finance irrigation. Opponents rested their case primarily on the conservation issue, arguing that the dams would destroy the Grand Canyon. For purposes of reviewing analysis in action, however, our focus is upon the original determination of the feasibility of the dams by the Department of Interior and the criticism of that feasibility determination by a Rand Corporation employee.

In May, 1966, the Subcommittee on Irrigation and Reclamation of the House Interior and Insular Affairs Committee heard a parade of witnesses on the plan. The testimony supporting the dams was based primarily on an Interior Department cost-benefit study.[10] Ignoring pages of nuances, the basic concept of the study was that the primary output of the project was electric power, which could be valued. Rather than seeking a buyer or developing a hypothetical price at which the power could be marketed, the Interior study based the valuation of this power upon what it would cost to provide a comparable supply to comparable locations. In other words, the first step of the Interior study was like an "economy" study in the technical sense, as it would answer the question: If one wanted x kilowatt hours of electric power at location C in time period z, what would be the most economical way to provide it?

In considering this question, if the private alternative
would be cheaper than the dam, presumably the project should
not be undertaken. If the private alternative appears more
expensive, the benefit used by the Interior Department is
assumed to be the "cost" of power if it had been produced
by the private plant. Thus, as the Interior Department put
it in one of its studies on the proposed dams,

> Benefits from power are . . . measured by
> alternative costs. In this analysis, power
> benefits have been assumed to equal the cost
> of providing equivalent power from fuel-fired
> steamplants. [11]

Criticisms of the Interior Department's proposals were
made in the hearings by Rand Corporation economist Alan
Carlin. The substance of Mr. Carlin's analysis as it related
to the question of measuring power benefits was that the
approach of treating the costs of other alternatives as the
measure of benefits of Interior's project was acceptable
but that the application of the concept had been faulty.[12]

The significance of these separate studies of the proposed
dams is that both adopted a method of measuring benefits
from a proposed project as the costs of alternatives to
achieve the same objective.

The London-Birmingham Motorway (M-1)

One of the first British attempts to build an American-
style superhighway was the London-to-Birmingham motorway, known in England as M-1. A comprehensive study of
the benefits and costs of this motorway was undertaken
(after the decision to build it had been made) by a group of
researchers from the British Road Research Laboratory
and the University of Birmingham. [13] Establishing the
construction and maintenance costs of the road did not
involve conceptual difficulties, but difficulties were encountered in seeking to measure benefits in monetary terms.
Clearly, the road would let some people get where they
were going faster and perhaps more safely, but what is
that worth? The basic answers of the study were:

Savings in tire (tyre) wear can be directly
estimated in dollars (pounds) worth of tires.

Saving the time of professional drivers can be
valued by multiplying the hours saved by
their wage rates.

Accident reduction can be valued primarily
in terms of the property damage prevented.

Traffic generated by the road (those who would
not travel at all on the older road) yielded
benefits half as great as time savings of
traffic using the older road.

The time savings of pleasure drivers were
given separate valuations of 2, 4, 6, and
8 shillings per hour (shilling /in 1963/ =
U.S. $0.14).

The study concluded that the rate of return on the original
cost was as high as 27.3 per cent when the highest estimate
of the value of leisure time and optimistic projections of
traffic growth were used.

Preventing High School Drop-outs

Considerable concern has been expressed in recent years
in educational and governmental circles about the problem
of the high school "drop-out," usually defined as a student
who voluntarily discontinues his education before completing
high school. An attempt to assess the benefits of a program
of preventing drop-outs is provided in a study by Burton A.
Weisbrod presented at a Brookings Institution Conference.[14]

Weisbrod's initial task is to define the "drop-out problem" in manageable terms. After considerable initial
discussion, he chooses to assume that drop-outs and high
school graduates have identical characteristics in all
respects except their education. He then takes earnings
data for each group and accepts the difference (discounted
to the present at two different interest rates for comparison

purposes) as the measure of the present value of preventing a drop-out. "External" benefits are treated in a narrative fashion, but no attempt to measure them is made. Costs of a drop-out prevention program and the effectiveness of the program (drop-outs prevented per $1,000 expended) are taken from a study conducted in St. Louis. These costs are then related to the benefits to produce the conclusion that the economic benefits from the program are less than the cost. The ultimate summary table, which in the actual study is surrounded by qualifications, is shown below--not as an instrument in forging educational policy, but to show the format in which the results are presented:

Summary of Benefits and Costs[15]

Resource Costs per Drop-out Prevented	
Direct Prevention Costs (the drop-out program)	$5,815
Additional Instruction Costs (because they stayed in school)	725
Total Resource Costs	$6,540
Internal Benefits per Drop-out Prevented	
Increased Present Value of Lifetime Income (unadjusted)	2,750
Improved Self Esteem of Student	+
External Benefits per Drop-out Prevented	
Increased Productivity of Cooperating Resources	+
Increased Social and Political Consciousness and Participation	+
Decreased Social Costs (e.g., crime and delinquency)	+
Decreased Social Costs of Administering Welfare	+
Intergeneration Benefits (better home education for next generation)	+
Total Costs per Drop-out Prevented Not Covered by Known Benefits	$3,800

Several points about this study are worth noting. First, there is no distinction made between private and public costs

and benefits. Second, transfers of resources among individuals and their government are not included in the table. For
example, a drop-out might require considerably more welfare payments than a high school graduate; that possibility
is reflected on the table--but as an entry for administering
the payments, not for the payments themselves which are
not found on the table. Distribution of benefits is discussed
in the report but is not a dimension in the cost-benefit
analysis made from the perspective of society as a whole.
From that perspective, transfers among individuals do not
create benefits or costs. Third, quantitative values are
not given for many of the benefits. In some cases, this
omission may be dictated by lack of information on the
relationships of two phenomena (e.g., dropping out by
fathers related to dropping out by their sons) and, in other
cases, by the fact that the quality being measured (e.g.,
political participation) does not possess a market measure.

Controlling Syphilis

At the same Brookings Conference, Herbert Klarman
presented a paper on syphilis-control programs.[16] Klarman
sought to put a dollar value on the output of the program.
The framework for the measurement is:

> The benefits of a particular disease program
> are the costs of the disease that are averted
> by it. Costs comprise three elements: loss
> of production; expenditures for medical care;
> and the pain, discomfort, etc., that accompany
> a disease. Commonly, the economist concen-
> trates on measuring the first two elements.
> The third is likely to be disregarded; if men-
> tioned at all, it is usually sidetracked.[17]

In the basic study, the production loss is shown to be highly
sensitive to the number of years of working life a person
would have had without the disease (his age). Future earnings
are discounted to present values by the same methods used
in the drop-outs study.

Carrying out these estimating procedures yielded values for the benefits per case of syphilis prevented. However, Klarman was unable to relate benefits to costs of control. As he put it:

> No attempt was made to calculate the direct costs of alternative control programs capable of yielding specified benefits. It is virtually impossible to estimate such costs in the absence of an adequate epidemiological theory on the spread of syphilis.[18]

SUMMARY

This chapter has sought to advance the study of the PPB approach by providing some samples of PPB analyses. Several examples were given of cost-effectiveness studies in which the benefits of a program were expressed in physical terms (commuters transported, fatalities prevented, military men and materiel moved, bombers over target, lives saved, and housing units provided). Some of these studies concentrated on alternative programs to achieve a fixed level of output (the airlift and commuter studies) while others (particularly the antimissile missile) arrayed pairs associating costs and outputs for the decision-maker.

Attempts to quantify benefits by converting program outputs into dollar values were described in four cases. An electric power study sought to utilize the cost of alternatives to develop a method of translating the value of a power-generating dam into money benefits. A highway study sought to convert time saved by commercial and private drivers into money benefits. Both the drop-out study and the syphilis study were designed to quantify the output of programs to improve human productivity through better health or education. Both focused upon earning power as a proxy for productivity gains.

NOTES TO CHAPTER 8

1. As attachment to U.S. Bureau of the Budget Bulletin
No. 66-3, Supplement (processed, 1966).

2. Ibid., p. 10.

3. U.S. Department of Defense, Statement of Secretary
of Defense Robert S. McNamara before a Joint Session of
the Senate Armed Services Committee and the Senate Subcommittee on Department of Defense Appropriations on
the Fiscal Year 1968-1972 Defense Program and 1968 Defense
Budget (processed, January 23, 1967), pp. 46-55.

4. Albert S. Wohlstetter et al., Selection and Use of
Strategic Air Bases, Rand Report R-266 (April, 1954,
reprinted in 1963).

5. P. A. Stone, "The Economics of Housing and Urban
Development," Royal Statistical Society Journal, Series A,
Vol. 122 (1959), Part 4, pp. 417-83.

6. U.S. Bureau of the Budget, Budget for Fiscal 1968,
p. 37.

7. The table reflects the health programs covered in
U.S. Department of Health, Education and Welfare, Office
of the Assistant Secretary for Program Coordination,
Program Analysis 1966-5, Selected Disease Control Programs (Washington, D.C., 1966).

8. J. R. Meyer, J. F. Kain, and M. Wohl, The Urban
Transportation Problem (Cambridge, Mass.: Harvard
University Press, 1965).

9. Ibid., p. 172.

10. During the hearings, many criticisms of this study
were made. The portion of the testimony used for this
example is only that relevant to a discussion of the role
of alternative costs in benefit measurement. For a rigorous
treatment of this subject, consult Peter O. Steiner, "The
Role of Alternative Cost in Project Design and Selection,"

Resources for the Future, Water Research (Baltimore:
Johns Hopkins, 1966), pp. 33-47, and also under the same
title in the Quarterly Journal of Economics, August, 1965.

11. U.S. Department of the Interior, Bureau of Reclamation, Pacific Southwest Water Plan Report (January,
1964), p. VII-2.

12. The analysis and testimony appear in U.S. Congress,
House, Committee on Interior and Insular Affairs, Subcommittee on Irrigation and Reclamation, Hearings on H.R.
4671 and Similar Bills, Lower Colorado River Basin Project,
Part II, Eighty-ninth Congress, 2nd Session (1966), pp.
1493-1539.

13. T. M. Coburn, M. E. Beesley, and D. J. Reynolds,
The London-Birmingham Motorway, Traffic and Economics,
Road Research Laboratory Technical Paper, No. 46, Her
Majesty's Stationery Office (London, 1960). The study is
also described in detail in C. D. Foster, The Transport
Problem (London: Blackie, 1963).

14. Burton A. Weisbrod, "Preventing High School
Dropouts," in Robert Dorfman (ed.), Measuring Benefits
of Government Investments (Washington, D.C.: The
Brookings Institution, 1965), pp. 117-71.

15. Ibid., p. 148, with simplifications. Costs minus
benefits should equal "costs not covered by benefits." They
do not. The mistake is carried from the original table in
the Dorfman volume.

16. "Syphilis Control Programs," in Dorfman, op. cit.,
pp. 367-414.

17. Ibid., pp. 367-68.

18. Ibid., p. 410.

PART II

PROBLEMS IN APPLYING
THE PPB APPROACH

CHAPTER **9** IDENTIFYING GOALS
AND OBJECTIVES

THE IMPORTANCE OF IDENTIFYING OBJECTIVES

This chapter begins a discussion of whether a PPB
system can discover goals, objectives, or criteria for identifying effectiveness or benefits. The problem is central to
the evaluation of PPB. As two of the leading exponents of
the PPB approach have put it, "Where there is no agreement
on criteria, we have nothing of general significance to say
about the efficiency of allocation decisions."[1]

One of the President's objectives for the PPB system
is that it "identify national goals with precision."[2] Other
objectives are clearly dependent upon the goal-identifying
objective. No output can be evaluated unless it is determined
that the criterion is that "more" or "less" of the given output
is a good thing. Such a criterion is not always obvious to
all concerned: For example, where output is percentage of
criminals in jail or number of miles of paved land or number
of welfare cases terminated, arguments can be made that
the quantity in question should be minimized or maximized
depending upon one's criterion. Such a criterion presumably
stems from whether increasing output is "on the way toward"
achievement of a goal. Thus, the comparison of outputs
necessary to achieve efficiency, to exercise informed judgment, to pinpoint programs to be expanded, and to evaluate
performance cannot be undertaken unless an objective is
specified.

To deal with the question of specifying objectives and
measuring achievement, it will be necessary to be precise
about a few words. No definition of any of these words is
the "correct" one in the sense that others would not be found

in standard dictionaries. However, to ensure precision,
definitions are here arbitrarily chosen. A goal, which will
be treated as synonymous with an objective, is a fixed attainable standard of accomplishment. This conforms with standard military usage (the next hill is the platoon's objective)
and with much civilian usage (the United Fund goal is to collect
one million dollars). A statement of a direction in which one
wants to move will be called an objective function, a notion
taken from linear programming. "Objective functions" en-
compass all statements of mere direction of improvement
such as "improve," "hasten," "minimize," "expand," and
"increase," as well as statements in the form of absolute
goals where it is clear from the nature of the phenomena
that movement toward the goal is all that is realistically
expected ("Our goal is to eradicate crime").

If the objective function is conceived of as having a
linear relationship with the status quo, which all one-
dimensional goals will have, then all goals/objectives will
lie on the objective function. More than one goal will thus
be possible. Sometimes these are labeled as short-term
and long-run goals and objectives. Sometimes they are
labeled intermediate and final goals and objectives. Such
terminology will be avoided here. The diagrams below
illustrate the concepts and the point that all goals establish
objective functions (the vector between the status quo and
the goal) and all objective functions are the locus of possible
goals.

Status quo ───►
          GNP - 700 billion   800 billion   1 trillion

In this example, the objective function is increasing gross
national product (equals prosperity, equals national economy,
etc.), and the objective/goal is a GNP of x, where x is any
GNP greater than 700 billion dollars.

There is no reason to assume that the special staff of
experts hired to perform PPB in the government will be
better qualified to make goals than those who hire the analysts.
In fact, the PPB approach does not pretend to claim the ability to "make" goals rather than find them. Thus, whether
goals can be found is key to the prospects of the PPB approach.

For goals to be found, they must exist. "Does the nation have any goals?" is a question that must be asked and answered long before the question of what those goals may be. It is generally presumed in most casual discussions of policy that the nation does have goals and objective functions (called by other names). The concept of national goals seems to stem from a syllogistic reasoning:

People act to achieve things
    People are acting
        Therefore they are trying to achieve something.

Alternatively, this can be phrased:

All behavior is purposive
    Governmental action is behavior
        Therefore it is purposive.

There are several logical difficulties with these formulations. First, whether behavior is, in fact, purposive in the sense of always being a means to an end rather than an end itself is debatable. Second, and more important, the syllogism is a serious example of the fallacy of composition. Government decisions and actions are outputs of a political system. That system is not a person and need not conform psychologically to the characteristic of a person. When more than one individual is involved, two important elements are added to consideration of purposive behavior. First, not all parties may have the same information; in fact, some information may be wrong. Second, not all parties may have the same motive. A nation may decide to establish a Civil Rights Commission, but the decision may reflect (a) a desire to get on with civil rights by group A, (b) a desire to forestall stronger legislation by group B, (c) a desire to get more facts on the subject before deciding on the merits by group C, (d) a desire to find jobs for one's relatives by group D, and (e) a desire to logroll for support for a group of home-town projects by group E.

Thus, it is possible for a group of individuals acting purposively to agree on a political system output without any agreement on the objective of that output. This is frequently recognized by comments that it is easier to agree on an action than on a philosophy. Thus, the first hurdle in identifying objectives is that there may exist no single set of objectives to be identified.

Assuming, arguendo, that national goals do exist, the hunt can begin. This hunt for objectives has in fact begun throughout the U.S. Government and in substantial academic literature on program analysis. As might be expected, it is a hunt undertaken by churches, business firms, and governments that are taking steps toward being true to their purposes or objectives by finding out what those objectives or purposes are. In many such bodies, however, it is possible to seek and find authoritative statements of objectives. For example, if the president of General Motors announces that the objective of General Motors is to increase its profit 10 per cent every year, that decision is authoritative, provided only that the stockholders have vested in the president the authority to make such decisions. An analyst in General Motors need take the question no further.

Under the U.S. Constitution, no single body or individual is empowered to state goals authoritatively. Laws may be passed by two houses of Congress with a majority vote and approved by the President or passed with a more sizable vote though not approved by the President. However, some areas of operation are left to state governments and some, under the Constitution, left to private citizens. The existence of the federal legislative power does not necessarily mean that Congress or the President will formulate objectives explicitly, nor do the limitations prevent either the President or the Congress from stating objectives (e.g., a stronger church system) beyond the "powers" of the federal government.

Many citizens, their leaders, and their elected representatives do talk of national goals. Unlike policies or political outputs, these words are not subjected to the tests of the political system. The President of the United States may state that equal opportunity to attend schools is a national goal, but the Congress will be confronted with a bill--not a goal. The Congress is not constrained to match its statements of objectives in a law to the actual decisions reflected in that law. In fact, it is not constrained to state objectives at all. Members of Congress may state their views in the form of a congressional committee report or "legislative history" made in floor debate, but the format for decisions does not permit the whole Congress to accept or reject such statements. Also, it is possible that while both House and Senate may reconcile their disagreements on operative language, they may not reconcile their differences on what legislation is supposed to accomplish.

In short, there is no single mechanism for the setting of U.S. national goals, objective functions, objectives, or national purposes. Even if such phenomena do exist in the abstract, they would not, and indeed could not, be stated authoritatively through our national political mechanism.

This is not to say that goals/objectives and objective functions are not stated. In fact, they are frequently stated and given considerable attention in practically all fields of human endeavor, both those directly involving the federal government and those not directly involving government. Individual researchers in the cost-benefit field have from time to time sought to use these goal statements of others as a direct indication of the dimensions of benefit measurement. [3] The basic technique in these studies is for the analyst to consult a wide variety of sources of potential goals. These include those stated by the agency itself, by supporters of the program, by the Congress in establishing the program, and by the President. Those statements frequently develop as a variety of loose generalizations about the projected effect of the program rather than a sharp indication of its goal. This makes it difficult to sort out what is a goal and what is a "by-product." Frequently an objective function will be discovered that doesn't make sense to the analyst, in which case it must either be interpreted to suit the analyst's understanding of what the decision-maker should have wanted or would have wanted if he had understood what he was about. [4] Finally, the analyst must, to make a meaningful study, direct his primary attention to objectives that he believes are subject to potential measurement and that are not inconsistent with other objectives. [*] All these problems place substantial hurdles in the path of PPB implementation.

---

[*] This is not as rare a problem as might be assumed. The public housing program, for example, is "designed" to (a) destroy the slums--thereby reducing the supply of housing and (b) to increase the supply of housing.

The remainder of this chapter represents an attempt to gather data on goals.

PROBLEMS IN DEPENDING UPON CONGRESSIONAL DECISIONS ON OBJECTIVES[*]

Programs Without Stated Objectives

Some legislation is adopted with no statement of objective or purpose. A sample studied by the author indicated thirteen such programs, including:

(1) Payments to farmers for milk made unfit for consumption by pesticide contamination

(2) The Civil Rights Commission established by the Civil Rights Act of 1957

(3) The establishment and programs of the Childrens Bureau

(4) Public Health Service programs of health surveys, traineeships, nurses training, vaccination, and collection of vital statistics

(5) Free treatment of seamen at U.S. hospitals

(6) The Medicare Program

(7) The Old Age and Survivors Insurance Program

---

[*] This section is a summary of a major portion of the author's doctoral dissertation which exhaustively considered statements of objectives appearing in laws codified in Titles 23, 24, and 42 of the United States Code. Those interested in a more exhaustive (and tedious) treatment with more complete citations should refer to that dissertation.

(8) Providing asylum for decrepit Navy officers

Obviously, Congress does not feel constrained to write a statement of purpose or policy to accompany and explain every law it passes.

The absence of a statement of objectives for each of these programs does not mean that one could not be discovered for each of them. Such statements could be found by searching through committee reports, words said in public and on the floor of Congress in support of the legislation, and in Presidential signing statements. However, whatever sources are selected, they represent (a) less than all of the participants in the decision to undertake the program and (b) a particular analyst's selection.

It is important to recognize, for the purposes of both PPB and normal policy formulation, that the search for objectives of these programs is not a trivial matter. Take the first example, the reimbursement to farmers for pesticide-contaminated milk.[5] Many farmers used pesticides, which the Department of Agriculture permitted to be marketed. These pesticides ultimately found their way into milk which, as a result, did not meet health standards. The dairy farmers involved sought reimbursement from the government. Because dairy-farm congressmen had nothing to lose by supporting such legislation, because there was no strong opposition from other groups or the White House, because most congressmen probably felt the case appealing, and because of the legislative gains for the poverty program associated with getting the farmers reimbursed, the Administration's poverty bill was amended to provide for reimbursement. This amendment gave the dairy-farm congressmen a better reason to support the poverty bill--which otherwise would have appeared to farm constituencies to be an "aid-to-city-folks package"-- and may have given the supporters of the poverty program the margin of votes they felt they needed for passage.

Suppose that the Congress had heard from public-relations experts of the need to state private goals in terms of "public interest," from lawyers about the concept that the best practice is to write separate pieces of legislation with a statement of purpose, and from PPB experts that one of the essential steps of reasoning about programs is to identify objectives.

What purpose or objective function could have been attached
to this amendment? The amendment was not designed to
stimulate agriculture. Even if it were, the political rules
would not have permitted saying so because the amendment
was being reported by the Committee on Education and Labor,
not the Committee on Agriculture. The legislation was clearly not designed to alleviate poverty--there was no necessary
correlation between the dairy farmers suffering the loss and
those with income below poverty levels. In fact, the pesticide
users were presumably the more progressive, higher-income
farmers.

The legislative statement of purpose could have been an
appeal to equity or the lawyer-congressman's common-sense
notion of tort liability. However, the notion that "the government told them it was OK to do something, they did it, they
lost" does not easily translate into a general statement of
objectives.

Even if one could be formulated, stating a more general
principle gives rise to a number of other situations that must
be covered as well, or favoritism (unequal treatment of
admitted equals) would have to be "admitted" by Congress.
Such an alternative is bound to be politically unappealing,
as favoritism unadmitted is known to the favorites and not
to the losers but favoritism admitted is a challenge to losers
and no better for the winners. A general government goal
of providing compensation to all those injured as a result
of their own or other's actions in following recommendations
of government agencies would (a) raise questions of policy
that might cause congressmen to prefer not to pass the legislation or (b) slow down the passage of the legislation while
its ramifications were considered. Such a general principle
of government liability would apply, presumably, to bad
meat that had passed Agriculture Department inspection,
action relying on stream flow data from the Environmental
Science Services Administration, all actions taken on the
basis of weather forecasts, all losses in commodity specu-
lation taken in reliance upon Department of Agriculture
crop forecasts, etc. Whether or not making the government
liable for these various losses would be good policy is not
of importance. What is of importance was that there was
no particular reason for any member of Congress to press

these knotty problems by trying to formulate a general
legislative purpose for the pesticide reimbursements.

In no sense can it be said that the absence of a statement
of objectives in this legislation was an accident or an over-
sight. In fact, the actors in the political process were probably not seeking to increase agriculture production, to alleviate poverty among dairy farmers, or to enact a general
principle of government liability for advice given by federal
agencies. In a certain sense, the objective of the program
may have been the program. When all the dairy farmers
are reimbursed, the interested dairy congressmen will feel
that their objective has been achieved. Perhaps when the
poverty bill passed, many urban congressmen thought that
the objective of the reimbursement program had already
been achieved.

The Civil Rights Act of 1957 presents a clear-cut example
of a circumstance where a majority of both Houses of Congress and the President of the United States can agree on a
set of words and actions embodied in a bill but cannot agree
on a policy. In 1957, there were politically potent calls for
sharply divergent actions on civil rights ranging on one side
from a roll-back of then recent Supreme Court decisions to,
on the other side, calls for immediate federal action to open
schools on an equal basis and enforce voting rights. There
were groups, with sufficient power to block action by the
Congress, who would not accede to a statement that "the
pact of achievement of civil rights (or any particular 'right')
needs to be speeded up" or to indications that rights were
being denied in some parts of the nation. Those same groups,
after considerable hesitation, were willing to avoid making
the sacrifices required in bitter opposition if the issue were
simply the creation of a commission. As a result, the Civil
Rights Commission was created with no statement of purpose,
no statement of objective, and no finding of "need." The
absence of an explicit objective in this statute is not legislative omission; it is a recognition that no authoritative statement of objective could secure the necessary support to
become law. An analyst may say that Congress passed the
Civil Rights Act of 1957 to further the objective (function)
of increasing attainment of equal rights of Negro and white
Americans, but, in such a case, it is the analyst, not the
Congress, speaking. If the authoritative statements are not

existent, the possibility of disagreement about objectives
among analysts arises, for who is to "prove" that any given
statement of objectives could have commanded the assent
of the United States of America "in Congress Assembled,"
when, in fact, it did not do so?

A second category of legislation lacking statements of
objectives is the group where the objectives of the program
appear to be obvious--collection of vital statistics, treatment
of seamen at U.S. hospitals, and providing asylum for decrepit
naval officers. The difficulty with apparently obvious purposes
of legislation is that they cannot provide a basis for rational
analysis of programs (by PPB or any other system), nor can
they make possible a determination of when a program is no
longer needed to achieve whatever objective the Congress may
have had in mind. "Obviously," seamen should be treated at
U.S. hospitals because they are sick and need care. However,
why single out seamen for treatment among the large group
of sick Americans? Did the measure simply fulfill a political
requirement imposed by Senators from states with large num-
bers of seamen--if so, does the political need still exist?
Perhaps the purpose was to assist U.S. flag carriers in
meeting competition of foreign carriers. If this is the case,
supplementing the operating differential subsidy administered
by the Maritime Administration might be another and perhaps
lower-cost method of achieving the same purpose. On the
other hand, the purpose may have been to provide patients
for government hospitals which might at the time the statute
was passed have had difficulty in finding doctors because of
the absence of normal patient load in facilities devoted primarily to research. If that were the objective of the program,
it might be possible to drop it as such a flow of customers is
now available in the course of meeting federal obligations to
provide medical services to members of the active armed
forces and veterans.

As this case illustrates, programs with purposes that
may seem obvious may in fact have been enacted for a wide
variety of sometimes overlapping reasons. This means that
it is not satisfactory simply to assume that any program's
objectives are obvious. The failure of Congress to state
objectives in the case of many programs thus forces an
analyst to find other forms of objective statements if the
objective of goal identification is to be fulfilled by the PPB
system.

Ambiguous or Vague Statements of Objectives

Some statements of purpose give no indication of the action expected to result from the program, the potential measures of program success, or the expectations of Congress in adopting it. While such ambiguous or vague statements may reflect politically useful bridges, permitting particular measures to pass despite underlying policy disagreements, they provide poor raw material for PPB. In these statements, instead of finding a criterion or objective, one finds words that themselves call for explanation in terms of criteria and objectives. The following examples give some indication of the problem:

(1) Manpower-development legislation "in order that the Nation may meet the staffing requirements of the struggle for freedom" and to "increase the Nation's capacity to meet the requirements of the space age."

(2) Atomic energy programs managed "so as to make the maximum contribution to the general welfare."

(3) Flood insurance as a "necessary adjunct" of preventive and protective means and structures.

(4) A program of assisting states "to provide the services and facilities essential to the health and welfare of the people of the United States."

"Needs" Formulations

Even those categories of statements that indicate a direction of activity desired by the Congress may not indicate clearly the purpose of that activity. Such a situation occurs when the Congress formulates its objectives in terms of meeting "needs." Frequently, "need" may imply a standard which may be the same for all observers. A husband could

adopt the policy of meeting all of his wife's "needs" for
clothing regardless of price, and the wife could adopt the
same standard. The resulting statement might obscure the
fact that the husband believed that the needs had already
been met three times over while the wife conceived needs
to be infinite. One water resource program, according to
its authorizing language, was to assure at all times "a supply
of water sufficient in quantity and quality to meet the requirements of its expanding population," and "to meet the rapidly
expanding demands for water through the Nation." This
formulation cannot guide policy-makers, because the demands
for water depend upon the price at which it will be sold. [6]
For this reason, statements expressed in terms of demand
or requirements are unsuitable for use as statements of
national objectives.

Intermediate Objectives

Some programs facilitate the operation of other programs, rather than fulfilling an objective themselves. This
is clearly the case for construction of public buildings but
may not be with the construction of public monuments. If
the world were so perfectly constructed that men reasoned
rationally from ends to means and stated their conclusions
and the steps in their logic carefully and completely, it
would be possible to identify which things were desired for
their own sake and which because they led to other things.
In fact, congressional statements of objectives do not necessarily meet this standard of perfection.

The link between an instrumental program and the final
objective is an explicit or implicit finding of fact that the
program will lead to the ultimate objective specified. This
creates for the analyst a difficult problem when the link is
in fact a false one. He is left with the problem of finding
"objectives" for a program which, by his logic, would not
be in existence if the truth about it had been known.

Some programs are not authoritatively stated to have
purposes of accomplishing x or increasing y. Instead, their
purposes are stated in terms of assisting some agency or
force in achieving x or increasing y. This difference means

that, assuming language is used logically, it is impossible
to say that a given program is a failure if x is not accomplished or y is not increased; it is logically possible for the
assistance to be given but the objective not to be achieved.
In a military example, the fire-support mission of an artil-
lery group may be accomplished, but the hill may not be
taken. Examples of these types of objective statements occur
frequently in legislative language authorizing programs of
federal assistance to states and local governments. The
juvenile delinquency, community relations service, and open-
space land programs incorporate this type of statement of
objectives. The Public Health Service objectives are stated
in "to further" terminology.

Hurdles to identifying objectives are most apparent in
the surprisingly frequent cases where the congressional
statement of purpose seems to express inaccurately what
Congress "must have" meant. For example, one of the
objectives of the Congress in enacting the juvenile delinquency legislation was "to encourage the coordination of
efforts among governmental and non-governmental educational, employment . . . and other agencies concerned with
such problems."[7] It is doubtful indeed that Congress would
be satisfied with a performance report indicating that coordination had been achieved, if nothing had actually been
done that moved toward solution of the juvenile delinquency
problem. A statement that makes "coordination" an objective can be read as a combination of a finding of fact (that
coordination would improve programs) and an implicit objective (less delinquency), but the rendering is not obvious; it
is possible that Congress believes coordination is in fact a
virtue.

Multiple Objectives

Conflicting or multiple objectives may also be found in
many enactments. These create difficult problems in applying the PPB approach, because it is impossible to find an
alternative to achieve a given objective when more than one
objective is given and their relative importance is unknown.

The school lunch program provides a good example of multiple objectives. The program provides school systems with food to encourage them to provide hot lunches to students. The legislation setting up the program states two objectives: (a) "to safeguard the health and well-being of the Nation's children" and (b) "to encourage the domestic consumption of nutritious agricultural commodities." Which one of these is the principal objective (function) of the program makes a great difference in how it is analyzed, funded, and administered. If the principal objective is the health of the nation's children, fish flour is an admissible alternative to milk and meat as a protein source. If the principal objective is increasing the market for agricultural commodities, fish flour is out, but a food-stamp program (for adults) is an admissible alternative.

When Objectives Are Stated

Usable objective statements are generally found in the form of an objective function. These usually indicated a national purpose or a direction for national policy but sometimes were directly tied to a program authorization in the form "authorize (program) to (achieve objective), or to (objective function)." These statements had two types of content: Those that specify beneficiaries and those that do not. Some samples of legislative statements that identify intended beneficiaries are shown below:

Group	Legislation
Unemployed	Manpower Development and Training Act
Mentally retarded	Mental Retardation Facilities, etc., Act
Low-income needy students	Work-study program of poverty legislation
Adult illiterates	Adult education program of poverty legislation

Deaf persons	Captioned films for the deaf
Low-income aged persons not receiving old age assistance	Medical assistance under the Social Security Act
Mothers and children, especially in rural areas and areas suffering from severe economic distress	Grants for maternal and child health services
Owners of farms and rural real estate	Farm housing program

The difficulties in using statements like these to establish objectives will be considered in a later chapter.

Some statements of objectives that appear in legislation passed by the U.S. Congress do provide relatively clear indications of what the program enacted was to achieve. Many of these are in the form of what we have called objective functions, that is, statements that merely indicate a direction for activity, not a particular goal to be achieved. Some examples from legislation currently in effect are: (1) strengthen small business, (2) expand human knowledge of space, (3) develop more effective measures for the prevention, treatment, and control of venereal disease and tuberculosis, (4) strengthen family life, (5) reduce the incidence of mental retardation.

Where Congress does state a goal or objective, it is not likely to be achievable within a reasonable time period given the present state of technology and the funds likely to be devoted to its achievement. Some examples of such statements in enacted laws include: (1) eliminate the paradox of poverty in the midst of plenty, (2) provide a decent home and a suitable living environment for every American family, (3) prevent the spread of slums, blight or deterioration, (4) achieve the prevention and control of air pollution, and (5) provide humane care and enlightened curative treatment of the insane.

Like these congressional statements, Presidential statements about objectives tend also to be formulated as objective functions (which by definition cannot be achieved) or in the form of an objective/goal that is not likely to be achieved within the political lifetime of those formulating it. *

The examples above show the incommensurability of the various objectives. The objectives do not readily relate to each other along a single scale of measurement in the same way that the number 1 relates to the number 2. Some express U.S. prestige goals, some compassion for certain groups or categories of persons, some research-and-development aims, and some consumption standards. Neither the words used nor the context in which they were formulated suggests methods by which these objectives could be related to each other, by which any conflicts among them could be reconciled, or by which priorities among them could be established.

Unambiguous measures of performance do not suggest themselves in all cases. For example, is the measure of performance of ending the paradox of poverty (a) reduction in income inequality--leveling--or (b) reaching a stipulated minimum for all families, regardless of inequalities with the highest incomes? Is the small business objective measured by the number of small businesses or by their profits on invested assets? Does prevention and control of air pollution mean (a) no contaminants in the atmosphere or (b) a level neither injurious to health nor offensive to smell or (c) an intermediate level that is aesthetically unpleasant but safe?

Henry Rowen has indicated that good analysis requires a precise statement of objectives; not, for example:

---

* This sentence summarizes a chapter in the author's doctoral dissertation. In that work, goal-oriented statements of the President's Commission on National Goals, a study on the costs of meeting national goals, and various scholarly material on the concept of the "public interest" were also analyzed. Nothing in any of that material suggested that it would be easy to formulate statements of governmental purpose in quite the form considered by some to be necessary to permit PPB to be applied.

"the development of a safer civil aviation
system," but rather, for example, "the
reduction of the civil aviation accident rate
by 10 percent annually over the next 5 years."[8]

The Supplement to Budget Bureau Bulletin 66-3 states:

Broad, general statements of national needs,
such as the "development of a safe and efficient civil aviation system" or the "elimina-
tion of poverty," though adequate for some
purposes, cannot form a basis of analysis.
The adequacy of specific programs cannot
be assessed unless their goals are stated
precisely--quantitatively wherever possible--
and the time span for their accomplishment
is specified.

This chapter has sought to show that these criteria are
not satisfied by the way goals are actually stated by political
decision-makers. This conclusion should not be surprising.
There is no legal reason why either Congress or the President must make clear statements of national goals. There
are, on the other hand, clear political advantages under
certain circumstances in ambiguity about, and even silence
concerning, goals and objectives. Likewise, the consistent
tendency to state purposes in terms of objective functions
rather than precise goals or objectives is probably attributable to a hesitancy by any participant in the political process
to accept anything less than perfection as his publicly stated
objective. It probably also reflects a reluctance by those
participants to subject their actions to the precise tests
available when performance is promised in specific terms
within specific time periods. The political repercussions
of a small increase in aircraft accidents are more easily
borne by a President committed to a safe and efficient civil
aviation system than by a President who has committed his
prestige to "the reduction of the civil aviation accident rate
by 10 per cent annually over the next 5 years." Thus, there
is considerable doubt that political decision-makers would
commit themselves to precise specifications of accomplishments even if their thought processes were consistent with
such precision.

There is some question, however, as to whether most
political decision-makers even think in the terms which the
PPB approach considers requisite to good decision-making.
For example, in an unusually personal speech in Baltimore,
Maryland, in the fall of 1966, President Johnson indicated
his thinking on objectives of some major programs:

> I should like for this period of the 20th century
> to be remembered as the period when we pro-
> duced more food to feed more people--because
> food is the necessary sustaining ingredient for
> all the other things--the period when we spent
> more money and more effort on educating more
> people; the period when we spent more time
> and more dollars on providing health for our
> bodies; the time when we did more planning
> and added more acres for conservation, recrea-
> tion and beautification. [9]

Such a formulation is not highly specific; it does not reveal
the relative "urgency" of achieving the various objectives;
time spans for accomplishment are not specified, nor is a
given level of achievement fixed. Such a formulation does
not provide criteria for evaluating programs--if the problem
is solely to spend more money on education, one million-
dollar program is as good as another. The statement suggests that a President will judge his own performance on
how much he spends to achieve an objective rather than on
what is achieved with the expenditure. Yet such a formulation is common, current, and, one suspects, an accurate
reflection of the feelings of many Americans. Certainly, it
is difficult by generally accepted standards of expression to
fault the President for statements of the type quoted above.
However, it must be noted that if such statements are an
accurate reflection of a President's (any President's) approach
to public issues, goal identification will not be a simple task
for PPBS purposes.

An even more vivid reflection of the difficulty inherent
in seeking to establish precise standards of accomplishment
are the concluding comments of the President's Commission
on National Goals. That representative group of American
leaders concluded in their report to President Eisenhower:

> Above all, Americans must demonstrate in
> every aspect of their lives the fallacy of a
> purely selfish attitude--the materialistic ethic.
> Indifference to poverty and disease is inexcus-
> able in a society dedicated to the dignity of
> the individual; so also is indifference to values
> other than material comfort and national power.
> Our faith is that man lives, not by bread alone,
> but by self-respect, by regard for other men,
> by convictions of right and wrong, by strong
> religious faith. [10]

It would be difficult to improve upon this statement of principles. Any approach (PPB or whatever) that sought to convert
such statements into quantifiable measures of accomplishment would probably encounter not only opposition to the
concept of changing such statements but also opposition based
upon the premise that certain statements will always have
greater value as inspiration than as objectives for a rigidly
defined management system.

Nonetheless, it is possible to make some of a political
decision-maker's objectives more specific by indicating
criteria of accomplishment. Such clarity communicates best
to subordinate officials what the chief really wants and provides the chief with criteria against which he can judge their
performance. Some examples of what can be done are indicated by the statements below, all of which came from comments of President Johnson made between January 1, 1966,
and July 30, 1966: [11]

(1) "A manned landing on the moon within the
present decade"

(2) "To create 1,000 school-to-school partner-
ships, to bring 5,000 exchange . . . in the
International Health and Education Program"

(3) "Eliminate illiteracy within a decade"

(4) "Extend special education help to 12 million
disadvantaged and handicapped children"

(5) "Bring public library services to 15 million
    more Americans"

(6) "Reduce by half the rate of high school
    dropouts over the next five years"

(7) "Not only slow, but stop--and ultimately
    reverse--the rate of crime increase"

(8) "So that the time will come when our life
    expectancy will not be 70 years, but
    materially increased"

The fact that most of these concern activities of one cabinet
department (Health, Education and Welfare) is probably not
unrelated to the fact that that department has a strong PPB
staff.

SUMMARY

        This chapter has presented a review of problems in
identifying objectives of government activities. Statements
of policy or purpose found in laws passed by Congress and
approved by the President were examined. In almost half
the cases studied, it was concluded that objectives could not
be unambiguously identified as a result of (1) no objective
being stated, (2) vague and ambiguous statements, (3) objectives expressed as "needs," (4) intermeshing of ends and
means, and (5) multiple objectives. The circumstances
under which the political system produces such statements
of objectives were explored.

        Cases in which objectives were stated were found to
fall into two indistinctly separated groups: (a) where a beneficiary group was indicated and the intention to aid it expressed
and (b) where the objective was stated in general terms. Objectives were found, almost without exception, to be stated
in the form of objective functions that could not readily be
compared with each other. Measures of performance were
not clearly available for all of the objectives. There is no
reason to suspect that state and local political leaders deal

with goals in a more specific fashion than do their national
counterparts.

The President said in his August, 1965, statement that
PPB would "identify objectives." To do so, the PPB analysts
will not get clear guidance from what political decision-
makers--the President and Congress--have said in the past.
If such precise specifications of objectives and criteria of
accomplishment are truly required for the success of PPB,
then PPB must either (a) permit the analysts to think up
objectives for themselves or (b) force decision-makers to
be explicit. These problems did not arise in the Defense
Department under McNamara because McNamara generally
knew what he wanted and certainly was not reluctant to communicate his objectives to others. In many domestic programs,
however, cabinet officers may be reluctant to seize such
power, and may be unsuccessful if they try.

NOTES TO CHAPTER 9

1. Alain C. Enthoven and Henry S. Rowen, "Defense
Planning and Organization," in Universities-National Bureau
of Economic Research, Public Finances: Needs, Sources
and Utilization (Princeton: Princeton University Press,
1961), pp. 364-417, 397.

2. Weekly Compilation of Presidential Documents,
August 30, 1965. This quotation is from President Johnson's
message introducing PPB.

3. Examples are Lowell E. Gallaway, "An Economic
Analysis of Public Policy for Depressed Areas," Industrial
and Labor Relations Review, XV (July, 1962), 500-509;
David A. Page, "Urban Renewal" (Paper presented to the
Bureau of the Budget Summer Seminar on Systems Analysis
and Program Evaluation, August 10, 1965); and Jerome
Rothenberg, "Urban Renewal Programs," in Robert Dorfman
(ed.), Measuring Benefits of Government Investments
(Washington, D.C.: The Brookings Institution, 1965),
pp. 292-366.

4. Examples are the rejection and change of the concept of "ending blight" found in Otto A. Davis, "A Pure Theory of Urban Renewal," Land Economics, XXXVI (May, 1960) 220-26; the treatment of the same concept in Rothenberg, op. cit., and the treatment of "reducing drop-outs" in Burton A. Weisbrod, "Preventing High School Dropouts," in Dorfman, op. cit., pp. 117-71.

5. The program was enacted as part of the legislation authorizing the poverty program. 42 U.S.C. 12 et seq.

6. This problem is discussed at length in Jack Hirshleifer, James C. DeHaven, and Jerome W. Milliman, Water Supply: Economics, Technology, and Policy (Chicago: University of Chicago Press, 1960). "Need" is often used to indicate gaps between a current situation and "standards" established by program officials. Such standards have a tendency to rise as they are nearly achieved.

7. 42 U.S.C. 2541.

8. U.S. Congress, Senate, Committee on Labor and Public Welfare, Subcommittee on Scientific Manpower Utilization, Hearings on S. 2662, Eighty-ninth Congress, 2nd Session, 1966, pp. 168-69.

9. Weekly Compilation of Presidential Documents, October 17, 1966, p. 1460.

10. President's Commission on National Goals, Goals for Americans (New York: Prentice-Hall, 1960), p. 23.

11. Precise citations for these and other statements quoted without citation in this chapter are available in the author's doctoral dissertation.

CHAPTER **10** CALCULATING COSTS
AND BENEFITS

Anything can be converted into dollars by a bold enough
analyst. An analyst can decide that the benefits from a 10
per cent increase in strategic bombing capability is worth
the cost of missiles that could not be procured or manned
because the limited funds were used for bombers. He could
place a value on the opportunity costs and on the benefit and
announce a ratio of costs and benefits. Such an analysis,
however, is not scientific, for a replication by another analyst
would not produce the same result. More important, it cannot be used as a guide to policy. The policy-maker does not
necessarily have the same values as the analyst and, if he
knew the valuation, would not have had to consult the analyst
in the first place.

This difficulty in valuation of estimates has forced cost-
benefit analysis into a mold of developing a "scientific" measure of benefit and cost. That measure is developed by
reference to an underlying reality--the willingness of persons
to pay. Benefit is defined as the composite of willingness to
pay--whether or not payment will actually be required. Cost,
conversely, is "benefits" foregone--the benefits which could
have been achieved by using inputs elsewhere. [*]

---

[*] Most of this chapter covers problems that are the
professional concern of welfare economists. The intent
of this chapter is not to contribute to this literature but
to remind readers that economic analysis has serious
problems which have long been recognized but not yet
solved.

USE OF MARKET PRICES

These concepts are hard to fault at a theoretical level
but difficult to use at a practical level. To apply them, PPB
analysts have moved to concepts that are easier to use but
harder to defend. Opportunity costs in the governmental
context tend in practice to be considered as opportunities
within particular programs. When quantified, these tend
to be equated with budgeted amounts. The PPB approach,
as Chapter 3 indicated, seeks to make sure that full-system
opportunity costs are considered. However, the significance
of information about square feet of office space, man-hours
of draftees' time, and gallons of water is not easily understood by either analysts or decision-makers. To improve
on the usefulness of this information, it is normally translated into dollars, using market prices to signal the proper
estimates of cost.

On the benefit side, willingness to pay is determined
by estimating what individuals would pay when confronted
with prices. What they will pay is in part determined by
(a) their income and (b) the prices of other goods--market
prices. Thus, the value of cost and benefit analyses rests
upon the assumption that market prices measure value.

The "Green Book," which was for years the bible (used
here to denote a document of high status, revered by a
designated group and frequently cited but less frequently
followed by that group) of cost-benefit analysts, makes the
following transition from the notion of benefit and cost to
market prices:

> The phrase "goods and services" as commonly
> used in the economic sense is utilized in this
> study to encompass all objects and activities
> which have the power of satisfying human wants
> and which may be increased or decreased in
> amount (or value) as a result of a project.
> Goods and services which fulfill human needs
> and desires and which are limited in supply
> have economic value. Any goods and services
> for which there is no need or demand have no
> economic value. In order for the effects of

a project to have economic value in terms of
benefits or costs it is necessary that there be
a need or demand for the goods and services
produced by or used for the project.

The most practicable measure of the relative desirability of goods and services for
meeting the various needs and demands which
exist is the market price in dollars. . . . To
the extent that project effects can be assigned
an actual or estimated market value, they
may be defined as benefits and costs in terms
of the market value in dollars of the increases
or decreases in goods and services that are
expected to result if a project is undertaken. [1]

Roland McKean's approach is comparable. After discussion of various reasons given for government's interest
in construction of water projects, he says:

In summary, the reasons for government
intervention in water-resource development
do not make cost-benefit estimates irrelevant
to the selection of projects. The government
is interested mainly in something akin to the
market values of projects' outputs. Our concern in such projects is not chiefly with outputs like justice, which cannot be vended to
individuals or valued at market prices.
Hence, it is urged here that it does make
sense to look at cost-benefit estimates in
which prices that would apply in the private
sector of the economy are extensively used. [2]

The equivalency of benefits and costs in the cost-benefit
framework is important. A benefit is frequently a cost
saved, so that one can speak of the benefits from flood control in terms of damage averted. A cost, on the other hand,
is a benefit foregone, as the resources used for a program
could always have been used for some other program. Because costs are usually expressed in dollars, this "opportunity cost" concept is sometimes forgotten. However, to
build a hospital for $1 million is to forego, say, a million-
dollar school. The costs of the hospital are the benefits

foregone by not having resources enough to build the school.
For these equivalencies to exist in the private and public
sectors, this marginal relationship must hold for all goods.
The cost of a ton of steel for hospitals must reflect the benefits from adding the ton to the production of autos or hospitals.
In a perfectly functioning market (with certain assumptions
soon to be considered), prices will reflect marginal costs.
In the example, car manufacturers will bid up to as much
for steel as steel is worth in benefits in the production of
cars. In the long run, if bids of car producers and hospital
builders are below the costs of steel production, steel will
not be produced and sold for these uses. On the other hand,
if the usefulness of steel is above production costs, it will
be produced and sold, if competitive forces operate, at a
price reflecting long-run marginal costs.

When this mechanism does not function, prices will not
reflect true marginal costs. In that case, cost-benefit analysis loses some of its significance for policy, because an
excess of benefits over costs does not necessarily signal a
worth-while activity. Also, in project and program design,
deviations between price and marginal cost distort the conclusions of both analysts and policy-makers from the economic
optimum. When a good is underpriced in relation to marginal
cost, the consumer buys too little of it and the analysts use
too little of it in project design. More important, they will
overvalue it as a benefit. For example, the Bureau of Reclamation values agricultural output at the price the Commodity
Credit Corporation (a government subsidy agency) will pay
for it, thereby continuing to construct projects to produce
surplus commodities.

WHY PRICES DON'T ALWAYS
REFLECT MARGINAL COST[3]

Subsidies

Sharp divergencies between prices and marginal costs
may occur as a result of government subsidies. If government builds roads and permits their use for a price (gasoline

tax) that does not fully reflect marginal costs, driving will be more attractive than if compensatory tolls were charged. Assuming that such a situation exists, is the benefit from a subway the value per customer (however calculated) times the number of customers who would use it "if roads cost what they should"? Or is it simply the value times the number of customers who will in fact use it, given the pricing policy in effect for roads? There is no correct answer to this question so long as the road and transit operations are separate. Unless the transit authorities or their superiors can control either the pricing of road services or new road construction, it can be argued that (a) the higher estimate of customers should be used and transit subsidized to reduce the need for more subsidized roads or (b) the lower customer estimate should be used, recognizing the public policy of free roads.

The problem of handling subsidized production is by no means confined to transportation, nor is it so specialized as to be a trivial problem in considering the usefulness of economic analysis of government programs. The Joint Economic Committee of the U.S. Congress periodically publishes a document that seeks to list all the subsidy and subsidy-like programs of the federal government. The recent version of this pamphlet is some 86 pages long. [4] In addition to granting subsidies, government may produce a comparable economic effect by producing goods and services itself--postal services and highways, for example--and making them available to users at prices not reflecting marginal costs.

Taxes

Taxes also distort the relations between marginal cost and price. Some of these deviations are substantial. For example, 22 per cent of the price of electricity purchased from a private supplier is attributable to federal, state, and local taxes. [5] A federal agency that values production at the full price to consumers (including the tax element) will produce a much higher estimate of benefit than if taxes were ignored in the calculation.

Uniform tax policies have differing impacts on the costs of particular goods and services in relation to other goods

and services due to different circumstances of particular
industries. For example, the federal income tax does not
fall on enterprises that do not make a "profit," even though
those enterprises may be conducting economic functions
comparable to profit-making enterprises. Substantial elements of the housing, medical, and education industries are
conducted on a not-for-profit basis. State and local property
taxes fall most heavily (tax as a percentage of sales) on industries with a high ratio of property to sales, such as railroads, utilities, and heavy manufacturing. They have less
impact (considered as a percentage of sales) on labor-
intensive industries such as textiles.

Other Government Policies

Besides taxing and subsidizing, government can cause
deviations of price from marginal costs through a variety of
other actions. By enacting a draft law, government can hold
the price of military labor substantially below what it would
be if it had to use compensation to lure recruits. Through
regulation, government may cause prices to be lower (at
least in the short run) than they would be if competitive
forces were allowed to operate. Through regulation, government may let prices drift higher by preventing the competition that would tend to drive them down toward marginal
costs.

No Competition

The economist's model of the free market assumes that
competition will drive prices to the level of marginal cost,
which is normally below the level at which sellers would
reap the most net revenue. However, it is not unusual for
sellers acting collusively, or simply following price leadership, to adopt pricing policies not consistent with this model.
While economics literature is filled with debate over the
subject of how actual pricing works, there are grounds for
belief that in many unregulated industries the pricing system
does not produce prices which reflect marginal costs.

Decreasing Cost Industries

Another important case of deviation between market price and marginal cost occurs in decreasing cost industries. In any industry where there are economies of scale or where new technology makes cheaper production processes available before the earlier equipment is fully depreciated, a situation of decreasing long-run marginal costs exists. If the industry charges a price reflecting the cost of production (including normal profit) from the new production facilities, it would have to operate at a loss. Assuming that all of a firm's prices for identical products must be identical regardless of the plant that produced the item, the price reflecting costs in the new low-cost plant would result in losses on the products manufactured at the older higher-cost facility. No firm can operate indefinitely at a loss. To avoid such losses, it must charge a price above the full costs of production at the new facilities. A cost-benefit analyst using market prices in such a situation will overestimate the cost to society of producing the item he is considering purchasing.

Externalities

Market prices also deviate from marginal production cost when externalities are present. Externalities exist when not all the costs of production are imposed on the producer, or when not all the benefits of consumption accrue to the consumer. Air pollution is a typical example of a production externality. A manufacturer may impose certain production costs on others by polluting their air. A typical example of a consumption externality occurs in the case of medical care for contagious diseases. Consumption of polio vaccine not only benefits the consumer; it benefits those who might catch the disease from him if he were not immunized. Externalities may be either positive or negative in both the production and consumption cases. Such negative production externalities as air pollution have positive counterparts such as lakes for recreation created by irrigation and power dams. To offset such positive consumption externalities as those of medical care, there are negative externalities--for example, those connected with the consumption of alcohol.

The importance of externalities is that they distort both market-place decisions and PPB analysis from the economic optimum. Because it excludes the cost of air pollution, the cost of steel might be too low, encouraging its consumption by government and private industry at the expense of pollution-less wood. Because the benefits of medical care do not all accrue to the consumer, medical care will (other things being equal) be underconsumed and the consumer's willingness to pay, which reflects itself in prices, will not fully reflect benefits.

THE ASSUMED SATISFACTORY DISTRIBUTION OF INCOME

Cost measurements using market prices are built upon the ultimate assumption that income is distributed in an ethically satisfactory manner. This assumption is inherent in cost and benefit analysis, because the welfare connotations of the price system exist only if this condition prevails.[6] To the extent that prices are dependent upon an income distribution deemed ethically unsatisfactory, they lose their significance in providing "correct" signals of real costs. The production of mink provides an example. If our national income were distributed equally among all Americans, it is reasonable to assume that no one would wish to purchase $5,000 mink coats. On the other hand, with present income distribution, a considerable demand exists for these garments. In a benefit analysis (for example, in calculating the benefits of increased water supply), the gross benefits of additional mink production would be the number of pelts produced times the market price of the pelts.* The value of the pelts depends upon the demand for the coats, and that demand depends upon how income is distributed in the United States.

A comparable problem develops on the cost side. Suppose converting a mink farm into a training school for boys

---

* In addition, the consumer surplus (amount above the sale price each customer would have paid for a good if it were only available at the higher price) would be considered as a benefit.

is being studied.* The costs of such action are the mink
pelts lost as a result of the decision times the unit value of
those pelts minus the costs of feed, etc., associated with
producing them. The higher the prices of mink (which depend
upon income distribution), the greater the price of the pelts
and the higher the costs in calculating the benefits and costs
of the school.

The same mechanism operates for private purchases, so
that market prices in fact reflect existing income distributions. If the school or any private party sought to buy the
mink farm in order to convert it, the price demanded by the
owner would have to compensate him for the lost profits of
growing mink--which, like the costs of abandoning the farm
in the example above, are the market prices of the product
minus the costs of producing it. If the income were, over-
night, redistributed equally among all Americans, the value
of the mink farm would drop (a) when measured as a benefit
in an analysis of whether to build one, (b) when measured as
a profit for an entrepreneur planning to build one, (c) when
measured as a cost for a government planning to replace one,
and (d) when measured as a price by someone trying to buy
one.

Americans do not hold special elections to determine
whether the existing income distribution in the United States
is optimal. It is clear, however, that a broad group of individuals and their elected representatives do not believe it is,
as is evidenced by the large number of income-transfer programs in the United States. Such programs, designed to
alter income distribution from that caused by market forces,
include a progressive income tax, unemployment compensation,

---

* It is important to remember that cost-benefit analysis
does not depend upon whether an activity is wholly, partly,
or not at all run directly by government. The conversion
could be from a government-owned farm to a government
school or from a private farm to a private school (required
by law through zoning, taxation, or condemnation of land
and sale to the school). The ownership question should be
irrelevant in the calculation of benefits and costs as noted,
for example, in connection with the urban transportation
study considered in Chapter 8.

welfare programs, and institutional care programs as well
as a variety of transfers in cash and kind made to the aged
and the poor. Despite these programs, there is no authoritative statement of a "proper" income distribution and no
reason to suppose that the one selected by any cost-benefit
analyst will be better than any other person's. These problems are the subject of the following chapter. For this
chapter, it suffices to note that they are substantial. The
only defense of using prices that reflect existing income distributions is that no better alternative is available.

CONSUMER SOVEREIGNTY

Ultimately, prices reflect what consumers decide to buy
and how they decide to sell their services as employees.
Economic analysis of government programs is thus dependent
upon consumer sovereignty, an assumption so basic to welfare economics that it is rarely questioned in cost-benefit
literature. When a consumer decides to buy two loaves of
bread rather than one quart of ice cream, the economist
assumes that his decision is worthy of respect and that reversing it cannot be justified on economic grounds. However,
government does not normally accord such significant stature
to the preferences of the consumer. Rejection of consumer
sovereignty and its implications for policy is inherent in a
number of long-standing governmental policies, many of
which are not even controversial. [7]

Laws exist which, if enforceable, would close some
consumer options entirely. The decision of life or death
itself, the ultimate in consumer sovereignty, is subjected
to legal restriction. Both suicide and euthanasia are crimes,
even when decided upon and carried out with knowledge and
sober deliberation. These are crimes even though the effects
upon others may be beneficial rather than harmful. Many
governments prevent their citizens from purchasing the services of prostitutes, prohibit homosexual acts among consent-
ing adults, and have, in the past, prevented the dissemination
of birth control information and devices. Hallucinogenic
drugs and narcotics cannot legally be purchased for nonmedi-
cal uses in the United States even when the customer knows

exactly what he is getting into and might be willing to create a situation where he would not injure others while using the drugs.   Sale of liquor is prohibited in some jurisdictions, perhaps because of alleged harm to innocent parties or per- haps because the public conscience is offended by drunkenness.

Certain categories of transactions, such as wagering and usurious loans, are prohibited entirely in many jurisdic- tions even though they may serve an economic function and neither imperfect knowledge nor significant externalities may exist in all situations in which the transactions are prohibited. Government may permit other transactions but limit the days on which they may take place by "blue laws" and Sunday closing requirements.   Consumers are sometimes prevented from taking risks, even when they have full knowledge of consequences.   Some jurisdictions prohibit plastic pipe, others gas heaters without flues and cleaning fluids with very low flash points.

Government also interferes with consumer decision- making by altering the price signals the economy gives to consumers.   For example, tobacco and liquor are sold only at prices far in excess of the costs of production, and some goods and services are distributed free by government.

Government, in short, is by no means committed to the implications of a policy of consumer sovereignty.   It is willing to prohibit certain types of consumer choices entirely, even when externalities and imperfect knowledge are not major considerations.   It is also willing to alter the composition of the shopper's market basket of goods and services by altering the price signals given the consumer from those which would prevail if prices were equal to marginal cost.

SUMMARY

This chapter has considered a number of more technical problems encountered in the application of the PPB approach to any real decision situation.   Both opportunity costs and willingness to pay--the signals of costs and benefits, respec- tively--are normally treated in terms of market prices.

These market prices may frequently be inaccurate measures because of taxes, subsidies, and other government policies and by virtue of competitive situations, decreasing-cost industries, and externalities. Another conceptual problem occurs because the current distribution of income must be assumed to be satisfactory for costs comparisons to signal preferred alternatives.

Given the current state of knowledge, to seek to correct prices to reflect all these distortions is an impossible undertaking. If economic analysis is to proceed at all, it must in most cases be based upon the assumption that market prices do reflect marginal cost and income is satisfactorily distributed. In all probability, analysis based upon this premise will not be perfect but will be better than no analysis at all. These difficulties, which may appear minor to lay readers, have very significant implications for the politics of program analysis. They leave room for legitimate differences of opinion among the analysts themselves and thereby make it more difficult to expect all analysts to give all decision-makers the same advice.

NOTES TO CHAPTER 10

1. U.S. Federal Inter-Agency River Basin Committee, Subcommittee on Benefits and Costs, Proposed Practices for Economic Analysis of River Basin Projects (Washington, D.C.: Government Printing Office, 1950), pp. 7-8.

2. Roland N. McKean, Efficiency in Government Through Systems Analysis (New York: John Wiley & Sons, Inc., 1958), p. 107.

3. This section is intended to raise some of the basic issues inherent in using market prices to signal costs and benefits. For an easily understood discussion of these issues, see Robert Dorfman, The Price System (Englewood Cliffs, N.J.: Prentice Hall, 1964). More advanced treatments will be found in Joe Bain, Price Theory (New York: Holt, 1952), and George Stigler, The Theory of Price (New York:

Macmillan, 1952). It may be possible to avoid the difficulties discussed in this section by using "shadow prices." For a discussion of the advantages and pitfalls of "shadow prices," see Roland McKean, "The Use of Shadow Prices," in Samuel B. Chase, Jr. (ed.), Problems in Public Expenditure Analysis (Washington, D.C.: Brookings, 1968), pp. 33-65.

4. U.S. Congress, Joint Economic Committee, Subsidy and Subsidy-Effect Programs of the U.S. Government, Committee Print, Eighty-ninth Congress, 1st Session, 1965.

5. U.S. Federal Power Commission, National Power Survey (Washington, D.C.: Government Printing Office, 1964), p. 22.

6. This is textbook economics. See, for example, Paul Samuelson, "Epilogue to Microeconomic Pricing," Economics (6th ed.; New York: McGraw-Hill, 1964), Ch. 30, pp. 616-31.

7. The questions involved raise difficult problems of political and economic theory. See, for example, Richard A. Musgrave, The Theory of Public Finance (New York: McGraw-Hill, 1959), particularly pp. 14-15; J. Roland Pennock, "Responsiveness, Responsibility, and Majority Rule," American Political Science Review, XLVI (September, 1952), pp. 790-808; Austin Ranney, The Doctrine of Responsible Party Government (Urbana: University of Illinois Press, 1954); Austin Ranney and W. Kendall, Democracy and the American Party System (New York: Harcourt, Brace, 1956); and Part Three (pp. 275-421) of S. I. Benn and R. S. Peters, The Principles of Political Thought (New York: Collier, 1964).

CHAPTER **11** WHO BENEFITS?
WHO PAYS?

BENEFITS FROM THE
REDISTRIBUTION OF INCOME

The preceding chapter considered conceptual questions involved in determining costs and benefits in terms of "economic efficiency." Programs that increase national income were said to have had net benefits--benefits measured by subtracting the value of goods and services consumed in producing the governmental output from the value of that governmental output. The resulting net benefit was considered to be a benefit regardless of to whom it might accrue. Implicitly, such a formulation assumes either that it makes no difference to whom the benefits might accrue or that the differences in income distribution resulting from a government program would be straightened out as a separate activity by a hypothetical branch of government known as a distribution branch. The mere transfer of resources from one person to another was considered to be both costless and benefitless. This approach, which simplifies the problems of benefit measurement considerably, has been used in essentially all cost-benefit studies both in present applications and in more theoretical treatments. [1]

The separation of redistribution effects and standard measures of economic efficiency is reflected in the writings of most economists concerned with public expenditures. The sharpest separation is made by treating government in three branches. One branch pursues policies of allocational efficiency (giving society what members of society are willing to pay for); one branch pursues redistribution policy (taking money away from those deemed to have "too much" and providing money to those having "too little"); and a final branch

172

pursues policies to prevent business cycles of alternating boom and bust. [2]

Without consideration of redistribution of income through a project, its benefits and costs can be stated in a relatively straightforward fashion. The benefits from a proposed new road can be measured, as in the M-1 study described in Chapter 8, in evaluations of time savings by personal and business drivers and in reduction in accidents, tire wear, and gallons of gasoline used. Costs consist of construction expenses plus planned upkeep. If benefits exceed costs, it may be concluded that the project would be economically efficient.

However, the income redistribution consequences of such a decision will be significant for the parties involved. These dimensions are the ones that frequently form the basis for both political controversy and political decisions. The owners of motels, gas stations, and stores along the old route stand to lose heavily, but their loss will be the gain of others who build along the new road. The parallel railroad will lose business to truckers whose driving time and costs have been lowered. Town A may now replace Town B as the shopping center for many customers who have had their access to A improved while their access to B remained unchanged. Cement manufacturers, sign painters, and highway contractors will have increased income, while manufacturers of railroad cars and mass transit may have less. The people in the area served by the road get the benefits, while the general taxpayer pays the costs.

Despite the conceptual neatness of working with distribution and allocation effects separately, in practice the two cannot be neatly divided. A cabinet officer or congressman considering a particular proposed policy is aware that no magical process will change distributional impacts of other programs and taxes to straighten out whatever inequitable distributions the program might cause. A new proposed subsidy to railroads will presumably benefit railroads and railroad workers and injure truck-owners and taxpayers. Distributional consequences of this type are frequently more significant (in terms of dollars involved) than net economic efficiency benefit consequences of government programs.

A layman looking at a government program to take money from A and give it to B would suggest that the program was conferring a "benefit" upon B. An economist in looking at the same program would label it a "transfer payment" and a tax. In the sense that the phrase "economic efficiency" has been used in the preceding chapters, such a transfer would be considered as neither a cost nor a benefit from the national point of view. In simple terms, such a transfer does not increase or decrease the size of the economic pie--it merely alters the size of pieces distributed to different persons. From the point of view of B, however, the funds will be considered a benefit. From the point of view of society, the transfer to B may also be considered to be a benefit, if society would rather B than A had the funds. We shall call this concept "redistribution benefits" and always use that term in the sense of altering the distribution of existing wealth rather than in creating new wealth. The remainder of this chapter will be devoted to the question of whether the U.S. political system makes it possible to talk of and analyze such benefits.

HOW CAN REDISTRIBUTION
BENEFITS BE TREATED?

Implicit in the concept of an allocational benefit or a redistribution benefit is a scale upon which such benefits can be measured--an objective function. In the case of allocational benefits, that objective function is economic efficiency--increasing the size of the economic pie obtainable from a limited endowment of resources. In the case of redistribution benefits, that function has not yet been defined for the nation as a whole, although it can easily be defined for an individual. The benefit from B's perspective of the transfer to him of $100 in cash or its equivalent (as he sees it) in goods or services is $100.

One way for PPBS practitioners to seek to define redistribution benefit measures for the nation as a whole would be to cumulate individual preferences. If one knew the utility of money or goods to every individual in the nation and could compare those utilities, it would be possible to redistribute income objectively to maximize total satisfactions. If, for example, John would get 5 "utils" of satisfaction from a new hat and Mary 10 from the same hat, the hat should go to Mary regardless of any of the other characteristics of the hat or the people involved. Interpersonal comparisons of satisfactions are made frequently in everyday life ("You don't need that; you already have two. Give it to Mary"), but no theoretically adequate method has been found to measure them.

In the absence of any objective method, a PPB analyst who is not prepared to make society's income distribution value judgment for it must seek guidance from "higher authority" about the income distribution consequences desired. The following sections are concerned with (a) in what form higher authority could provide this guidance if it were disposed to do so and (b) why it is not disposed to do so. [3]

A Redistribution Constraint

The benefits of a policy or project to any group may be measured in a fashion similar to that employed in measuring the benefits of the policy to the nation as a whole. The universe is simply restricted to include only the target group, and the policy's benefits can be measured as the group's willingness to pay for the policy output. Thus, it is possible to choose policies on the basis of their relative value to any potential target group, i.e., the sick, the ill-housed, the middle-income residents of Los Angeles, or pretty redheads. This type of calculation frequently appears in actual political processes. It is, conceptually, the definition of "special interests" which is relevant to the conception that sometimes "special interests" gain over "the general interest" due to some feature of the political process like stupidity, corruption, or lobbies.

Even assuming that political leaders would agree on a target group to be assisted (say, Group A), it would be impossible to develop government programs on the sole criterion of undertaking policies that benefit Group A the most. The policy developed to fulfill that criterion would be to transfer all program funds to Group A and seek more such funds. There are, however, other less radical methods

by which redistribution preferences could be included in the
policy formulation process.

It is possible to determine that any particular program
or project shall be designed to yield maximum net benefits
subject to a requirement (constraint) that the target group
get particular benefits. An example is an irrigation program
under guidance to maximize efficiency with a constraint that
a group of Indians receive increased annual income of at
least $20 million as a result of the project. [4]

This concept of a redistribution constraint normally does
not have an explicit counterpart in the actual political process
of program and project design and approval. Guidance to design an irrigation project as efficiently as possible, consistent
with transferring $20 million to the Indians, is not likely to
appear in actual program design. First, to state the constraint
explicitly is to state that the project is a special benefit one.
This is politically possible only if there is a consensus on benefiting the particular group. Such a consensus may exist for
low-income Indians but not for Indians living on oil royalties.
If the redistribution objective is left unstated, government
agencies, congressmen, and private groups can talk in terms
of general objectives such as increasing the food supply.

Equally important, to state a constraint is, by definition,
to state a condition where overfulfillment is presumed worthless. Those beneficiaries not familiar with linear program-
ming--a group large enough to be politically significant--will
not be pleased with a determination that the benefits of x
program are to be held to $20 million. Their response, no
doubt, would take the form of "Well, if the best irrigation
project the experts can design yields more benefits for us,
why not adopt it?" Thus, there may be a political penalty
in stating redistribution desires in the form of constraints
(e.g., the beneficiaries should get $20 million but you don't
need to give them more) rather than objective functions (e.g.,
the project should help beneficiaries).

Combining Redistribution and Economic Efficiency

The notion that benefits are equal no matter to whom
they accrue is not representative of the views of various

groups in American society nor of the views of political decision-makers, who are normally concerned more with the welfare of certain identifiable groups--for example, themselves and their constituents. It is possible, at least in theory, to convert these preferences into mathematical expressions which can be utilized in program formulation and evaluation.

Suppose, for example, that in the preceding example it was discovered that society, through its decision-makers, was willing to sacrifice $20 in efficiency benefits in order to obtain $200 of redistribution benefits to the Indian tribe, as indicated by the opportunity cost of the constraint. Suppose further that society was not willing to sacrifice $21 in efficiency benefits to obtain $200 in redistribution benefits. These facts permit inferences about the added value accorded funds or project outputs in the hands of the Indians. Specifically, $220 in the hands of outsiders is considered equivalent to $200 in the hands of the Indians, as society is willing to "spend" $20 in efficiency benefits to get the transfer accomplished. The same inference stated in another way is that any project that puts $200 in efficiency benefits in the hands of Indians is worth $220 to society. Thus, the benefits from a project can be stated as follows:

Where water is valued at $100 per acre foot and 100 acre feet produced

Benefit from 50 acre feet to non-Indians is (50 x $100)	$ 5,000
Benefit from 50 acre feet to Indians is (50 x $100) + 10% of (50 x $100)	$ 5,500
And the total benefits from the project would be	$10,500

The common-sense notion of the same concept is the statement: "I would rather see a dollar given to him than a dollar and ten cents to anyone else." The weighting of distributional consequences in connection with the measurement of efficiency benefits is mathematically simple if the value of redistributions does not change as redistribution

increases.* It is possible to consider a planner's ideal
world, where properly qualified decision-makers would make
value judgments that could be arrayed on a scale similar to
the one below:

Where x is the value of a good or service
    accruing to or being taken from any
    individual directly or indirectly

When the individual is	for x use
Persons with income below $3,000	110% of x
Veterans	105% of x
Add for combat service 15%	
Add for service-connected disability 20%	
Persons in Appalachia, regardless of income	105% of x
City dwellers	95% of x
Residents of Vermont	80% of x
Negroes	110% of x
Redheads	78% of x
Elderly persons (regardless of income)	120% of x

Such a value table would permit additions and subtractions to
find the exact value of any project with known distributional
effects. A project to construct housing in West Virginia for
elderly combat veterans would be "worth" to society about
40 per cent** more than the willingness of the beneficiaries
to pay the economic costs associated with it. Although
political decision-makers and most citizens who talk about
policy make such value weight judgments implicitly, they
are rarely made as explicit as in the table above.

---

    * It probably does. For example, a dollar distributed
to Appalachia might seem less desirable to society after $1
billion had already been distributed.

    ** Taking into account the fact that some occupants
might also have service-connected disabilities or be Negroes
(tending to increase the differential), and some might be city
dwellers, residents of Vermont, or redheads (tending to
decrease the differential).

To assume that members of Congress, Presidents, and other political decision-makers would commit themselves to weights such as these would be naive indeed. Besides the political problem inherent in trying to identify one group as "worth more" than another, such weightings would imply that appropriate policy would always be to take from those with low weights (through taxation) to benefit those with high weights (through programs). Thus, conceptually, unless provision is made for constant readjustment of weights, such a weighting is not a practical guide to policy.

Discovering What Decision-Makers Want

An intriguing aspect of redistribution weighting is the concept that decision-makers' weightings are inherent in every decision and that the weights can therefore be established merely by looking at the decisions. For example, the welfare weights implicit in a progressive tax system can be determined and even attributed to various states of the Union.[5] If an analyst is aware of the beneficiaries of any given policy, he can infer that Congress chose to prefer those beneficiaries over the population at large, thereby permitting the inference that their welfare weights would presumably be above average.[6] What can be done for the parts could presumably be done for the whole if enough academic resources could be devoted to the task--and the welfare weights implicit in each federal program could be derived.

In fact, however, the political decision-making process is such that this procedure would be (a) impossible as a practical matter and (b) unsound as a theoretical matter. One can well imagine a corps of researchers after each examining a separate federal program returning with inconsistent sets of distribution preferences inferred from various programs. Two examples are given to illustrate the problem.

Example 1

Distributional Weights Implicit in Federal Programs
Distinguishing Characteristic:
Geographic Location--States

Policy	Favors
Cotton subsidies	Southern and Southwestern states
Income tax (per capita incidence)	Southern states and Appalachia
Sugar beet subsidies	Western states and Maine
Reclamation program	All states west of Mississippi River
Ship construction subsidies	All states with shipyards, primarily ocean-bordering states
Tidelands oil legislation	Western ocean and Gulf-bordering states
Urban renewal	Non-Southern states
Some grants-in-aid formulae	Low-income states
Some grants-in-aid formulae	Low population-density states
St. Lawrence Seaway tolls less than costs	States bordering Great Lakes
Corps of Engineers beach erosion projects	Eastern seaboard states
Corps of Engineers bay pollution, etc., program	Eastern seaboard states
Peanut support program	Eastern seaboard states
Appalachia program	Appalachia

Example 2

Distributional Weights Implicit in Federal Programs
Distinguishing Characteristic:
Income Levels

Policy	Favors
Progressive taxation	Low income
Cigarette taxes	High income

Excise tax on furs	Low and medium income
Repeal of excise tax on furs	High income
Cabaret tax repeal	High income
Auto excise repeal	Medium income
Non-taxation of inputed income from owner-occupied housing	Medium-high income
Working wives, child care deduction	Low-medium income
Subsidies to performing arts	High income
Subsidies to rapid transit	Low income
Subsidies for open space, parks, etc.	Medium income
Airport construction (personal travel)	High income

The above examples make no attempt to define "favor" rigorously, nor do they purport to be based upon substantial studies of the program described. Regardless of whether particular readers may agree with all the examples, the point is clear that the distributional value weights implicit in federal program decisions are frequently not consistent. Even if this practical problem could be surmounted, important conceptual problems would remain. For the redistribution weights implicit in congressional policy decisions to have normative meanings, several conditions must hold.

First and most important, "the Congress" must have been aware of what it was doing. Not only did congressmen need to be aware that a given project was going to be voted upon, they needed to be aware of the redistribution consequences of their action in approving it. It is theoretically possible that in approving a project or program "the Congress" (a) was aware of the redistribution consequences, (b) had a false notion of redistribution consequences, or (c) didn't know the redistribution consequences. Inferring general redistribution preferences will always be incorrect when situation b prevails and is no more likely to be correct than incorrect when situation c prevails.

Second, it must be presumed that members of Congress based their decisions on the known redistribution considerations. Even if redistributional consequences were known, inferring them to each member of Congress who did not vote against a project or policy totally misperceives the nature of the legislative process. There are many perfectly logical decision rules that would explain a failure to vote against a project or policy and have nothing to do with income redistribution preferences of individual congressmen. For example, a decision rule to vote for any measure reported from committee with the support of a majority of one's own party would not be an illogical response to the flood of new legislation, constituents, and other pressures upon a congressman's time.

The third fallacy inherent in inferring redistribution preferences from actual program decisions originates in the fact that a decision under consideration is never the first affecting the distribution of income. A Corps of Engineers recreation and flood control project near Cleveland, Ohio, may be considered to redistribute income to Ohioans but could also be considered to "compensate" Ohioans for large reclamation projects in the West. The Cross-Florida barge canal may--in the calculations of individual congressmen-- be included conceptually with the St. Lawrence Seaway when redistribution effects are being considered. In short, it is incorrect to infer redistribution preferences from the selection of an individual project or policy unless it is shown that the decision-maker has considered that project or policy in isolation. Political decisions, however, are not made in isolation.

The fourth fallacy in seeking to infer any kind of redistribution preferences from actions of "the Congress" rests in the fact that Congress is nothing more than a collection of individuals. While the phrase "the Congress works its will" is in common use, there is no such thing as a "congressional will." Congress does what a voting majority wants it to do, and procedural matters can prevent even that statement from being entirely accurate. A majority decision may incorporate individuals' preferences based upon entirely different perceptions of what a given policy would do and entirely different attitudes toward various subpolicies inherent in the legislation.

In short, the decision rules implicit in congressional decisions cannot be taken as policy guidance for analysts seeking to fulfill the PPBS objective of "identifying objectives." Similar comments could be made about noncongressional decision-makers' decisions.

Getting Decision-Makers To Say What They Want

Policy-makers in the United States have traditionally shied away from direct transfers of cash to program beneficiaries. Instead of adopting European-style income maintenance plans such as family allowances, national poverty programs stress job training, food stamps, public housing, and health programs. These transfers in kind are comparable to transfers in cash, but it can be shown that they are less efficient economically (assuming that the objective is maximizing the satisfaction of the recipient) than cash transfers. To the extent that society transfers in kind goods and services with an economic cost greater than the consumer's willingness to pay (given the redistribution payment as a lump sum), society will be acting inefficiently--spending more satisfactions (equals economic resources, equals money) than it needs to in order to give the desired level of benefits to the recipient of the goods and services. [7] Thus, the economic logic of redistribution benefits leads to the conclusion again that, economically speaking, if such a benefit exists, a policy of direct cash transfers should be pursued. Clearly, however, such a policy is not being pursued in the United States nor does its adoption seem likely in the near future. This forces the further question of why no such transfers are being made.

One reason is clearly political. That is, it would not be unreasonable for an analyst, and certainly not for a congressman, to develop the idea that Americans just don't like the idea of transferring money. The very idea is described by trigger words of distaste like "handout" and "dole" which have become associated with the transfer concept. Thus, there may be a constraint in the United States against direct transfers of resources or at least an aversion to such direct transfers and a preference for indirect methods like food stamps, public housing, and free medical treatment for the indigent.

If such an aversion does exist, its existence seems to suggest that a redistribution weight could never exist. The weight accorded to redistribution of income through a project might then be seen to vary with the type of project involved. A project to redistribute income through improved clothing might be preferred to a method of redistribution through free street dances that provided equal recipient satisfaction at lower cost. In the same sense, irrigation projects might be preferred to rent supplements--or vice versa.

A second plausible explanation for an aversion to direct transfers is aversion to the consequences of consumer sovereignty. As previously pointed out, "government" does not accord particular sanctity in many cases to the consumer sovereignty concept despite the assertion by many economists that it should. Many Americans cherish a concept of "he who pays the piper should call the tune." This is not unusual in a society where the voter of average age has spent about half of his entire life in a situation where his consumption decisions (spending) were dictated by others (parents) and where political leaders are in loco parentis in their own homes and have grown up in a legal system that recognizes such concepts as "wards of the State."

Violating consumer sovereignty in the abstract may sound unfair and undemocratic, but in the real world it appears as a series of politically attractive propositions. As a policy, it sometimes reflects externalities--particularly externalities associated with children. Mother might prefer candy to housing, and the child may not be consulted if funds are redistributed to mother. Mother may prefer dresses for herself to dental care for her child, but the ultimate costs of the decision to society may be significant. A willingness to violate consumer sovereignty may also appear even when externalities and innocent victims (in or out of a household) are not apparent. What sacrificing, frugal, teetotaling taxpayer wants to see his hard-earned money turned over to other people so that they can buy beer? Why should we give people money when they would spend it on movies and lipstick instead of improving those awful houses? What is the point in making welfare payments to lift people out of poverty when all they do is give most of the money to churches instead of lifting their standard of living? All of these questions imply a willingness on the part of the questioner to override the preferences of consumers even though, presumably, this would reduce the recipient's total satisfaction derived from the economic resources society is willing to commit to improve his welfare.

To the extent that this phenomenon exists, it makes a single redistribution objective impossible to formulate. A program that redistributes income by making money available may not be considered as desirable as a program to make housing available even by those who have no aversion to direct transfers as such. A program to redistribute food may be preferred to a program to distribute housing, and within the food program bread may be preferred to steak. The potential preferences are as unlimited as the government policies available to redistribute income.

THE CONSEQUENCES OF INABILITY
TO DEAL WITH REDISTRIBUTION

The absence of any reliable method for PPB analysts to ascertain the redistribution preferences of their superiors in Congress and the executive (as well as the public) is probably the most significant hurdle to success of the PPB approach. It was probably insufficiently considered in the drafting of initial PPB guidance in the U.S. Government because the problem did not arise to any significant degree within the Defense Department. Almost without exception (save for the costs of involuntary military service), the costs of Defense are borne by the general taxpayer. Ignoring occasional windfall profits, the benefits of defense also accrue to all taxpayers in equal (common) measure.

In civilian programs, however, costs may be imposed upon small, readily identified groups. They may be forced through user charges to pay more for government services they currently receive or may have costs imposed upon them by pollution control, zoning, building codes, rent controls, and a wide range of other policies. Likewise, benefits can, unlike the benefits of defense, be concentrated on some persons and denied to others in domestic programs. Few domestic policies are justified solely on an alleged contribution to national income. Most are related to specific groups of beneficiaries and have as one objective some measure of assistance to the beneficiary groups.

Under these circumstances, analytical techniques that
cannot cope with policies of taking from some to benefit
others are sterile techniques indeed. Yet, in this chapter,
we have sought to show that the PPB approach does not offer
a politically feasible way of determining benefits from redistribution of income or of identifying program objectives
precisely where income redistribution is involved. If a
decision-maker has no known redistribution preferences and
there is no way to infer any from his past decisions, then
alternatives obviously cannot be designed to maximize
achievement of his objectives. The result is that, to a large
degree, where redistribution is at stake, the PPB approach
develops into conveying the redistribution implications of a
decision to the decision-maker without any attempt to relate
redistribution effects to economic efficiency effects.[8] Such
information is unquestionably useful and leaves the decision-
maker better informed than he would be in its absence. However, it does not leave him as well off as those who expect
wonders from the PPB approach may assume.[9]

                          SUMMARY

In this chapter, we have considered the various methods
recommended for the program analyst to consider policies
that redistribute income among individuals. The distinction
between the layman's conception of a benefit (which incorporates the economist's "transfer payment" concept) and
national income or economic efficiency benefits was pointed
out. Redistribution of income was found, in effect, to offer
another dimension of benefits and costs. This second dimension can be treated analytically in a variety of ways, all
of which are unsatisfactory from either a theoretical point
of view, a political point of view, or both. First, a consistent system of redistribution preferences cannot be found in
actual political decisions. Second, any general desire to
weight benefits and costs to reflect income distribution preferences can be most readily reflected in direct income-
transfer programs. The absence of such programs carries
some implication for the existence of the weights. Third,
the thought of directly taking from some groups and giving
to others is less palatable politically than the thought of

spending without explicit identification of the groups providing the funds. Finally, the basic concepts of treatment of redistribution of income values presume that those values are related solely to the amount distributed. In fact, it would seem that redistribution preferences depend upon the method chosen as well as the amount involved.

Income distribution consequences are an important portion of the design, evaluation, and administration of programs through the political process. "Who gets?" and "Who pays?" may frequently be more controlling than "How much is gotten?" and "How much is paid?" Yet, it has been argued in this chapter that these income redistribution consequences cannot be readily evaluated using the PPB approach. Political decision-makers will not make these determinations explicitly, and they cannot validly be inferred from decisions previously made. In offering programs and alternatives for decision and in evaluating past programs, PPB analysts may point out redistribution consequences for the decision-maker's review. However, in designing and administering programs, and in suggesting alternatives, PPB analysts must proceed on the basis either of their own (or their superior's) income distribution preferences or act on the assumption that society is indifferent to the income distribution effects of economically efficient programs, an assumption that is clearly wrong.

NOTES TO CHAPTER 11

1. Existing water resource cost-benefit studies exclude distributional consequences and measure "benefits to whomsoever they may accrue." See U.S. Federal Inter-Agency River Basin Committee, Subcommittee on Benefits and Costs, Proposed Practices for Economic Analysis of River Basin Projects (Rev. ed.; Washington, D.C.: Government Printing Office, 1958), and U.S. President's Water Resources Council Policies, Standards, and Procedures in the Formulation, Evaluation, and Review of Plans for Use and Development of Water and Related Land Resources (Washington, D.C.: Government Printing Office, 1962), Eighty-seventh Congress, 2nd Session, Senate Doc. 97. A limited exception is the

inclusion of "secondary" or "indirect" benefits by the Bureau of Reclamation in its irrigation project studies. However, the Bureau treats these benefits as though they were allocational benefits, a practice that has given rise to considerable criticism. See U.S. Bureau of Reclamation, Report of Panel of Consultants on Secondary or Indirect Benefits of Water-Use Projects, Washington, D.C., June, 1962 (Mimeograph), and S. V. Ciriacy-Wantrup, "Benefit-Cost Analysis and Public Resource Development," Journal of Farm Economics, XXIX (November, 1947), 1181-96. The same viewpoint is taken in transportation studies where distributional consequences are not called either benefits or costs. For excellent samples of the literature, see John R. Meyer et al., The Urban Transportation Problem (Cambridge: Harvard University Press, 1965); Tillo E. Kuhn, Public Enterprise Economics and Transport Problems (Berkeley: University of California Press, 1962); and E. L. Grant and C. H. Oglesby, "A Critique of Some Recent Economics Studies Comparing Alternate Highway Locations," Proceedings of the Thirty-Ninth Annual Meeting, National Academy of Sciences, National Research Council (National Research Council Publication 773; Washington, D.C., 1960), pp. 1-8.

2. This separation appears in a widely used book on public finance theory--Richard A. Musgrave, The Theory of Public Finance (New York: McGraw-Hill, 1959).

3. The design of a policy is conceptually similar to the design of a dam, so it was possible to base this section upon the excellent discussion by Stephen A. Marglin, "Objectives of Water-Resource Development: A General Statement," Ch. II of Arthur Maass et al., Design of Water Resource Systems (Cambridge, Mass.: Harvard University Press, 1962), pp. 17-87.

4. Marglin, op. cit., pp. 63-85.

5. This exercise is undertaken in Robert Haveman's Epilogue, "The Measurement of Economic Welfare: An Empirical Experiment," in his Water Resource Investment and the Public Interest: An Analysis of Federal Expenditures in Ten Southern States (Nashville, Tenn.: Vanderbilt University Press, 1965), pp. 125-51.

6. An attempt to justify and provide an example of such a procedure appears in Burton Weisbrod's "Income Redistribution Effects and Benefit-Cost Analysis," in Samuel B. Chase, Jr. (ed.), Problems in Public Expenditure Analysis (Washington, D.C.: Brookings, 1968), pp. 177-209. The Weisbrod effort is criticized by Robert Haveman and Ruth Mack on pages 209-22 of that volume for reasons comparable to those given in this chapter.

7. Proof of this proposition using indifference curve analysis can be found, for example, in Donald Watson, Price Theory and Its Uses (Boston: Houghton-Mifflin, 1963), pp. 93-94.

8. For an interesting attempt to identify the distribution effects of government expenditures, see W. Irwin Gillespie, "Effect of Public Expenditures on the Distribution of Income," in Richard A. Musgrave (ed.), Essays in Fiscal Federalism (Washington, D.C.: Brookings, 1965).

9. For example, it has long been known that farm price support programs heavily concentrate their assistance on higher-income farmers, yet this knowledge alone has not caused significant program changes. For a recent study of the distribution impact of one subsidy program, see James T. Bonnen, "The Distribution of Benefits From Cotton Price Supports," in Chase, op. cit., pp. 223-48.

CHAPTER **12** AGENCY STRATEGIES FOR
DEALING WITH PPB

How the PPB approach is implemented depends upon the
agencies whose programs are being reviewed through this
tool. Ultimately, the success of the system in federal, state,
and local governments will depend not only upon whether its
underlying economic concepts are sound but also upon how
agencies apply those concepts to their own programs. This
chapter considers the bureaucratic environment in which PPB,
and any other management system, must be implemented.
Drawing examples from the economic analysis of water resource projects, it seeks to show how economic analysis
using what appear to be approaches comparable to PPB can
produce justifications for continuing programs that many
believe are economically unsound. These examples are included not to show that any given analytical technique is
wrong, but to show that the framework for economic analysis
is sufficiently loose so that analysis alone is not likely to
inform the decision-maker precisely which programs should
be cut back and which increased. As agencies and private
interests begin to hire their own analysts, the conclusions
from analysis will tend to become as diverse as the interests
of the groups hiring the analysts. Leaders in PPB have
recognized this possibility but have suggested that the ensuing
debate will be carried out at a higher informational level
than if analysts were not used.

PPB MAY THREATEN AGENCY POLICIES

In order to consider potential agency reactions to PPB,
it is necessary first to consider the functioning of an agency
within the political system. For this purpose, it is reasonable

AGENCY STRATEGIES FOR DEALING WITH PPB

to use the general approach adopted by Aaron Wildavsky in
The Politics of the Budgetary Process.[1] Wildavsky considers
an agency's budgetary activities as directed toward its survival and toward increasing its budget. To perform this function, the agency seeks support of various groups in the political system, forms alliances, and pursues various budgetary
strategies.

Agencies--a term used broadly here to connote any
government activity, from branch to department, large enough
to have its own budget--tend to develop loyalties among their
employees toward both the organization and the program it
administers. Employees of the Soil Conservation Service
tend to have a greater interest in soil conservation and a
somewhat different view of its importance than those who
work in the space program.[2] There are three major reasons
for this loyalty. First, in their occupational choices, people
tend to follow their own interests and their sense of what is
important. Thus, those who believe most strongly in soil
conservation are more likely to seek employment in that field
rather than the space program. Second, their program and
organizational orientations are reinforced by associations
with others of comparable beliefs. Third, their personal
future welfare is intertwined with the future of the programs
they administer.

Thus, the staff of any agency can be expected to have a
substantial commitment to the agency's program. This
commitment will usually be couched in programmatic rather
than survival terms. The concept of bureaucrats as individuals who reason explicitly, "I will fight for my agency's
survival because I desire my own advancement and, failing
that, want to make sure I still have a job" is a naive one.
Instead, the PPB approach will encounter government employees fighting for "their" programs simply because they
believe sincerely that it is in the national interest that the
program be continued and expanded. It can be said that the
staff of agencies tend to support the continuation of the program they administer at levels necessary to fulfill the "needs"
of the clientele for the program and to fulfill the public interest, as that interest was expressed by the Congress when it
established their program. Phrased another way, and viewed
from another perspective, this can be stated: Agencies act
to protect and expand their budgets.[3]

Upon the announcement of PPB (or any new management system), agency staff members naturally will wonder what effect it will have on the programs they administer. That effect must be one of three:

(1) The system will help the agency achieve expanded budgets because under the PPB approach the agency's programs will appear desirable.

(2) The system will not affect the agency's programs, except insofar as it requires more paper work.

(3) The system will retard the agency in achieving its objectives.

In the first case, the agency will cooperate readily with the implementation of PPB. * In the second case, the agency would initially be indifferent to PPB at least until it appeared that PPB would have an effect on its programs. ** In the third case, the agency has something to lose from PPB. Even in the first case, it may think there is more to gain than most PPB practitioners might concede is "legitimately"

---

* The author suspects that the rapid and relatively complete implementation of PPB in the Department of Health, Education and Welfare and the slower and less complete implementation in Agriculture and Interior may reflect this phenomenon. If one gathered impressions about the likely effect of PPB from what economists tend to say about program issues, it would have been possible to infer that human resource programs might gain substantially and certain Agricultural and Interior Department programs (particularly land management and reclamation) might be adversely affected by greater involvement of persons with economic training in the decision-making process.

** Simply by reorganizing the information presented for decision-makers, PPB is likely to have some effect on every agency in any government that adopts it. When the information presented to decision-makers is changed, it is unreasonable to expect that decisions would not be affected.

there. This chapter considers what agencies can do under these circumstances and the implications their options have for the PPB approach.

At the outset, it should be noted that when a program manager is presented with an analysis that his program is not the best alternative for achieving a given national purpose, he quite logically can conclude that the problem arises from one of two causes:

(1) There is something wrong with his program, or

(2) There is something wrong with the analysis.

It is naive indeed to assume that the first alternative will be explored before the second.

HIRING YOUR OWN ANALYST

It is probable that PPB expertise would be developed by major agencies in any government adopting the system even if for no other reason than defense against PPB experts outside the agency. The question is academic in the U.S. Government because the PPB guidance requires agencies to develop "in-house" program analysis capability. In an airtight, perfect system, whether or not analysts were employed by particular agencies, or by universities, or were on the President's own staff would not affect their conclusions. For the reasons discussed in this chapter and the two preceding ones, PPB is not such a system. As a result, the forces of self-selection and reinforcement described in the preceding section will tend to affect PPB analysts just like everyone else. This has already happened in the Defense Department. Charles Hitch, after his experience as Assistant Secretary of Defense (Comptroller), has commented:

> There is no question but that the systems
> analysis groups working within the defense
> establishment tend to take on the philosophi-
> cal coloration of their sponsoring organiza-
> tions, if for no other reason than that they

are exposed to the same environment and same
influences. [4]

This tendency, combined with a directive that each major
agency within the federal establishment hire its own analysts,
seems reasonably likely to produce the possibility that the
PPB approach will generate differing information and recommendations depending on where the analysis is done.

When Analysts Disagree

Some PPB experts have considered the development of
competing analysis groups to be a virtue of the new system.
For example, John Haldi--who for some time had headed
the PPB office in the Bureau of the Budget--told the Joint
Economic Committee:

> To me, the ultimate state of affairs is the
> healthy dialog that can be brought into existence
> through having other analytical groups vie with
> each other. Analysts are not perfect. They
> err sometimes. And they may make different
> assumptions. I believe that competition in
> analysis can lead to a much healthier discus-
> sion. [5]

Arthur Smithies has also suggested that there is virtue
in having a variety of analyses on any given issue. As he
put it:

> I conceive of effective government decision
> making as consisting of adversary pro-
> cesses. . . . The correctness of the deci-
> sions can rarely be judged by any objective
> standards. Their validity depends on the
> methods by which they are reached. [6]

He has explicitly drawn a parallel between the courtroom
situation and the government decision processes. In his
"Conceptual Framework for the Program Budget," he
commented:

There is a useful parallel to be drawn between
political and legal processes. The decisions
of judges or juries cannot be appraised by
objective standards. They depend on adversary
procedures that follow well-established rules.
If those rules are violated, decisions are upset
on appeal. Otherwise, they stand.

A programming approach to government
decision making can be thought of as an adversary process. Decision making is arranged
so as to permit the competition of ideas, in
the light of which decision makers make choices
among relevant alternatives. [7]

The suggestion that decision-makers function best when
experts disagree may not be entirely out of place when applied
to a courtroom situation. Such a circumstance deviates
sharply from decision-making processes in government.
The judge in a courtroom is a former expert, a member of
the experts' (bar) association, a graduate of the experts'
technical schools, and usually has long experience in his
specialized subject. He reaches decisions under relatively
leisurely conditions. Sometimes a cabinet member or other
political decision-maker may fulfill these conditions.
McNamara did. He was an expert in applying quantitative
techniques to military problems--having been employed to
do this long before he became Secretary of Defense. He
also managed to buy enough time to permit relatively careful consideration of at least some complex issues. [*]

Will all decision-makers be able to do this? Will they
even want to? To assume so presumes a great deal on the
part of the lawyers, newspapermen, businessmen, and others
who assume cabinet and subcabinet positions in the executive
branch of the federal government and hold congressional
seats. It is assuming even more to expect our state legislators, state department heads, and local mayors and coun-
cilmen to be able to react to analysts advocating differing

---

[*] To make this time available, he had to sacrifice leisure and many traditional activities of the Secretary of
Defense such as annual appearances at the war colleges.

positions in the way that judges react to lawyers advocating differing positions. Analysts can produce different conclusions for various reasons explored in this chapter and the preceding one and for other reasons too complicated to be considered in a book of this type. Some possible controversies involve:

... Comparative merits of the rate of return
    and the cost-benefit ratio as a ranking
    function

... Social time preference or opportunity
    cost of capital as a measure of the price
    of money

... Differentiating risk and uncertainty

... Tracing pecuniary spillovers

... Longer amortization periods or higher
    salvage values

... Appropriate uses for shadow prices

It is unrealistic to expect the political decision-maker to cope with these complex issues unless we are to recruit all of our decision-makers from the ranks of the analysts. [8] A more probable decision-maker's response to analysts who disagree is to ignore both of them and decide on the same bases that have traditionally been used. [9]

The Importance of Ground Rules

When my lawyer disagrees with your lawyer, we can go to court and get the matter solved. When the Interior Department's PPB analyst disagrees with the Bureau of the Budget's analyst, to whom is the disagreement to be taken? The President is the lowest-level official with responsibility for officials in two different cabinet departments, so, assuming that the analysts are supported by their superiors, only he can resolve the dispute. In the federal government, the odds are very good that such issues will not be considered

important enough to merit consideration by the President, so
that disagreement will be permitted to persist indefinitely
without resolution of the conceptual issues underlying the
difference.

It is at this point that PPB can differ markedly in civilian
agencies from the situation in the legal profession or in the
Defense Department. The significance of the American legal
system is measured not by what goes on in the courts, but by
what never gets taken to court. The value of the system is
that it provides a reasonable amount of certainty to all participants in society. Thus, when one car hits another, when
one party is damaged because another does not fulfill his
contract, or when ownership is in doubt, Americans do not
go to court under normal circumstances. There is enough
consensus on what the rules are and how they are enforced
that people pay damages and admit title without advocacy and
the need for a judge. To a major degree, litigation is unnecessary because analysts (lawyers), regardless of by whom
consulted, will normally be in a position to determine who
would win were the case taken to court. Given this knowledge, contestants do not resort to the court. The point of
this legal discourse is that the strength of PPB will ultimately be tested not by how the controversial cases are resolved,
but by how well the issues too unimportant to be taken to the
President or department head are resolved.

If the PPB approach is sufficiently well defined so that
PPB analysts in Agency A will reach about the same conclusions (on alternatives, suboptimizing, costs, etc.) as analysts
in Agency B, then PPB can have an effect on decision-making
and on the framework in which argumentation takes place.
To a certain extent, this has happened in the Pentagon, where,
for example, analysts from the military departments and
Office of the Secretary of Defense have agreed on such things
as a set of numerical representations of the outcome of
nuclear war under alternative assumptions and on a numerical
representation of the world-wide rapid deployment problem. [10]
Whether it will happen in civilian agencies will depend upon
(a) the extent to which the President or the Bureau of the
Budget can establish common ground rules and standards and
(b) the skill with which analysts can devise techniques to
support programs that they themselves prefer.

The key question, in relationship to the future of PPB, is what happens when an agency's basic program is inconsistent with the level indicated (to any specified decision-maker) through PPB. To what extent will the existence of program analysis affect the outcome within the political process? Will analysts, like lawyers, frequently advise their employers that they "don't have a case?"

Conceivably, the political bargaining process could be affected by analysis. Such analysis could alert decision-makers to the full impact of their alternatives, thereby influencing their decisions. Whether or not this mechanism can operate depends upon whether an agency can be induced to produce an analysis which (a) reveals any inconsistencies between its programs and the President's criteria and objectives and (b) uses proper assumptions and models. If an analysis can be produced which shows in substance that an agency program is consistent with these higher level criteria even if, in fact (by any single individual's judgment of fact), it is not so, then it is clear that the impact of analysis on bargaining in government will be negligible. Whether it will be possible for the "experts" on agency PPBS staffs to produce "objective" analyses to support nearly any position is the key to the value of PPBS.

This basic problem may be examined with respect to agencies where it has arisen in the past. For the purposes of this discussion, the water resource agencies will be taken as examples because cost-benefit analysis has been carried out in an elaborate fashion in those agencies for some years. Thus, they present a much better sample for analysis than those agencies where the analytical procedures are just beginning to be applied, and the Bureau of the Budget's attempts to apply its criteria may, in part, be considered unsuccessful by virtue of the short time in which the Bureau's pressures have been operative. The persistence in water project analysis of what many economists consider to be poor analytical techniques serves as a warning to those who believe that cost-benefit analysis and PPB are self-implementing systems which inevitably and inexorably will improve governmental decisions.

The following section is written in the form of advice to the agency that seeks to avoid the impacts of the PPB

approach on its program. Examples are provided from non-
water projects if they appear to indicate an interesting
strategy--even though the problem may be transitory. The
examples should not be interpreted to mean the author objects to all of the practices being considered. In some cases,
the strategies (e. g. , no objectives) are inevitable results of
the political system; in other cases, it is the diversity of
defensible viewpoints (say, on the applicable interest rate)
and not any particular viewpoint which is being pointed out.

SOME TECHNIQUES TO MAKE PPB WORK
IN YOUR FAVOR OR NOT WORK AT ALL

Can't Find Objectives

The fundamental requisite for analysis through the PPB
approach is the identification of objectives. It has been
suggested in Chapters 9 and 11 that it is difficult indeed to
determine what lawmakers intend when they establish a
program. Furthermore, many programs have multiple
objectives, where the relative emphasis on each is unknown.
Under these circumstances, PPB analysts will have considerable difficulty in establishing the objectives of government
programs. It is, therefore, equally difficult to identify what
might be an alternative to the present program. Contrary
to the assumptions underlying the PPB approach, it is possible to operate programs indefinitely in pursuit of no identified objective or where different participants have markedly
different views of what the objectives are. Thus, the Interior
Department's PPB chief could report to the Joint Economic
Committee two years after PPB was established that "we
have had our most difficult problems internally in trying to
identify our specific goals, particularly where, say, in the
water field, we have talked to about seven bureaus having
direct interests. "[11]

Can't Identify Criteria of Accomplishment

In previous discussion, it was indicated that most objectives tend to be stated in the form of essentially unachievable
objective functions, rather than in terms of goals that are
capable of immediate achievement. It was also suggested
that potential political losses occur when political decision-
makers promise specific achievements in specific time periods. Thus, while output is being measured, there seems
to be little effort underway toward setting criteria of accomplishment for federal agencies. In the 1967 PPB hearings
before the Joint Economic Committee, it was Senator Proxmire
(supported to some extent by Harry Shooshan of Interior) who
took the position that precise goals should be stated. [12] The
suggestion that such goals were difficult to establish and probably not desirable came from PPB experts from the Department of Housing and Urban Development and the Department
of Health, Education and Welfare. Obviously, if targets or
goals are not specified in precise, quantitative terms, PPB
does not provide a mechanism for performance evaluation.

Pick the Right Interest Rate

A critical question in connection with the determination
of the feasibility of projects and programs is the matter of
interest rates. It can be argued that federal funds are made
available at 0 interest rate--that is, that a dollar two years
from now is as valuable as a dollar now. Many analyses proceed upon this assumption either explicitly or implicitly.
For example, for many years highway benefits accruing in
the future have been assumed to be equivalent with costs
accruing today, in effect, assuming a 0 per cent interest
rate. [13] The Defense Department cost-effectiveness studies
have on occasion presented the same problem. [14] For water
resource projects, instead of 0 per cent, the interest rate
used in evaluating projects is based upon a formula that
currently yields a rate of about 3-1/8 per cent. * This rate

---

* This situation is changing; the President's budget
released in January, 1968, indicated that projects were being
reanalyzed at a higher rate.

is substantially less than the actual borrowing costs of the Treasury, as that department itself is quick to point out. [15] It is also substantially below the cost of borrowing comparable funds in the private sector.

Some scholars have argued for an even higher interest rate than the Treasury borrowing rate. [16] The dispute is in no sense academic. Recent studies have indicated that if a higher interest rate were used, most water resource projects could not be justified under cost-benefit criteria, even if all other factors, including the actual assumptions about benefits and costs, were accepted. [17]

The urban transportation study described in Chapter 8 shows the impact of choosing a uniform higher rate of interest. It used an interest rate of 6 per cent and assumed that this interest rate applied to all those involved in transportation decisions. This was done despite the fact that the various participants in transportation decisions have markedly different borrowing costs. Municipalities can usually borrow at a rate of 3 to 4 per cent because the interest on their bonds is exempt from federal income tax. The federal government borrows in the 4-1/2 to 5-3/4 per cent range. Federal and local governments would presumably be constructing either the regular road alternatives or the mass transit alternatives in the transportation study. On the other hand, private bus companies raise both debt and equity capital in the open market. They, like other public utilities, tend to find themselves confronted with an over-all rate of interest and dividend cost on their investment in transit plant of 7 to 8 per cent. The individual who purchases automobiles frequently pays for his automobile on delayed-time payments at a rate approaching 10 per cent true annual interest and frequently pays even more for other forms of consumer credit. If the Meyer transportation study had used these interest rates, rather than a uniform interest rate of 6 per cent for the various alternatives, it is reasonably clear that the private automobile alternative would have been evaluated much less favorably.

The conceptual question involved is the extent to which one wishes to utilize the lower borrowing rates of some activities in comparison to others (e.g., those of local governments by comparison to private individuals) to reflect

benefits in any given line of governmental policy such as
transportation. In fact, it does cost cities less to borrow
funds to build mass transit than it does individuals to borrow
to buy cars. The differences stem in part from the public
policy of exempting interest on municipal bonds from federal
income taxation. It can be argued that the analyst must take
policy decisions of other programs as he finds them (recognizing the lower rate as a public preference for public investment) or that he should ignore such differences. The second
major cause of the difference in interest rates reflects the
fact that it is riskier to loan to an individual than to a government, a difference not necessarily relevant to transportation
choices. Economists differ on whether the interest rate used
for analysis should reflect risks of project failure. Reflecting risks would, in the transportation example, introduce a
whole new set of rates (related to project failure risk, not
lendor's risk) for each of the alternatives.

The water resource agencies sometimes use different
interest rates in considering a single project. Occasionally,
interest rate differentials alone will be used to justify a project, as the Interior Department's Palmetto Bend economic
analysis illustrates. [18] This irrigation project was designed
to provide water for municipal and industrial uses to a city
in Texas. The estimate of benefits was based on what it
would cost if the same quantities of water were derived from
another source. For the Department's purpose, the other
source was a physically identical dam to be constructed by
the city being served. Interior assumed that capital funds
cost the federal government 3-1/8 per cent and would cost
the city 4-1/2 per cent. It also assumed that the city would
amortize the facility faster than the Department. On the
basis of these accounting differences alone, it was possible
to construct a cost-benefit ratio of 1.9 to 1 for the project,
in effect, by comparing it with itself.

Count Your Consumer's Surplus
But Not the Other Guy's

The benefits measured in water resource project analysis
include a substantial ingredient of "consumer's surplus,"
the difference between the willingness to pay for a commodity

and the price for which it would sell in a market. For
example, the measure of recreation benefits is based upon
willingness-to-pay estimates even though consumers will
not, in fact, be asked to pay these amounts to secure the
benefits of recreation at water resource projects and may
not be shown to do so at other privately financed recreation. [19]

Use of the consumer surplus concept presents a number
of opportunities for any agency to avoid the implications of
market-directed cost-benefit analysis tests. Most important,
it is difficult to test in any way any estimate of presumed
surplus, because the amount will never be ascertainable
through market pricing processes. Also, it is possible to
develop benefits based upon consumer surpluses that assume
that no consumer surpluses are foregone on the cost side.
Assume, for example, that the Bureau of Reclamation and
the Bureau of Land Management are competing for funds
within the Department of Interior budget. Land Management
seeks to enhance the profitability of ranching by preventing
the growth of deleterious weed species on the range land,
while the Bureau of Reclamation seeks to establish new irrigated farms. If consumer surpluses will be generated by
both programs--and they are mutually exclusive because the
budget can only accommodate one of them--then the costs
appropriate for cost-benefit analysis will include an element
of consumer surplus as the benefits already do, because
part of the opportunity cost of each project is the consumer
surplus of the other. [20]

Count Benefits Regardless of Cause

Frequently, a government project, and even more frequently a government policy, will not have benefits or effects
that occur in isolation from other actions and programs. It
is, therefore, difficult to disentangle the project benefits
from the benefits of other programs. Such problems can be
resolved in favor of attributing all such benefits to the project that is the subject of cost-benefit analysis. This procedure is not unknown in the water resource field. For example,
the Soil Conservation Service and the Bureau of Reclamation,
in calculating the increases in agricultural production due to
their projects, count the benefits from "better utilization" of

surrounding cropland. This better utilization depends upon
at least three factors: (a) the project itself, (b) the efforts
of the private farmer, and (c) consulting provided by the Soil
Conservation Service and the Agricultural Extension Service
(county agents). Of these benefit-creating activities, only
the first is considered a cost of the project, though the benefits created by all three are considered benefits of the project.[21]

Assume Optimal Distribution of Benefits

A frequently noted difficulty in the analysis of water
resource projects is the difference between the benefits
measured in project formulation and the benefits realized
by actual operation of approved projects. Part of this gap
between promise and performance is inherent in the distribution of benefits. The notion of benefits implicit in a consumer surplus concept is that those with the highest willingness to pay do in fact receive the benefits even though they
are distributed free. Actual distribution of the project's
benefits may not proceed in this fashion. An example is
the analysis of hydroelectric power projects. In calculating
the benefits from installation of a dam that stores water and
releases it to generate electricity at the time of peak utilization, the water resource agencies measure "benefit" by
what it would cost a supplier to produce comparable amounts
of power at comparable times. Such "peaking" power is
very valuable, and this high value shows up in the benefits
claimed for it. In actual operation of such facilities, however, the power is sometimes marketed and generated on a
different basis. Instead of being released only during short
periods in large quantities (a policy that makes it, in effect,
suitable only for large privately owned power companies),
it is released in longer periods in smaller quantities (giving
it characteristics which permit providing its benefit to small
rural electric cooperatives and publicly owned power systems), reducing its market value--as measured by what
these systems could have provided it for by themselves.[22]

Find Unemployed Resources

Economists who have studied calculating benefits and costs in government project analysis generally agree that the opportunity cost of using otherwise unemployed resources in a project is zero. From this conclusion, water resource agencies have developed the concept of an "area redevelopment" benefit which allows as a project benefit some of the costs (pay rolls) expected to be incurred in construction of the project. This procedure creates the potential of rather substantial benefits resulting from actual costs incurred in constructing projects. In other words, it permits costs to be converted into benefits. The procedure, however, does not recognize the possibilities of alternative public expenditures which would utilize similar unemployed labor. Thus, the water resource agencies, in effect, can use the cost-benefit framework to compete with agencies not using it and count as benefits what other agencies must count as costs--namely, the amounts paid to persons who would otherwise be unemployed. The opportunity cost of unemployed labor is not zero if some other public program could use the same labor.

Count Income Redistribution as a Benefit

As previously discussed, economists separate the allocational efficiency and the redistribution context when calculating benefits and costs. However, the water resource agencies may from time to time be in a position to combine both types of benefits while using only one type of cost. Water resource projects' cost-benefit studies conducted by the Bureau of Reclamation do claim "indirect" benefits from the business stimulated near projects which would otherwise take place somewhere else. These merely represent benefits attributable to moving business from one part of the country to another and are truly redistributional. The costs of such redistribution are not calculated in a category of indirect costs--no such category is recognized. [23]

Optimistically Project Use

Water resource projects (like many other important physical construction functions of government such as highways, mass transit facilities, and utilities) operate over a long period with a value highly sensitive to anticipated use. That use in the future can never be known with certainty and, therefore, presents one of the most difficult problems of determining the appropriate benefits in cost-benefit analysis. In the water resource field, there has always been, and probably will always be, a continued debate over whether expected usages, of navigation facilities particularly, are overestimated. The importance of the point is, however, that results of such analyses can be manipulated by small changes in anticipated future utilization--a point that can never really be checked by reviewing agencies until and unless they allow the project to be constructed. (In fairness to the Corps of Engineers, it should be noted that its record on this point is not bad.)

Omit Alternatives

PPBS calls for agencies to consider all alternatives to a given governmental action. However, in our pluralistic society, many alternatives to action by one federal government agency are not within the jurisdiction of that agency. The flood control functions of the Corps of Engineers provide an example, one where the criticism for failure to consider relevant alternatives has been particularly strong.[24] The Corps is authorized to deal with downstream flooding problems by (a) systems of levies which, because of legal requirements for local contributions to the cost, are often rejected by local interests in favor of (b) large upstream dams. Alternatives not within the jurisdiction of the Corps include a variety of public actions such as (a) better flood warning systems (Environmental Science Services Administration), (b) upstream treatment works of smaller size (Soil Conservation Service and Forest Service), and (c) flood insurance measures.

Local governments can practice systems of flood-plain zoning as well as information programs designed to warn persons about the flood danger before they buy or build houses and business buildings on the flood plain. Privately financed adjustments to flood dangers include: flood-proofing buildings, changing location decisions or uses of existing facilities, and evacuation programs. However, in the existing procedures for the analysis of water resource projects, these nonstructural alternatives are not considered. [25]

Though the objective of the Bureau of Reclamation is presumably to increase agricultural production, its programs do not consider the alternative of seeking ground water through wells rather than damming surface water flows. There is considerable evidence to indicate, if one did consider alternatives, that increased irrigation using ground water in the East would be preferable to using surface water in the West. [26]

Ignore Costs

The federal government's programs like many private activities, can have external effects not reckoned in the analysis of project costs. Project benefits measurement devices are intended to reflect positive externalities, but project cost-measuring devices do not measure negative ones, even though the costs involved may fall upon the federal government itself.

In the water resource field, several examples are classic. The benefits from construction of a reservoir include the additional fishing values associated with providing a larger body of water. These fish develop only because of other costs--not attributed to the project--for stocking the reservoirs. On the other hand, the type of fish, such as trout, that flourish in freely flowing fast water do not thrive in reservoirs, but the loss of these fishing values is not considered in project analysis of benefits and costs. [27]

Also in the water field, the Bureau of Reclamation, as has been mentioned, includes a category of indirect benefits roughly approximating the regional (not national) benefits of projects. It does not include as costs, however, some of

the increased public costs required as ancillary to such
benefits. For example, the federal government's "impacted
areas" school assistance program provides assistance to
school districts in areas in which a dam is being built to
recognize the extra load thrown on local school systems by
the families of construction workers. These federal costs
are not counted as part of the costs of constructing a project
because they are paid for out of appropriations to the Department of Health, Education and Welfare, not the Bureau of
Reclamation. The problem is by no means confined to water
resource projects; the urban transportation study discussed
in Chapter 8 has been criticized for failing to attribute pollution costs to the automobile alternative. [28]

Other Methods

There are various other devices available to agencies
that wish to use the program analysis framework for their
own ends--failing to include data with which to evaluate their
programs, seeking to discover new objectives or categories
of benefits for existing lines of activity, and underestimating
total costs or overestimating benefits even while using the
appropriate ground rules. The data problems are particularly severe where program inputs (i.e., FAA controllers)
do not relate through known data to precise quantities of
program outputs (measured in holding time or accident
rates).

As the water resource development analytical procedures
so aptly illustrate, it is possible to develop program analysis
in a variety of ways and "get away with it." Program analysis
in the water resource area has been criticized continuously
since 1958 in academic literature, but changes in procedures
and practices have been in the direction of loosening the
standards rather than tightening them. [29] This water resource
experience should not encourage those who expect that program analysis and PPBS will provide analyses from the
agencies themselves that will offer suggestions for cutting
down on programs of low priority (however defined).

COUNTERSTRATEGIES FOR GOOD ANALYSIS

While, as the above sections have indicated, there is clearly considerable room for maneuvering within the general approach of cost-benefit analysis, there is something of an underlying consensus on what constitutes "good" program analysis. This consensus, for example, can be found among the economists who have considered cost-benefit analysis in the water resource field. [30] Presuming that the Bureau of the Budget and the President wish to avoid letting PPB become simply another set of key words and justification material for established policies, whether or not they can adopt counterstrategies to force "good" analysis becomes a central question for the political viability of PPBS.

Competition

Establishing program analysis in an environment of inter- and intra-agency competition has a certain appeal. The theory is that competitive forces, operating because of nearly unlimited demands upon a limited budget, will force agencies into review of each other's planning assumptions and programs. The theory is also that this competition will bring to the attention of central decision-makers the advantages or disadvantages of various programs in a fashion that, though not "objective," would tend to provide relatively complete information at these levels. There have been instances in the government where such forces might have been felt; the results do not support the theory.

In the water resource field, there has been a tendency for a kind of Gresham's law of project analysis to operate. Because key elements in getting one's own program selected when competition with another agency for the same body of water to dam are both high cost-benefit ratios and low local cost-sharing requirements, there is a competitive pressure to reduce the quality of analysis rather than improve it. [31] When this competition results in pressure from central control agencies for more uniform procedures, the resulting agreements among agencies (all of which have vested interests in program continuation) have been most liberal in

terms of maximizing the projects meeting the criteria. [32]
There is also a tendency for any benefit-increasing innovation
by one agency to be copied by the others, as has been the case
with recreation benefits. [33]

The most fruitful testing ground for the competition
theory was probably within the structure of the three military
departments contesting for the limited quantities of funds
available to the Defense Department during the 1950's. The
impact of the competition was, however, not careful analysis
of the programs of each service by other services. Instead,
it developed into mutual and reciprocal endorsement of programs, resulting in transferring the key decisions to civilian
budgeting authorities in the Office of the Secretary of Defense
and the Bureau of the Budget. [34]

Independent Review

Another frequently recommended solution in the water
resources field is the independent review of project analyses
by groups other than the portion of the agency responsible
for the formulation of basic programs and program levels. [35]
The basic notion that those who analyze should be independent
of those who implement is one long argued in both theory and
practice. The theory is that the independent reviewers--
with no vested interest in whether projects are constructed
or not--will be objective in applying predefined guidelines
to actual factual situations.

The most difficult problem with this approach in the
practical world of program analysis in the late 1960's is that
no such central guidelines currently exist--a separate problem to be considered later. However, even without such
guidelines, many of the basic criticisms of cost-benefit
analysis as applied to the water resource project analytical
procedure would not be met merely by establishing independent review boards. Such boards would presumably serve
well in preventing falsifications of data and stretching of
data to make a favorable cost-benefit ratio. However, they
could not cope with "honest" analysis following guidelines
widely rejected by outside authorities but not rejected by
any political authority. For example, if a project were

found to be feasible merely because of utilization of a 2 per cent interest rate according to uniform agency guidelines uniformly applied, an independent review panel would not be in a position to reject it, unless it were also empowered to set guidelines for project formulation and review.

The basic problem in deciding on the utilization of an independent review function is whether the function shall be located in the agency constructing the projects. If it is, it would seem unlikely that the independence of review within the agency would yield substantial program eliminations, as the independent review staff would have as much vested interest in the continuation of the agency's program as the original project formulators.

Central Guidelines

The question of central guidelines for program analysis is key to the future role of program analysis and PPBS in the political process. The advance planning mode and budget format instructions of PPB are little different from nostrums for government which have been proposed and supposedly implemented in the past. The analytical mode--we have sought to show--can be met by a variety of agency counterstrategies working within the flexibility available in analysis. These flexibilities present the prospect of leaving the studies of PPBS in the status of "studies," which to some observers always seem to be available to support all positions taken in the political arena. [36]

The interest rate assumption alone controls the outcome in many analyses of projects involving the creation of longlasting physical assets. There is no logical reason why it should be assumed that budget funds used for highways have any different cost to society than those used for urban renewal or for water resource projects. Likewise, there is no reason to assume that the Bureau of Public Roads is in a particularly good position to determine the appropriate interest rate for all government projects. Under current procedures, the Bureau of Public Roads and all other agencies are left on their own to determine what interest rate to use and what other planning assumptions to make.

In this circumstance, it would not be unreasonable for
an agency head to decide that the interest rate for PPBS
analysis in his agency would be no less favorable to agency
projects than that used by other agencies. Thus, the tendency
would be for the lowest interest rate and worst assumptions
in use in the government to control what is used for project
analysis.

Most of the opportunities for "fudging" cost-benefit
analyses--though not the problems of seeking and finding
objectives--could be prevented by clear and enforced central
criteria for cost-benefit and cost-effectiveness analysis
formulated and issued in the name of the President by the
Bureau of the Budget. Such standards could control all
matters in which the judgments of individual agencies would
not be based upon information uniquely available to their
agencies. Thus, the guidelines could cover such matters as
the appropriate interest rate for use in analysis, future
population growth assumptions, treatment of taxes, and costs
imposed upon other agencies.

Issuance of such guidelines is likely, however, only if
sufficient interest is taken in them by the Congress, or the
President, to provide the force to initiate them and implement
them in the face of opposition by agencies that stand to lose
by their application. Whether such interest exists is problem-
atical.

User Charges

One of the most obvious responses to some of the problems of cost-benefit analysis in the public sector and economic
analysis in the private sector is to alter the signals given by
the economic system to the decision-makers. In the case of
private actions, this process simply consists of shifting the
actual costs and rewards patterns to reflect both previously
internal and previously external gains and losses. This is
the basis, for example, of the idea of user charges for pollution.

In the public sector, the same mechanism can be achieved
by several accounting devices and by actual program decisions.

In the first category, a good example is seen in the efforts
of President Eisenhower's budget directors to seek to realize
some of the costs of asset consumption, to adopt accrued
expenditure accounting, and to shift some of the previously
central costs--such as the civil service retirement fund contributions and franking privilege costs--to individual agencies
so that they would appear as part of the costs of agency operations.

The other action that can be taken in public sector decision-
making is to bring the distribution of benefits from public
investment into line with comparable decisions in the private
sector. This is the basis of the user-charge position taken
by the Bureau of the Budget under Eisenhower's Presidency
particularly. [37]

The user charge performs both a resource allocation
and a redistribution function and, when used in connection
with project planning, may also perform a function of checking
and scaling down anticipated future benefits. The basic notion
is simple. Take a waterway built and maintained with federal
funds. Under existing procedures, the users of the waterway
pay nothing for its construction or maintenance, while those
shipping their goods by rail or road do pay (through private
ownership in the first case and gasoline taxes in the second).
This situation tends to make the waterway more attractive
vis-à-vis the other modes of transportation and, significantly,
to create a demand for more waterways. The user charge in
such a circumstance would (a) tend to force users of the waterways to pay some of the costs of constructing and maintaining
them, (b) reduce traffic on the waterways, other things being
equal, as the user charge would presumably be reflected in
the price of shipping by barge, and (c) reduce the benefits
from new waterways in cost-benefit calculations because
less traffic would use the waterway. *

The user charge, while not inconsistent with PPB, is
not itself a part of the PPB system but is one of the methods
designed to yield compatible results.

---

* The example is a real one, since President Johnson
has for the last several years proposed a tax on diesel fuel
used to propel barges. Similar proposals were made in previous administrations, but Congress has never acted on them.

COUNTERSTRATEGIES BY
AGENCIES AND CLIENTELE

E. E. Schattsneider has recognized that the political process is the resort of those who are losing outside of it. [38] An agency or agency's clientele who lose or appear to be losing within the executive branch on the question of centrally imposed analytical standards may seek to "lock in" by legislation the standards they find beneficial. Whether such legislative action precludes all of the strategies open to the President is a separate question. * However, it is clear that such legislative standard-setting can present significant hurdles for lower-echelon central agency personnel--such as Budget Bureau personnel seeking to apply the PPB approach.

The water resource field provides an example of how this process can work. For many years, the Corps of Engineers followed a procedure for calculating navigation benefits that was widely criticized in the academic community and by railroad interests. A change in that procedure to respond to these criticisms produced storms of protest that the new standards would preclude substantial further development of the nation's waterways. [39] After considerable debate, the political solution was a provision in the act authorizing the new Department of Transportation. [40] This provision in effect locked the older standard into law.

SUMMARY

This chapter has been devoted to the strategies agencies may pursue to avoid any impact by program analysis and PPB upon their programs.

---

* The President may presumably use any standards he chooses in reviewing the recommendations of his subordinates within the executive branch in connection with the formulation of his budget.

The precedent of the water resource construction agencies was utilized to identify and illustrate these strategies for dealing with analysis. Analytical strategies include use of low interest rates and long amortization periods, assuming consumer surpluses, assuming benefits independently caused, assuming optimal distribution of benefits, creating unemployed resources benefits, treating income redistribution benefits as allocational benefits, overestimating future growth, omitting alternatives and ignoring costs, in addition to basic problems of "incorrect" or "fudged" analysis. The combination of these strategies, it can be concluded, are sufficient so that analysis--unless done by those who share the objectives and perspective of the ultimate decision-maker (whatever those may be)--will not be likely to produce recommendations for curtailed programs.

However, counterstrategies are available to combat many of these analytical strategies. These counterstrategies include competition, independent review, central guidelines, and user charges. One already developed mechanism for repelling central guidelines is to resort to the legislative process to freeze standards and criteria for project and program analysis into legislation.

NOTES TO CHAPTER 12

1. Aaron Wildavsky, The Politics of the Budgetary Process (Boston: Little, Brown, 1964).

2. In addition to Wildavsky, this discussion draws upon a substantial literature of political sociology beginning with Max Weber's functional approach to bureaucracy. See pp. 18-29 of Talcott Parsons' Introduction to Max Weber, The Theory of Social and Economic Organization (New York: The Free Press, 1947), and H. H. Gerth and C. Wright Mills, From Max Weber: Essays in Sociology (New York: Oxford University Press, 1958), pp. 228-29.

3. The approach here follows V. O. Key, "A Politics of Self-Preservation," Politics, Parties and Pressure Groups

(4th ed.; New York: Crowell, 1958), pp. 746-47. See also, in addition to the work of Parsons and Weber cited above, Robert K. Merton's comments on the shared views of participants, "Bureaucratic Structure and Personality," in Robert K. Merton et al. (eds.), Reader in Bureaucracy (New York: Free Press, 1952), pp. 361-71. See also Merton's Social Theory and Social Structure (Rev. ed.; New York: Free Press, 1957), pp. 195-206. Fritz Morstein Marx discusses "stake in programs" in "The Social Function of Public Administration," in Fritz Morstein Marx (ed.), Elements of Public Administration (2nd ed.; Englewood Cliffs, N.J.: Prentice-Hall, 1959), pp. 89-109. A sophisticated approach to the linkage of personal and organizational survival will be found in Talcott Parsons' concept of "legitimation" in "Authority, Legitimation and Political Action," Ch. 12 of Carl J. Friedrich (ed.), Authority, Nomos I (Cambridge, Mass.: Harvard University Press, 1958), p. 201.

4. Charles Hitch, Decision-Making for Defense (Berkeley: University of California Press, 1965), p. 57.

5. U.S. Congress, Joint Economic Committee, Subcommittee on Economy in Government, op. cit., p. 221.

6. "Government Decision-Making and the Theory of Choice," Rand Corporation Paper, P-2960, 1964.

7. In David Novick (ed.), Program Budgeting (Washington, D.C.: Government Printing Office, 1965), p. 25.

8. Not a bad idea, perhaps, but an old one. See Plato's Republic.

9. This is not the only presumption about the attitudes and intelligence of decision-makers underlying the PPB approach. It also presumes that decision-makers want to consider alternatives. In Alain Enthoven's words:

> I believe it is fair to say that the staff system
> that was in operation before PPBS, for the
> most part, was designed to suppress alterna-
> tives as the paper or issue worked its way up
> the chain of command in the staff so that the
> Chief of Staff or the Secretary of Defense was

presented with a staff position which he could
accept or reject. That was the classical concept of staff work. One of the innovations that
Secretary McNamara emphasized, and that we
made a part of the PPBS approach, was that
the top officials would see the various interesting alternatives explicitly stated and they,
themselves, would apply their thought to the
major alternatives.

Now the various available alternatives are
systematically analyzed and presented to the
Secretary of Defense and the Joint Chiefs of
Staff.

The principle that the men at the top will
see all the important alternatives, so that they
can exercise some choice, rather than just
accepting or rejecting a staff position, is
fundamental to the system.

(U.S. Senate, Committee on Government
Operations, Subcommittee on National Secu-
rity and International Operations, Hearings,
"Planning-Programming-Budgeting," op. cit.,
Part II, p. 137.)

Does this mean that PPB is of no usefulness when the President believes--as President Eisenhower is said to have
believed--in a military staff system?

10. Testimony of Alain Enthoven, ibid., p. 96.

11. U.S. Congress, Joint Economic Committee, Subcommittee on Economy in Government, op. cit., p. 82,
testimony of Harry Shooshan. Interior's way out has been
to study demand for water--setting the implicit objective
that all water demands should be met (presumably without
regard to price, and presumably by programs of that
department as distinct from other departments of the
federal government, local government, or private action).

12. Ibid. As noted in Chapter 9, the PPB guidance
initially provided by the Bureau of the Budget stressed
setting such goals.

13. C. Oglesby and E. Grant, "Economic Analysis--
The Fundamental Approach to Decisions in Highway Planning
and Design," National Academy of Sciences, National Research
Council, Highway Research Board, Proceedings of the Thirty-
Seventh Annual Meeting (Washington, D.C., 1958), pp. 47-57.

14. See the general discussion of the problem in B.
Sobin, "Some Interest Rate Aspects of Weapons Systems
Investment Policy," Institute for Defense Analyses Research
Paper P-171 (Arlington, Va., 1965), and Charles Hitch and
Roland McKean, The Economics of Defense in the Nuclear
Age (Cambridge: Harvard University Press, 1960), Ch. 11.
The situation has been resolved for investments not based
primarily on military necessity by requiring a 10 per cent
rate through Department of Defense Instruction 7041.3 of
December, 1966.

15. See letter of November 17, 1964, from Secretary
of Treasury to Secretary of Interior, U.S. Congress, House,
Conservation of the Natural Resources of New England,
Eighty-ninth Congress, 1st Session, 1965, H. Doc. No. 236,
pp. 33-35.

16. Jack Hirshliefer et al., Water Supply: Economics,
Technology and Policy (Chicago: University of Chicago
Press, 1960), argued for a 12 per cent rate on the grounds
that this was the rate applicable to capital in private enterprises of comparable risk. Also, see testimony of a group
of economists in the Joint Economic Committee's PPB
Hearings, op. cit., pp. 129-79.

17. Irving Fox and Orris C. Herfindahl, "Attainment of
Efficiency in Satisfying Demands for Water Resources,"
American Economic Review, LIV (May, 1964), 200-206,
and Robert Haveman, Water Resource Investment and the
Public Interest (Nashville: Vanderbilt University Press,
1965). Senator Proxmire has encouraged the Corps of
Engineers to make these same calculations. The results--
see pp. 5226-27 of the Congressional Record (daily edition),
January 22, 1968 --are striking.

18. U.S. Congress, House, House Document No. 279,
Eighty-ninth Congress, 1st Session, 1965, particularly
p. 45.

19. This is not intended as a criticism of the method of measurement since insufficient comparable private recreational opportunities exist to make such a comparison feasible. See Marion Clawson, Methods of Measuring the Demand for and Value of Outdoor Recreation (Washington, D.C.: Resources for the Future, 1959), Reprint No. 10.

20. The same problem arises when private alternatives are considered. See M. M. Kelso, "Economic Analysis in the Allocation of the Federal Budget to Resource Development," in Stephen Smith and Emery Castle (eds.), Economics and Public Policy in Water Resource Development (Ames, Iowa: Iowa State University Press, 1964), Ch. 5.

21. This point is made in Edward Renshaw, Toward Responsible Government (Chicago: Idyia Press, 1957), p. 77. This procedure also makes the benefit estimate too large if the independent forces do not act as expected, as noted in George S. Tolley and Ralph A. Fruend, Jr., "Does the State of the Data Suggest a Program for Modifying Planning and Evaluation Procedures?" in George S. Tolley and F. E. Riggs (eds.), Economics of Watershed Planning (Ames, Iowa: Iowa State University Press, 1961), p. 136.

22. This particular example is from Panel of Consultants to the Bureau of the Budget (Maynard M. Hufschmidt, John Krutilla, and Julius Margolis, with assistance of Stephen A. Marglin), Standards and Criteria for Formulating and Evaluating Federal Water Resources Developments (Washington, D.C.: Bureau of the Budget processed, June 30, 1961), pp. 48-49. The panel was concerned with future policy rather than the accuracy of past calculations. The problem lies not in this "preference" policy or any other method of benefit distribution, but in the assumption of one distribution in cost-benefit analysis and implementation of another.

23. For a full discussion of this question, see U.S. Bureau of Reclamation, Report of Panel of Consultants on Secondary or Indirect Benefits of Water-Use Projects (June 26, 1952, processed).

24. William G. Hoyt and Walter B. Langbein, Floods (Princeton, N.J.: Princeton University Press, 1955).

25. An excellent discussion of nonstructural alternatives is Gilbert F. White, Choice of Adjustments to Floods (Department of Geography Research Paper No. 93; Chicago: University of Chicago, 1964).

26. Vernon Ruttan, The Economic Demand for Irrigated Acreage (Baltimore: The Johns Hopkins University Press, 1965).

27. This situation affects about half of all projects according to representatives of the Bureau of Sport Fisheries and Wildlife. U.S. Congress, House, Committee on Interior and Insular Affairs, Subcommittee on Irrigation and Reclamation, Policies and Procedures Applicable to the Planning of Water Resource Development Projects, Eighty-eighth Congress, 1st Session, 1963, p. 78.

28. The New York Times Book Review, September 4, 1966, p. 3.

29. Particularly noteworthy developments in this connection were the revocation of Budget Circular A-47 and its replacement by Senate Doc. 97, Standards and Criteria, and the sharp expansion of the use of recreation and fish and wildlife benefits. President Johnson may be reversing this trend.

30. It is evident in the material cited in the bibliography on this subject and in the summary presentations such as Julius Margolis, "The Economic Evaluation of Federal Water Resource Development: A Review Article," American Economic Review, XLIX (March, 1959), 96-111; C. L. Barber, "Water Resource Development," Canadian Journal of Economics and Political Science, XXVII (November, 1961), 533-40; and A. R. Prest and Ralph Turvey, "Benefit-Cost Analysis: A Survey," Economic Journal, LXXV (December, 1965), 683-735.

31. This phenomenon was discovered for example by Arthur Maass in Muddy Waters: The Army Engineers and the Nation's Rivers (Cambridge, Mass.: Harvard University Press, 1951).

32.   Robert River, "Benefit-Cost Evaluation as a Criterion for Federal Resources Development" (Unpublished
Master's dissertation, University of California, Oakland,
1952), is particularly critical of water resource agencies
on this point.   See also the comments of an ex-Agriculture
Department employee Jesse T. Sanders in Tolley and Riggs,
op. cit. , pp. 124-25, and Lawrence G. Hines, "The Hazards
of Benefit-Cost Analysis as a Guide to Public Investment
Policy," Public Finance, Vol. XVII, No. 2 (1962), pp. 101-17.

33.   See U.S. Congress, Senate, Committee on Interior
and Insular Affairs, Hearings, Water Project Recreation
Act, Eighty-ninth Congress, 1st Session, 1965.

34.   Charles Hitch, op. cit. , describes the basic problem.

35.   This approach is taken, for example, in Eckstein,
Water Resource Development: The Economics of Project
Evaluation (Cambridge, Mass.: Harvard University Press,
1958); Fox and Herfindahl, op. cit.; and Huburt Marshall's
Chapter 22 in Smith and Castle, op. cit.

36.   An example of a somewhat strong statement of this
view is the following from Edward C. Banfield, Political
Influence (New York: The Free Press, 1961), p. 283:

> A common, indeed an almost invariable, feature
> of the process by which an issue is prepared for
> settlement is a ceremonial appeal to the author-
> ity of "objective facts" and "technical experts."
> Although the issue must, in the last analysis,
> always be settled on grounds that are political, in
> the broad sense, and although the crucial judg-
> ments that are involved--judgments not only
> about values but about facts and probabilities
> as well--cannot possibly be made in a purely
> scientific or technical way, nevertheless the
> almost unvarying practice is to make it appear
> that the decision rests upon "objective" and
> even "factual" grounds.

37.   Eckstein, op. cit. , mentions this possibility,
as do Fox and Herfindahl, op. cit. , and Edward Renshaw,

"A Note on the Measurement of Benefits from Public Invest-ment in Navigation Projects," American Economic Review, LXVII (September, 1957), 652-62. Added user charges in the transportation field are recommended periodically; for example, they are advocated in President Johnson's fiscal 1969 budget recommendations.

38. E. E. Schattsneider, The Semi-Sovereign People (New York: Holt, Rinehart and Winston, 1960).

39. A readable discussion of the assumptions involved will be found in Chapter V of Edward Renshaw, Toward Responsible Government, op. cit. Some supported the change; for example, see Senator Proxmire's remarks on June 28, 1966, Congressional Record (daily edition), pp. 13794-96. Typical of the criticisms were Representative William C. Cramer's remarks, Congressional Record (daily edition), March 30, 1966, pp. 6872-73.

40. Section 7(a) of the Department of Transportation Act, 80 Stat. 931.

PART III

CONCLUSIONS

CHAPTER **13** THE PLANNING-PROGRAMMING-
BUDGETING SYSTEM:
AN EVALUATION

THE EVALUATION OF PPB

In Part I of this book, readers were exposed to the PPB
approach in the best light in which the author could present
it. The basic elements of the approach were presented along
with reasons why they represent improvements over earlier
decision-making mechanisms and information systems.
Examples were presented to show that PPB could force important questions out into the open and thereby improve the
information available to the political decision-maker. Assuming that the fundamental criterion for evaluating an information system is whether it permits the decision-maker
to make choices which best help him get whatever he may
want, it is difficult to fault the PPB approach. It is even
more difficult to suggest alternatives to it. The PPB approach clearly offers the best thing on the horizon to make
government decision-making a little more rational and the
public sector of our economy a little more efficient. For
this reason, it has tremendous appeal.

In Part II, readers were exposed to four chapters of
argument suggesting serious problems on both the conceptual
and operational level of the PPB approach. It could have
been longer; many difficulties were left unexplored because
they have been adequately covered elsewhere or were considered too technical for complete discussion in the space
available.[1] If it served the author's purpose, Part II left
the reader with the conclusion that many of the elements of
the PPB approach would not work well in real world situations.

The purpose of this part is to seek to synthesize the promises of the PPB approach described in Part I with the problems described in Part II to reach conclusions about the contributions the PPB approach can and cannot be expected to make. It seems only fair that the PPB approach itself be evaluated in its own terms--namely, by first determining the objectives it is intended to achieve. For this purpose, the example of the U.S. Government will be considered. The authoritative source of specification of objectives for the planning-programming-budgeting system in the federal govern- ment is, of course, the President who ordered its adoption. These objectives for the new system are to be found in four Presidential statements on the system.[2]

At the outset, it should be noted that some of these statements, particularly the August 25 statement announcing the new system, reflect a speech writer whose zeal for the new and exciting exceeded his knowledge of government budgeting. The high hopes raised by this statement have been difficult for PPB practitioners to live down, and in some cases have given rise to direct contradictions of the President by members of his administration. For example, in his August, 1965, statement, the President told the world that he was introducing "a very new and a very revolutionary system of planning and budgeting." In the same year that the President introduced this "very revolutionary system," his Budget Director told a congressional committee:

> In giving such a presentation /of PPBS/, I do not want to leave anybody with the idea that what we are doing is some revolutionary change. It really is an improvement in what we are doing now, a systemization and rou- tinization, if you will; that is what it is, a substantial improvement, but not a revolu- tion. It is not as if we are not doing any- thing right now, and we will be getting every- thing right. I want to stress this, that it is evolutionary and not revolutionary.[3]

THE OBJECTIVES OF PPB

In considering four different statements of President
Johnson on the advantages and purposes of introducing the
Planning-Programming-Budgeting System in the federal
government, reasonable men could no doubt arrive at different formulations of what the President expected the new
system to do for him. The following seven objectives, however probably reflect reasonable conclusions about the objectives of the system as stated by the President.

Identify Goals

One objective stated by the President was that the system would "identify our national goals with precision" and
on a continuing basis. This will be called the goal identification objective. *

Establish the Priority of Goals

Not all goals of individuals or nations can be achieved
simultaneously, and, in all probability, some are mutually
exclusive. Thus, the President indicated that PPB would
enable the Administration to "choose among those goals the
ones that are most urgent." This will be called the goal-
ordering objective.

Promote Efficiency

Some of the Presidential objective statements indicate
an efficiency (fixed input, maximized output) objective. The

---

* The difference between seeking the federal government's
goals--thus presuming that other institutions (e.g., churches,
charities, local governments, businesses) in a pluralistic
society would identify their own goals--and seeking the nation's
goals is significant.

objectives indicated in these statements were "greater benefits from every tax dollar"; "fullest value for each dollar
spent"; "insure a dollar's worth of service for each dollar
spent"; and make certain that programs are "operated at a
maximum level of efficiency and effectiveness." Thus, the
third objective of the Planning-Programming-Budgeting System is to achieve maximum output from any given level of
inputs, or, in more meaningful terms, maximum output
from each dollar spent. This will be called the efficiency
objective. *

Promote Economy

Economy, one of the concepts most prevalent in the
President's PPB statements, has always been a popular word
to use in the same sentence with government spending. In
the Presidential statements, the concept is used consistent
with a technical definition of economy as minimizing cost
to produce any fixed output. This definition of economy
corresponds to common-sense notions of dominant solutions
for both household and government management. Men can
surmount their objections to particular undertakings by
their governments or their wives to argue that, "If you're
going to do it, at least you ought to do it as cheaply as
possible."

In his statements on PPB, the President evokes the
standard of economy six times. He seeks to bring "the full
promise of a finer life" to every American "at the lowest
possible cost." He seeks a system to permit us to find the
most effective and "the least costly alternative to achieve
American goals." The system will, according to one statement, help find ways "to do jobs less expensively." It is
said to "enable us to fulfill the needs of all the American
people with a minimum amount of waste." An objective of

_____

* Efficiency is sometimes called the reverse twin of
economy as an efficient solution (maximum output A for fixed
cost C) is also an economical one (least cost C to achieve
fixed output A) so long as comparable magnitudes (A and C)
are involved.

the system is to "search for alternative means of reaching those goals most effectively at the least cost." The system is also lauded for its contribution to cost reduction.

One notable feature in these six statements is that the exact goal or objective of government activity is not precisely specified. Logically, the economy criteria can and should be applied to achieve particular program outputs regardless of one's valuation of the goal or objective which the particular output may help to achieve. Thus, the governmental outputs are called various names in the statements--namely, "the full promise of a finer life," "American goals," "goals," "the needs of all the American people," and simply "jobs." Thus, the fourth objective of the Planning-Programming-Budgeting System is to achieve any given governmental output target at least cost. This will be called the economy objective. *

Spotlight Program Changes

The President also suggested in his statements that the system would pinpoint "those things that we ought to do more" and spotlight "those things that we ought to do less." This formulation, unlike the others related to judgment, seems to indicate a more active role for PPBS than simply throwing up pairs of outputs and costs to the decision-maker. Mere collections of outputs and costs, like collections of apples and oranges on a supermarket shelf, do not pinpoint or spotlight the choices that should be made.

To a minor extent, implementation of programs to achieve economy and efficiency objectives will satisfy an

---

* The President's statements, it should be noted, do not claim that the system will result in reduced budgets. The economy concept has no necessary relationship to the extent of government activity in any particular field. Because that activity can and does change from year to year, PPB cannot be said to have failed in achieving its objectives simply because budgets rise or to have succeeded simply because budgets fall.

objective of spotlighting programs to be cut back and expanded.
However, the bulk of situations faced by the government
decision-maker do not involve dominance of one solution by
another (e.g., Program A will do exactly what Program B
will do and cost less). When programs achieve different
objectives, or even different mixes of the same objective,
such comparisons are impossible. However, other portions
of the PPB approach, particularly cost-benefit analysis, do
have the potential to identify worth-while and less worth-
while programs, assuming that benefits and costs can be
measured. Therefore, this objective stated by the President
is considered separately from economy and efficiency. The
fifth objective, then, of the PPB approach in the federal
government is to pinpoint programs that should be expanded
and spotlight programs which should be contracted. This
will be referred to as the output-determining objective.

Improve Judgment

A number of the President's statements about the new
system are expressed in terms of better information and
sounder judgment. The President stated that the system
"will insure a much sounder judgment through more accurate
information"; indicated that "we will be able to make sounder
decisions than ever before"; and claimed that "this system
is primarily a means of encouraging careful and explicit
analysis of Federal programs"; and that "it will substantially
improve our ability to decide among competing proposals
for funds." He also noted that "this system will improve
our ability to control our programs and our budgets rather
than having them control us." There is a temptation to write
these statements off as nonsense or mere puffing for the
system, devoid of substantive objectives. However, to
treat them in this fashion would be to write off some of the
more significant claims being made for the PPB approach.

The principle of equal marginal returns provides a
basis for considering these Presidential statements. The
concept is basically that of a consumer confronted with a
variety of consumption options. Each commodity has a
price, and the consumer is presumed to have a budget set
by the level of his income or his allowance. The principle

of equal marginal returns indicates that the consumer will arrange his purchases of commodities so that the gain in satisfaction from an additional dollar expended upon one commodity would be equivalent to that gained from a dollar expended on some other commodity. A situation other than this may properly be deemed inefficient as, by definition, the consumer could increase his satisfaction derived from his fixed budget by changing his market basket of goods.

The importance of this formulation of equal marginal utilities is that no common denominator has been used to measure the relative satisfactions derived from the consumer goods. The analogy to federal budget decisions is clear. The federal government is presumed to be acting rationally when "it" allocates funds among competing programs, such as defense, space, health, and research so that the marginal utility (however implicitly or explicitly defined) of the last dollar expended on each program is identical. Until such time, if ever, as PPBS shows it to be possible to provide common measures of the benefits of these various programs, the choice among them, like the consumer's choice between apples and oranges, will be labeled "judgment." Such judgment can be improved by better knowledge of relationship between costs and program results and by fuller knowledge of alternatives.

Judgments based upon relatively complete information on costs and probable results are more "rational" than those that are not.[*] They are more "rational" in the sense that any person (or government) who does not get as much of what he wants as he can get is "irrational." Thus, the sixth objective of the Planning-Programming-Budgeting System is to permit decisions to be made with knowledge of the incremental costs and outputs connected with the programs being considered. This will be called the informed-judgment objective.

---

[*] Assuming that this information is free. When information costs are considered, they must be weighted against probable increases in satisfaction resulting from having added information.

Improve Performance Evaluation

An interesting objective was included in the budget
message of January, 1967, that did not appear in the earlier
Presidential statements on PPBS. That was that the system
would assist in "evaluating actual performance." In most of
the literature and discussion of PPBS, it has been considered
as a method for ex ante (prospective) analysis of proposed
future courses of action rather than a system for reporting
performance of past programs and evaluating that performance. However, the prospect that the system may be utilized
in performance reporting and the fact that the President has
indicated this as an expected system output indicates that it
can properly be stated as a system objective. Thus, the
seventh objective of the Planning-Programming-Budgeting
System is to help evaluate actual performance. This will
be described as the performance evaluation objective.

Other Statements

Some of the President's statements on PPBS merely
state general unverifiable expressions of preference for the
new system without stating separate program objectives.
These statements indicate that the system will get jobs done
"faster" and "better" and offer "better" achievement and
"excellence." Likewise, the statement that the new system
would make decision processes "modern" is construed to
reflect a mere by-product of the system rather than an
objective and is, in effect, a self-fulfilling prophecy when
applied to any newly introduced system.

CAN THE PPB APPROACH
ACHIEVE THE OBJECTIVES?

This section considers the extent to which the PPB
approach described in Part I can, in light of the problems
and difficulties discussed in Part II, achieve the objectives
specified for it by the President as summarized in the
preceding section.

Identify Goals

President Johnson's August, 1965, statement that PPB would identify national goals with precision identifies a key prerequisite to the success of the PPB approach. Goal identification is central to measuring the costs of inputs and benefits from outputs, as outputs are increments of goal achievement and costs, broadly defined, are sacrifices of capabilities to achieve other goals.

The obvious criterion for measuring whether the PPB approach is identifying goals with precision is whether all of the goals of the nation are identified. Clearly they are not. Earlier chapters showed that goals are not precisely stated anywhere in the political process. In fact, there is no single set of national goals lying somewhere waiting to be found through PPB. Men may act without explicit goals or with only vague notions of the goals they seek. Some activities and policies may not be related to a single goal but rather fulfill different purposes for differently motivated individuals and political groups. Thus, no analyst, no President, no single member of Congress, not even Congress as a whole can be looked upon as the sole authoritative source of such goals for all Americans. Indeed, some Americans would, no doubt, consider some areas of goal setting as beyond the proper sphere of governmental action and, perhaps, even governmental consideration.

One problem in stating goals is that there may be conflicting objectives for a single program. Such a situation makes it difficult for any analyst, and even the program's partisans, to state a single or multiple objective that will command universal acceptance. Also, intermediate political objectives affect the types of programs pursued. The objectives urban Democrats may have had in supporting the reimbursement to dairy farmers for pesticide losses would not serve as a criterion for program evaluation. It would be impossible to alter the substance of the program to attempt to meet such political objectives, because such objectives were not related to the substance of the program in the first place.

Objectives can, however, be handled by the PPB approach
if one sets one's sights considerably lower than the objectives
stated by the President. Specifically, analysis can be useful
if one is willing to allow the analyst to proceed on the basis
of assumptions about objectives. Some of the most useful
cost-benefit and cost-effectiveness studies have been made
on this basis. For example, the British Housing Study
described in Chapter 8 proceeded on the assumption that
if one wanted simply to provide housing units at least cost,
then such and such a program would be preferable. Acting
in this framework, the analyst puts forward his conclusions
in this fashion: "If you, Mr. Decision-Maker, want value x
or want this combination of values x and y and z, then you
should select program A. If, on the other hand, you want
only value y, then you should proceed on the basis of program B."

An alternative method for handling goal identification
is to induce new goal-oriented decisions. The same analysis that breaks down in discussing economy and efficiency
until goals are identified provides great incentive to have
decisions on the goals or objectives of the agency or the
government made prior to the analysis. Such decisions
can be made by persons whose decisions are authoritative
vis-à-vis the analyst even if they are not authoritative
for all branches and levels of government. Perhaps the
best example is the airlift-sealift study discussed in Chapter 8. For this study to have been successful, the objectives had to be specified with some concreteness. In fact,
the objectives of airlift and sealift were specified very
concretely on the basis of three separate scenarios of
limited war. These separate scenarios presumably were
based, in turn, upon a determination by cabinet-level
officers of the types of response U.S. objectives would
call for under certain circumstances. Thus, even though
the political process does not render statements of objectives which will permit the kind of analysis the PPB approach
contemplates, it is possible for individual cabinet officers
and individual Presidents to undertake this objective-setting

function to give drive and purpose to the particular federal agencies they administer. *

Clearly specifying agency or business objectives and communicating them to lower echelons has traditionally been a basic function of leadership. PPB adds to this concept only insofar as it may help force those who head government agencies (and Presidents of the United States) to think seriously about the trade-offs between various alternative objectives open to them and force them to identify objectives. To the extent that PPB does this, it will have made an accomplishment, though not so grand an accomplishment as many may have envisaged for this system.

Establish the Priority of Goals

Even if they could be identified, ordering goals would be politically unrealistic. What politician would argue that it was more important to assist the poor than to assist the aged (or the reverse)? It is simply not good politics to announce to any group concerned about any problem that a decision has been made to put that group's objectives on a lower priority rating than some other group's objectives. The alternative, equally viable as an apparent logical thought process and politically much more sensible, is simply to state that the complete achievement of the goal is not possible in the year in question because of resource limitations. The question of trading off one goal against another need not even be mentioned. [4]

---

* The limitations of this approach are substantial. The goal set by the cabinet member may not be the same as goals of other participants in the political process, such as members of Congress. The Fast Deployment Logistic Ships suggested by the Defense airlift-sealift analysis were not accepted by Congress, largely because some congressmen, not being sure that they wanted U.S. forces to intervene in such situations at all, were not enthusiastic about getting them in quickly.

Promote Efficiency

One criterion for determining whether the efficiency
objective--getting maximum possible output for any given
input--is likely to be met by PPBS is to determine whether
the alternatives available to maximize output for any given
input are considered before any action is taken. If the
decision-making process succeeds in doing this, it presumably will fulfill the efficiency objective at least to the
extent that decision-makers are, in fact, willing to choose
efficient alternatives.

Measuring Output

The problems of identifying goals give rise to very
serious problems in measuring output and, therefore, in
applying the efficiency criterion. For example, the food
stamp and the school lunch programs can be conceived as
means of providing food to those who would not otherwise
have food, as means toward child and adult health, and as
means toward maintaining demand for agricultural commodities. Comparing equally costly alternatives to achieve
valued outputs is impossible for such programs.

There are some circumstances when the objective
function of an activity may seem obvious. For example,
health programs are designed to improve health, and pro-
motion of U.S. travel can produce output functions measured by the number of people traveling in the United States.
Thus, there are at least some programs where one can speak
meaningfully of the efficiency concept. Even in these examples, though, there are problems when one seeks to formulate more specific measures of effectiveness (e.g., Is the
travel program's success best measured in foreign exchange
or people?). Particularly in "lower-level" questions (e.g.,
operations research questions rather than systems analysis
and over-all PPB questions), efficiency studies may be
carried out. If the problem is maximizing access to trees
that can be harvested, one can speak more meaningfully
about a single valued objective function (in terms of how to
best spend $50 million for forest roads) than one could in
determining, for example, whether or not to add additional
segments to the national park system in rural areas or in
urban areas close to population centers.

Fixing Input

A second test for the achievement of the efficiency objective is inherent in the nature of the objective itself. The objective is to maximize output for a fixed input. For these calculations to be performed, the input must be fixed. That is, the analyst or the agency operating to achieve the efficiency objective must be aware of the resources that will be made available. In the short run, of course, an agency budget informs it of the sum total of resources available to it, but most government planning deals in the future and not in the current budget year. To be useful in efficiency studies, an agency's financial projections should reflect the resources likely to be available. When its expectations of financial resources are substantially overexceeded or underfulfilled, then the agency's efficiency studies will no longer be relevant.

Such a condition is likely to arise if agencies consistently base their planning on larger budgets than they are likely to get. In the absence of central guidelines, they may well do this. In fact, the Budget Bureau's decision (reflected in the revised PPB guidance in Bulletin 68-2) seems to abandon any concept of requiring realistic assumptions about future appropriations and even fails to require agencies to expose their unrealistic assumptions. The Bulletin (unlike its predecessor and the practice in the Defense Department) requires that the future implications of present decisions be indicated but does not require that expected future implications of future decisions be recorded.*

However, operating in ignorance of future agency plans is not an inherent part of the PPB approach. In the Defense Department, while Secretary McNamara could legitimately quote guidance from the President to the effect that he need

---

* As a result, it will produce "irrational" decisions when a decision-maker accepts future costs of present decisions only to find that he is not willing to incur those costs when the time comes (e.g., procure large quantities of B-58 aircraft) because budgetary limitations will not permit both implementation of previously approved programs and new programs which look attractive.

not use arbitrary budget ceilings, Defense decision-makers have had quite precise concepts of resources available for the programs. In fact, the Five Year Force Structure and Financial Program gave very specific ideas on the resources likely to be available for particular activities and therefore permitted analysts and decision-makers to use the right order of magnitude of resources in considering how to improve outputs.

Organization

The organizational limitations of PPB appear particularly in the achievement of the efficiency objective. Maximizing the return on one's budget presumes that the various alternatives for maximizing return can be purchased with that budget. If, in fact, an objective is being achieved by an agency's program and several other programs outside of the agency, it is clearly impossible for the agency head to allocate among the programs so as to maximize return. Perhaps the strongest exposition of this problem is Secretary of Defense McNamara's frequent comment that "dollar for dollar" the nation gets more return from military-assistance expenditures than from money spent within the regular Department of Defense budget. The existence of such a situation implies that total efficiency of the program could be increased by transferring dollars from the regular budget to the military-assistance budget, yet in fact these transfers do not take place because the two budgets are separate--one is defense; the other is foreign aid. [5]

The problem in domestic affairs is even greater than in Defense. Education programs, for example, are funded not only through the Office of Education but also through the Public Health Service within the Department of Health, Education and Welfare and by the Veterans Administration and the Office of Economic Opportunity. Under these circumstances, one cannot maximize the return on a given budget for education objectives unless there is transferability, at least in the budgeting process if not in the spending process, between various budgets achieving the same objective. As a practical matter, given difficulties in communication among agencies and the tendency for an agency to identify with its own program, the existence of the same

function in various organizations can frustrate achievement
of the efficiency objective.

Organizational changes, therefore, can become a
necessary requisite to achievement of the efficiency objective. The result of not making such changes is that no
official short of the President is in a position to balance
programs designed to achieve similar objectives. Defining
what should be balanced with what, however, is not simple.
Frequently, organizational changes facilitate comparison
of some programs at the price of obscuring other comparisons. For example, urban transportation planning and mass-
transit functions were for years lodged in the Department of
Housing and Urban Development and its predecessor agencies.
They were not transferred to the new Department of Transportation when it was established but were transferred later
after long study. The basic question is whether or not mass
transit is so inextricably related to city planning and housing
structures as to be properly included in the Department of
Housing and Urban Development. Alternatively, it can be
considered as a transportation program. There is obviously
no "correct" answer, and one's emphasis on one side of the
question or the other simply reveals one's own concept of
the objectives that ought to be served by mass transit. In
these circumstances, without a "right" answer, organizational decisions will in fact have a great deal to do with the
program decisions, and organizational decisions can by no
means seem perfect to individuals who do not agree on objectives and program concepts.

The problem that arises if organization is not perfect
(and it cannot be) in pursuing an efficiency objective is
indicated by one budgetary strategy used by the Johnson
Administration. In the initial year of PPB, the basic concept was that departmental budgets would be presented by
cabinet officials in terms of "bands."[6] One band was the
budget level of the prior year. Within this, however, the
cabinet officer could make recommendations for cutting
some of his programs and increasing others. Thus, for
example, within the Department of Housing and Urban
Development, the budget for mass transit was competing
with the budget for administration of single-family home
loan mortgage programs and the budgets for water and
sewer loans and college housing. If one considers mass

transit to be transportation, this budgetary competition
within the band was wrong; the competition should have been
with the rail corridor concept, with maritime subsidies,
and the like. Comparable debatable competitions arise
within other departments. It may be that if the nation gets
more roads it will need less airports, but it is not obvious
that more health should result in less education or "welfare."
Thus, achievement of the efficiency objective (and economy
objective to be discussed in the next section) will in fact be
conditioned by the organizational arrangements for the review of budgets. [7]

Promote Economy

The economy objective (producing any given output for
the least cost) presents many of the same difficulties in
analysis as the efficiency objective, as both costs and output
must be measured in terms of some basic concept of what
governmental policy is to achieve. However, to a very
major degree, many of the outputs of government are generally agreed upon or sufficiently fixed so that one can seek
to examine alternative ways to reduce dollar costs of
achieving them. Thus, the applicability of economic analysis to government programs is probably most feasible in
the economy-type study, which avoids both significant value
judgments on the part of the analyst and the presumption
of participation by high-level decision-makers in the planning
process.

The output of many governmental programs is set by
the fact that they involve public-utility functions. Thus,
the Tennessee Valley Authority supplies all the electricity
demanded by the customers of the system. The Bureau of
the Mint seeks to supply all the money required to keep
coinage in circulation without serious supply shortages.
The Post Office seeks to supply mail service to all who
deposit letters in its boxes. Other programs involve a
fixed level of payments, as in aid to families with dependent
children, social security, public assistance, unemployment
compensation, and many Veterans Administration programs.
The level of these programs is set by forces outside the
programs themselves, although the dollar cost can obviously

be increased or reduced as benefit levels are increased or reduced.

Certain other functions satisfy derived demand. The General Services Administration, for example, provides paper, buildings, transportation, supplies, etc., to other agencies. The disbursement offices within Treasury have their work load set by the activities of other agencies, and in many of the grants-in-aid programs a tradition has developed whereby the funding levels are set by the level of demand of those who seek to use funds. While not all persons would agree on all programs on a given list of programs with fixed output, it is obvious that there are major government programs where the level of output is known with relative certainty, and the problem is simply to minimize cost for that given level of output. The PPB system, with its emphasis on economic analysis, is well suited to this situation.

Spotlight Program Change

The objective of utilizing PPBS to pinpoint potential contractions or expansions in government programs is the area where economic analysis of governmental programs has received the greatest attention. This is the one area where it is generally presumed that the PPB system will do more than simply highlight decisions for potential decision-makers to make in light of their own objectives. Here, by measuring both benefits and costs, the PPB approach may indicate preferred courses of action for the decision-maker to adopt.

The achievement of the output-spotlighting objective is, like the other objectives, tied very closely to the ability to specify goals and objectives. If goals and objectives cannot be clearly specified, then the concepts of benefit and cost have a very narrow and not necessarily important meaning. If, for example, the maximizing of human choice is one of the objectives of our nation, a program with major economic benefits might have very serious "costs" in terms of human choice that would not be measured if benefits and costs were reckoned solely in economic terms.

This having been said, however, there is much potential for cost-benefit analysis, particularly in areas where the major output of the project or program has market value. In transportation, postal services, water resources, housing, and perhaps in other areas as well, it may be possible to apply market tests and to treat governmental output, in essence, as though one were making decisions for a firm or a business, seeking only to satisfy consumer wants at a price that consumers are willing to pay but subsidizing output or seeking to capture the natural profits from the functions involved for public use rather than private purposes.

It may be possible for agencies to escape economic analysis of their programs when they have objectives other than pure economic efficiency. Of course, simply because an agency claims that noneconomic values are involved is no reason for central decision-makers to assume that such values do exist or to take them into account. In fact, the most fruitful kind of PPB program review can occur in those old programs that have strong clientele and agency support but which perhaps could no longer stand the test of a general political desire to fund the programs. Such programs may persist on the basis of economic arguments for continuing them. If PPB could foil agency strategies previously described, it could have an impact on these programs by exploding their "economic" rationalizations. At the same time, it could encourage more rapid expansion of programs of real economic value.

However, the prospects for successful cost-benefit analysis will depend on the political strength and tenacity of those who wish to resist the application of this type of analysis to their programs relative to that of the President and the central control agencies (or departmental strength vis-à-vis component bureaus).

There is a second way in which the output-determining objectives of PPBS may be achieved. This is in the examination of achievements toward intangible goals. It is very difficult to estimate the value of a human life, the value of a given amount of health care, or an income supplement for a family. It may be possible, however, to analyze existing programs to determine the weights implicitly given to such values in program decisions. For example, a decision not

to put a guardrail on a highway may involve an assumption
that saving a human life is worth only $5,000. A health pro-
gram or clinic program may involve saving human life at
$2,000 per life. Given these assumed facts, it would be
clearly inconsistent to pursue all programs simultaneously
at the same levels.

Analyses like these can be conducted without the analyst
himself making value judgments. He may simply point out
the implicit values given in the different programs by fac-
toring out the known economic costs and values. By this
method, he may be able to provide the decision-maker with
some idea of inconsistencies among his own decisions, which
will highlight those decisions that most further the objective
he desires. The extent to which decision-makers will respond
to this type of analysis will undoubtedly vary. However, it
does seem fair to conclude--with respect to both cost-benefit
analysis and the analysis of inferred values accorded to
various intangible objectives--that the very knowledge of
these various factors can influence the political bargaining
process by altering the information available to the participant.

Improve Judgment

The difficulties in achieving other objectives (as a result
of a lack of clear statements of national goals and objectives)
occurs with respect to the informed-judgment objective. In
essence, the informed-judgment objective required that the
decision-maker, whether Congress, the public, the President, or an agency, be confronted with pairs of costs and
outputs so that he could determine policy as a consumer would
determine whether or not to buy apples or oranges. This
was found to require knowledge of incremental costs and
outputs, knowledge that can only be gained if the continuum
on which costs and outputs are to be measured can validly
be determined. To the extent that it can, it is possible that
the informed-judgment objective can be furthered by PPB,
as PPB focuses attention on differing ratios of output to
input at various program levels.

By focusing upon open and explicit analysis, and indeed
by encouraging analysis itself, the PPB approach will certainly not cause decision-makers to have less information
than they would have without it. How much better information becomes as a result of PPB will vary with the skill and
resources with which the PPB approach is applied. At a
minimum, it would seem that a probable major accomplishment of the system in the federal government will be to focus
more attention on models. Early PPB studies, even though
they did not produce decisive answers, have reminded government decision-makers that such important relationships as
that between Federal Aviation Agency controllers and air
safety, and health programs and morbidity, are not understood with any certainty. [8] By showing that current knowledge
is insufficient to permit informed judgment to operate, the
PPB approach will no doubt cause a considerable effort to
identify more precisely how (and whether) added resources
employed in various government programs produce social
and economic results that political decision-makers consider
worth-while.

Improve Performance Evaluation

Evaluation of program decisions made in the past is, of
course, possible through the PPB approach, but only with
the same caveats and difficulties as have been noted for the
possibility of approving proposed future programs. Few
conclusions can properly be drawn from evaluation of past
programs in many cases because "suboptimizing" a program
cannot have been undertaken when the program was implemented before the objective was discovered. You cannot
blame a manager (or a government program) for failing to
achieve objectives that he (or its managers) had not been
made aware of. For example, the public-housing program,
in retrospect, can be faulted for seriously aggravating problems of racial isolation. However, public-housing administrators in the late 1930's and 1940's were pursuing objectives
of (a) eliminating substandard housing and (b) building
minimum-standard housing for low-income persons as
rapidly as consistent with their fund limitations. They cannot be faulted as managers if they did a good job of achieving
objectives as communicated to them. The program itself

cannot be said to be "bad" by a criterion of racial isolation unless redesign is considered in light of the newly discovered objective. As the public-housing example shows, the program can be restructured to take the newer objective into account. This example merely highlights a more general proposition that specifying what is desired must precede performance evaluation.

IMPROVING PPB PERFORMANCE

The preceding evaluation of the prospects for PPB in terms of objectives stated by President Johnson may leave an unduly pessimistic impression. Measured against the high hopes evidenced in the President's statements, prospects for the system in the federal government are none too favorable. However, measured against the somewhat more realistic expectations of leading PPB practitioners, the outlook is not nearly as unfavorable. Accomplishments will not come easily or quickly. One test of the PPB approach will be whether its supporters and practitioners can use their analytical training to cope with problems of acceptance and implementation as well as problems of finding "right answers." To this end, the following recommendations are offered, based upon the conclusions of the study and upon the author's preparations to write it. They stem from a belief that the assumptions implicit in PPB are, on the whole, sound and that the impact of PPB is likely on the whole to be "in the public interest." They are treated as though directed toward a staff of the President for application throughout the federal government but can easily be converted to recommendations for departmental officers and for state and local officials.

Setting Program Objectives

To a significant degree, objectives are not going to be "found." To make analysis meaningful, it will be necessary to set objectives, not find them. The President's tolerance for making decisions before practical problems appear should be stretched to the limit to obtain guidance on as

many substantive points as possible. In cases where a program, project, or activity is being carried out in response
to nonrelated objectives (for example, in response to cam-
paign commitments or as part of a logrolling process), the
central control staff should understand this point, even though
it might not be expedient for them to publicize it. Formulating statements of purpose and objectives to give an apparent public purpose to programs adopted for other reasons is
inevitable but should not be permitted to confuse the decision-
makers themselves. Much of McNamara's success in the
Pentagon came because he was willing to face hard issues
and choices early in the planning stages.

Dollar Guidelines

    Although establishing arbitrary resource limitations
before all the facts are in is foreign to the basic concepts
of PPB, to make it work in practice some ball-park resource
guidelines may be necessary. Perhaps, after one or two
rounds of reviewing program memoranda, resource limitations should be established (with the approval of the President) on a broad program basis. The importance of setting
ceilings on a program basis must be stressed. Ceilings on
an agency basis can lead to false trade-offs among unrelated
programs (such as between education and health and between
mass transit and housing). One value of the Defense Department's program structure is that it provides the framework
for allocating resources between strategic offensive capability and limited war capabilities regardless of the military
department in which a particular program might appear.

Attacking Externalities and Hidden Costs

    "Shadow pricing" will probably always remain a concep-
tual mystery to most people analyzing government programs.
It certainly can never be expected to become intelligible to
the nonspecialists whose reactions trigger political action
in a democracy. However, some steps can be taken to relate more closely the real costs of a program or policy to

the costs considered by those who propose and adopt it.
These steps include:

(a) Continuing to press for user charges in all
cases but those where the President would
be willing to make direct transfers to the
beneficiaries comparable to the benefit from
a zero price or subsidized price policy.

(b) Reflection of all governmental costs caused
by an agency in that agency's budget. This
should include apportionment of central
overheads (e.g., Civil Service Commission
administrative costs) and specialized costs
(e.g., navigation clearances for highway
bridges). Implementation of this approach
will require widening existing statutory
authority for one agency to achieve its purposes by transferring funds to another for
program implementation.

(c) Using shadow prices in those cases where
actual payment is inappropriate. For example, the cost inputed to agencies using
government-owned office space in Washington, D.C., should be the costs that the
government pays in leasing space, not the
zero price implied by existing budgetary
procedure. In some cases, actual payment
rather than shadow pricing may seem desir-
able--for example, in the case of payments
to state and local governments in lieu of
taxes on federal real property.

Finding Program Issues That
Are Not Budgetary Issues

The budgetary cycle tends to focus the bulk of analytical
effort upon programs with consequences for the expenditure
side of the federal budget. As a result, the most fruitful
areas for analysis are probably those without budgetary
impact but which have comparable impact on the nation's

248   THE PPB APPROACH

welfare. Conceptually, tax concessions are equivalent to expenditures and should be reviewed at least as eagerly and often. The regulatory agencies and portions of regular departments exercising regulatory authority have opportunities to cause expenditures (by both the regulated industry and its customers and suppliers) without being held accountable for those expenditures through any budget review procedures. Many administrative decisions (for example, in the allocation of grants-in-aid) also require analysis with PPB techniques. There is no reason why the PPB approach could not be applied to these programs and activities.

Planning and Analysis Guidelines

The conclusions of this analysis do not bode well for PPB's reliance upon analysis performed within existing agency structures. To the extent that the central control authorities and the agencies share objectives and program interests, this will not be a problem, but in the really important cases the two interests are not identical. The Defense Department solution relied heavily upon (a) analytical staffs at the top level of the organization and (b) outside consultants. This solution would seem equally necessary in the case of domestic programs of government.

The establishment of separate PPB staffs in each agency presents the possibility of creating ties of loyalty between such staffs and other analysts in other agencies and in the Bureau of the Budget. Such ties could be strengthened by the emergence of "professional" standards, a professional literature, and organizations emphasizing communality of interest among PPB personnel. Particularly if a group outside of the agencies--say the Bureau of the Budget--maintained considerable indirect control over hiring for these staffs and sought to find employment for those analysts being replaced for not adequately representing their agency's position, it is possible that the system might work (as judged from the perspective of the central control agencies). However, it should be noted that the original concept of the agency budget officer--which is as old as the Budget and Accounting Act of 1921--had implicit in it the notion that the budget officer might play such a role within agencies. Those expectations have not been achieved fully.

A second approach would be to seek to ensure as much responsibility in agency analytical work as possible through utilizing the central guideline device. Because a reasonable response of any agency head will always be to use the most flexible approach (worst from the standpoint of the central control agency) that the President and Bureau of the Budget will permit, these institutions must crack down early and often if they expect analysis to show anything but what the agency's normal processes would have produced. This problem can be alleviated by central guidelines prescribing such factors as:

(a) Planning assumptions such as population
    increases, expected growth in GNP, etc.

(b) Utilization of real prices, without the
    potential to assume inflation in either
    costs or benefits

(c) A cost-of-money assumption reflecting
    the opportunity cost of money

(d) A requirement to avoid illusory benefits
    or costs stemming from differences in
    tax liabilities or borrowing costs result-
    ing solely from type of ownership (pri-
    vate, local, or federal) rather than the
    nature of the enterprise being considered.

Full Funding

The lament that x per cent of the budget is uncontrollable is heard with great regularity, but steps within the legal powers of the executive branch to increase controllability have been lacking. There is little reason why, for example, "full funding" should not be adopted for such domestic programs as civil works. Under today's procedure, a budget item may simply represent the funds required to finish a project first funded two years earlier. Under "full funding,"

the entire cost of the project would be budgeted in the first
year, meaning that full costs would be apparent to all decision-
makers and each year's budget would be more controllable.

Transferability

Increasing transferability of funds among departments
and within departments among sharply differing programs is
as much a question of the relative power of executive and
legislative power as one of better budgeting. However, it
must be noted that, at least from the executive branch point
of view, relatively complete transferability among appropriations is essential if the economy criterion is to be applied consistently to program implementation so long as
(and this will always be the case) the means to any given
end are found in many different government agencies.

Those familiar with the problems of financial management in the federal government will recognize that these
proposals are not new. It should also be understood that
they are not aseptic, value-free, neutral procedural recommendations for "better administration," devoid of program
impact. If these recommendations were implemented, certain government agencies, certain industries, and certain
categories of individuals would be substantially worse off
than they otherwise expect to be. Conversely, other groups'
positions would be improved. One of the tragedies that
could easily befall program analysts in the federal government would be the failure to recognize that these groups
will not abandon their beliefs, their jobs, their industries,
and their welfare (not to mention their own views) just because some "experts" in policy analysis say that their programs are not in the national interest.

A CONCLUDING COMMENT

If supported by an enthusiastic chief executive, sought
and supported by an inquiring and open-minded legislative
body, implemented by McNamara-like political executives

and well-trained analysts, the PPB approach can cause major improvements in the way government goes about its business. However, in a world where one man's objectivity is another's bias, one man's truth is another's falsehood, one man's benefit is another's cost, and one political leader's success is his opponent's loss, no analytical system producing tests of government programs will command ready public acceptance. Ultimately, as has always been the case, better government must be achieved through politics by politicians.

NOTES TO CHAPTER 13

1. There is considerable debate in the economics journals over social preference functions; many important issues in the pricing area were not considered (see Roland N. McKean, "The Use of Shadow Prices," in Samuel B. Chase, Jr. (ed.), Problems in Public Expenditure Analysis (Washington, D.C.: Brookings, 1968), pp. 33-77. The implications of the PPB approach for centralization-decentralization, the assumptions about the proper role of expertise, the presumed relationship between politics and program decisions, etc., are all important. These have been considered by Aaron Wildavsky (a political scientist) in his article "The Political Economy of Efficiency: Cost-Benefit Analysis, Systems Analysis, and Program Budgeting." The article appears both in the PPBS Symposium, Public Administration Review, XXVI (December, 1966), pp. 292-310, and in The Public Interest (Summer, 1967), pp. 30-48. The relative roles of U.S. legislative and executive branches in their use of the approach will itself become a topic for a book-length study.

2. Reported officially in Weekly Compilation of Presidential Documents, August 30, 1965, pp. 141-43, 143; November 21, 1966, pp. 1705-6; and in the President's fiscal 1968 budget message from The Budget of the United States Government for the Fiscal Year Ending June 30, 1968 (Washington, D.C.: Government Printing Office, 1967). The Presidential statements can be found in U.S. Congress, Senate, Committee on Government Operations,

Subcommittee on National Security and International Operations, "Planning-Programming-Budgeting, Official Documents," Ninetieth Congress, 1st Session, 1967.

3. U.S. Congress, Joint Committee on the Organization of Congress, Hearings, Eighty-ninth Congress, 1st Session, 1965, Part 12, p. 1799.

4. There is also a logical fallacy in the concept of giving one objective priority over another. This is discussed well by Charles Hitch and Roland McKean, The Economics of Defense in the Nuclear Age (Cambridge, Mass.: Harvard University Press, 1960), pp. 122-23. The basic point is that when we give "priority" to guns over butter, we don't mean all guns and no butter, and it's impossible to tell exactly what we do mean.

5. Detail on this example is provided in the author's United States Military Assistance: A Study of Policies and Practices (New York: Frederick A. Praeger, 1965), pp. 275-76.

6. The procedure is described in the Testimony of Charles Schultze, U.S. Congress, Joint Economic Committee, Hearings, Fiscal Policy Issues of the Coming Decade, Eighty-ninth Congress, 1st Session, 1965, pp. 59-96.

7. This has been recognized by George A. Steiner in David Novick (ed.), Program Budgeting: Program Analysis and the Federal Budget (Cambridge, Mass.: Harvard University Press, 1965), p. 348; by Melvin Anshen in the same volume, pp. 358-62; and by Aaron Wildavsky, "The Political Economy of Efficiency: Cost-Benefit Analysis, Systems Analysis and Program Budgeting," Public Administration Review, XXVI (December, 1966), 304-5.

8. On aviation, see Gary Fromm, "Economic Criteria for Federal Aviation Agency Expenditures" (prepared for the FAA by United Research, Inc., Cambridge, Mass.: 1962). On health programs, see testimony of William Gorham before the Joint Economic Committee, Subcommittee on Economy in Government, op. cit.

BIBLIOGRAPHIC COMMENT

BIBLIOGRAPHIC COMMENT

There is no shortage of bibliographies on the PPB approach. That maintained by the staff of the Bureau of the Budget library, Program Analysis Techniques: A Selected Bibliography, is comprehensive, kept relatively current by a knowledgeable staff, and well organized. Single copies of the Bureau's Bibliography are, when available, provided free by the Bureau's publications office. That bibliography currently lists nine other bibliographies, a number bound to grow rapidly as implementation of PPB spreads from the federal government to state and local governments. This bibliographic comment is no substitute for those documents, which will continue faithfully to reflect the burgeoning literature on program analysis. The strength of these bibliographic endeavors, their exhaustive coverage, is also their weakness, as exhaustiveness and a high degree of selectivity are mutually exclusive. Furthermore, it is understandably difficult for a government employee to criticize privately published books as not worth reading, even if the employee feels he has the competence to make such an evaluation. Already, it is probably impossible for any single individual to read everything written on PPB.* An individual outside the government knows no such constraints on criticisms, evaluations, and conclusions. Thus, the purpose of this essay is to help others to gain an appreciation of PPB without suffering through repetitive, dull, and even incorrect writing on the subject.

---

* This bibliographic comment is based upon an attempt to do so. The author has read and taken notes on all documents on PPB reflected in the Bureau's bibliography through the end of 1966 and has managed to follow new publications reasonably well since that time. This was probably an ineffective approach when undertaken and would be ridiculous now.

Background

At the outset, it should be noted that PPB is not necessarily the preserve of the highly trained technician. In the
words of Alain Enthoven:

> The advanced mathematical techniques of
> econometrics and operations research have
> not proved to be particularly useful in dealing
> with the problem I have described. Although
> a good grasp of this kind of mathematics is
> very valuable as intellectual formation, we
> are not applying linear programming, formal
> game theory, queuing theory, multiple re-
> gression theory, nonlinear programming
> under uncertainty, or anything like it. The
> economic theory we are using is the theory
> most of us learned as sophomores. The
> reason PhD's are required is that many
> economists do not believe what they have
> learned until they have gone through grad-
> uate school and acquired a vested interest
> in marginal analysis. *

Nor is a strong quantitative background necessarily essential.
Budget Director Charles Schultze has suggested that law is
good training and that "lawyers tend to make good PPB
analysts."** Henry S. Rowen, who helped introduce PPB
when he was an Assistant Director of the Bureau of the Budget, has commented:

> PPBS requires people who are tough-minded,
> analytical, and not frightened by numbers.

---

* Alain Enthoven, "Economic Analysis in the Department of Defense," American Economic Review, LIII (May,
1963), 422.

** In testimony, U.S. Congress, Senate, Committee
on Government Operations, Subcommittee on National
Security and International Operations, Hearings, "Planning-
Programming-Budgeting," op. cit., Part I, p. 39.

Although complex methods of quantitative analysis will not generally be used, some knowledge of these methods is useful. Most important is the desire and the ability to question, to compare, to quantify--and to select, from among alternatives, those programs that will produce the greatest benefits from Government expenditures. [*]

While it may be possible to understand PPB solely on the basis of economics we learned as sophomores, as Enthoven implies, it is clearly impossible to approach the subject seriously without at least that much knowledge of economics. Also in evaluating Enthoven's comment, it is well to bear in mind that he may have been considerably more brilliant and diligent as a sophomore than the rest of us. Specifically, I believe that anyone who cannot handle sophomore-level microeconomics (supply, demand, price, choices of means of production, marginal utility, indifference curves, production functions, etc.) will waste his time if he begins to read material on the PPB approach without first improving his economic background. The parts of Paul Samuelson's text which deal with microeconomics--Parts 3 and 4 in the sixth edition of Economics: An Introductory Analysis (New York: McGraw-Hill, 1964)--or Robert Dorfman's The Price System (Englewood Cliffs, N.J.: Prentice-Hall, 1964) fulfill this need. For those interested in such criteria, the Dorfman volume costs less and is shorter.

On the subject of economic background, Otto Eckstein has a volume of slightly more than one hundred pages in the Prentice-Hall Foundations of Modern Economics Series (various editions) which is good background. For those intending to pursue the theory of benefit measurement at a rigorous level (but only for them), an understanding of the relevant parts of Richard Musgrave's The Theory of Public Finance: A Study in Public Economy (New York: McGraw-Hill, 1959) is essential. Readings in welfare economics and the logic of collective action are also helpful background. See the Budget Bureau's bibliography for

---

[*] "PPBS: What and Why," Civil Service Journal (January-March, 1966).

citations of material by James Buchanan, William Baumol, Jerome Rothenberg, and Paul Samuelson.

Those whose exposure to government has been limited and whose academic background is primarily in economics, engineering, or natural sciences will profit from improving their understanding of the governmental process before seeking to apply economic analysis to governmental problems. The Inter-University Case Program in Public Administration produces useful case studies, some of which are collected in a public administration case book edited by H. Stein, Public Administration and Policy Development (New York: Harcourt, 1952). Useful case material will also be found in such studies as Robert Dahl, Who Governs? Democracy and Power in an American City (New Haven: Yale University Press, 1961); Edward C. Banfield, Political Influence (New York: The Free Press, 1961); Arthur Maass, Muddy Waters: The Army Engineers and the Nation's Rivers (Cambridge, Mass.: Harvard University Press, 1951); and Richard E. Neustadt, Presidential Power (New York: Wiley, 1960). For those who prefer a form of exposure less direct than case studies, Charles S. Hyneman, Bureaucracy in a Democracy (New York: Harper, 1950), is useful for the executive branch; and Charles L. Clapp, The Congressman: His Work as He Sees It (Garden City, New York: Doubleday, 1963), and Richard Fenno, The Power of the Purse: Appropriations Politics in the Congress (Boston: Little, Brown and Company, 1966), are useful for the legislative branch.

For background on planning, I have found George A. Steiner (ed.), Managerial Long-Range Planning (New York: McGraw-Hill, 1963), a good approach to the subject and one which considers business and government together. On budgeting, try Jesse Burkhead, Government Budgeting (New York: Wiley, 1965); Arthur Smithies, The Budgetary Process in the United States (New York: McGraw-Hill, 1955); Frederick C. Mosher, Program Budgeting: Theory and Practice with Particular Reference to the Department of the Army (Chicago: Public Administration Service, 1954); and Aaron Wildavsky, The Politics of the Budgetary Process (Boston: Little, Brown and Company, 1964).

The PPB Approach

For individuals who feel that their economics background is adequate and that they are familiar with the governmental process through experience, education, or both, the following sequence would not be an unreasonable way to expand knowledge of the PPB approach.

Black, Guy. The Application of Systems Analysis to Government Operations. Washington, D.C.: National Institute of Public Affairs, 1966.

Budget Bureau Bulletin 68-3 (single copies available on request from the Bureau of the Budget). Or George Washington University, State-Local Finances Project. PPB Note No. 3. Development of Initial Instructions to Inaugurate a Planning-Programming-Budgeting System. Washington, 1967.

Grant, Eugene, and Ireson, W. Grant. Principles of Engineering Economy. New York: Ronald Press, 1964.

Hatry, Harry P., and Cotton, John F. Program Planning for State, County, City. State-Local Finances Project of George Washington University, 1967.

Lyden, F. and Miller, E. (eds.). Planning-Programming-Budgeting: A Systems Approach to Management. Chicago: Markham, 1967.

Maass, Arthur. "Benefit Cost Analysis: Its Relevance to Public Expenditure Decisions," Quarterly Journal of Economics, LXXX (May, 1966), 208-26.

McCullough, J. D. "Cost Effectiveness: Estimating Systems Costs," RAND Corporation Paper No. P-3229 (1965).

McKean, Roland N. Efficiency in Government Through Systems Analysis. New York: Wiley, 1958.

_____, "Evaluating Alternative Expenditure Programs" (and comment by Jesse Burkhead), in Universities-National Bureau of Economic Research, Public Finances:

Needs, Sources, and Utilization. Princeton: Princeton University Press, 1961. pp. 337-64.

Merrett, A. J., and Sykes, Allen. The Finance and Analysis of Capital Projects. New York: Wiley, 1963.

Novick, David. "Origin and History of Program Budgeting," RAND Corporation Paper No. P-3427, October, 1966. Reprinted in Senate Government Operations Committee, Subcommittee on National Security and International Operations, Planning-Programming-Budgeting: Selected Comment, Ninetieth Congress, 1st Session, 1967 (committee print).

_____ (ed.). Program Budgeting: Program Analysis and the Federal Budget. Cambridge, Mass.: Harvard University Press, 1965. Also published by the Government Printing Office in an abridged version.

Prest, A. R., and Turvey, R. "Cost-Benefit Analysis: A Survey," Economic Journal, Vol. 75, pp. 683-735. Reprinted in American Economic Association, Surveys of Economic Theory, Vol. 3, Resource Allocation. New York: St. Martin's Press, 1966.

U.S. Congress, Joint Economic Committee, Subcommittee on Economy in Government, Hearings, "The Planning-Programming-Budgeting System: Progress and Potentials," Ninetieth Congress, 1st Session, 1967.

U.S. Congress, Senate, Committee on Government Operations, Subcommittee on National Security and International Operations, three planning-programming-budgeting publications: "Official Documents," "Initial Memorandum," and "Selected Comment," Ninetieth Congress, 1st Session, 1967.

Wildavsky, Aaron. "The Political Economy of Efficiency: Cost-Benefit Analysis, Systems Analysis, and Program Budgeting," Public Administration Review, XXVI (December, 1966). Reprinted in U.S. Congress, Senate, Committee on Government Operations, Subcommittee on National Security and International Operations, "Planning-Programming-Budgeting, Selected Comment," Ninetieth Congress, 1st Session, 1967, pp. 50-72.

Testimony of key federal government officials on PPB will be found in the hearings cited above. Additionally, most of these officials have given speeches, written articles, and testified before other committees; see citations to this material in the Budget Bureau's PPB bibliography.

Specific Applications

The following are citations to good examples of program analysis in particular subject-matter fields.

Housing, Urban Development, and Social Programs

Hirsch, Werner Z. "Cost Functions of an Urban Government Service: Refuse Collection," Review of Economics and Statistics, XLVII (February, 1965), 87-92.

Institute for Defense Analyses, Science and Technology (Task Force Report to the President's Commission on Law Enforcement and Administration of Justice). Washington, D.C.: Government Printing Office, 1963.

Margolis, Julius (ed.). The Public Economy of Urban Communities. Baltimore: Johns Hopkins Press, 1965.

Morse, Philip (ed.). Operations Research for Public Systems. Cambridge, Mass.: MIT Press, 1967.

Rothenberg, Jerome. Economic Evaluation of Urban Renewal. Washington, D.C.: Brookings, 1967.

Schaller, Howard G. (ed.). Public Expenditure Decisions in the Urban Community. Baltimore: Johns Hopkins Press, 1963.

Health, Education and Welfare

Conley, Ronald. The Economics of Vocational Rehabilitation. Baltimore: Johns Hopkins Press, 1965.

Hirsch, Werner Z., et al. Spillovers of Public Education Costs and Benefits. Los Angeles: Institute of Government and Public Affairs, University of California, 1964.

Kershaw, Joseph A., and McKean, Roland N. Systems
Analysis and Education. RAND Corporation Research
Memorandum RM 2473-FF (1959).

Klarman, Herbert. The Economics of Health. New York:
Columbia University Press, 1965.

U.S. Department of Health, Education and Welfare, Program
Analysis (series of analyses of various HEW programs
available, if in stock, from the Department).

Weisbrod, Burton. Economics of Public Health. Philadelphia:
University of Pennsylvania Press, 1961.

Transportation

Ferguson, Alan, et al. The Economic Value of the United
States Merchant Marine. Evanston, Ill.: Northwestern
University Press, 1961.

Foster, C. D. The Transport Problem. London: Blackie,
1963.

Fromm, Gary. "Civil Aviation Expenditures," in Robert
Dorfman, Measuring Benefits of Government Investments
Washington, D.C.: Brookings, 1965.

Kuhn, Tillo. Public Enterprise Economics and Transport
Problems. Berkeley: University of California Press,
1962.

Meyer, John, et al. The Urban Transportation Problem.
Cambridge, Mass.: Harvard University Press, 1965.

Mohring, Herbert, and Harwitz, Mitchell. Highway Benefits:
An Analytical Framework. Evanston: Northwestern University Press, 1962.

Defense

Enke, Stephen (ed.). Defense Management. Englewood
Cliffs, N.J.: Prentice-Hall, 1967.

Goldman, Thomas (ed.). Cost-Effectiveness Analysis. New York: Frederick A. Praeger, 1967.

Hitch, Charles. Decision-Making for Defense. Berkeley: University of California Press, 1965.

_____, and McKean, Roland. The Economics of Defense in the Nuclear Age. Cambridge, Mass.: Harvard University Press, 1960.

McKean, Roland (ed.). Issues in Defense Economics. New York: Columbia University Press, 1967.

Quade, E. S. (ed.). Analysis for Military Decisions. Chicago: Rand McNally, 1964.

U.S. Industrial College of the Armed Forces. A Modern Design for Defense Decision: A McNamara-Hitch-Enthoven Anthology. Washington, D.C.: ICAF, 1966.

Water Resources

Eckstein, Otto. Water Resource Development: The Economics of Project Evaluation. Cambridge, Mass.: Harvard University Press, 1958.

Hirshleifer, Jack, et al. Water Supply: Economics, Technology and Policy. Chicago: University of Chicago Press, 1960.

Kneese, Allen. The Economics of Regional Water Quality Management. Baltimore: Johns Hopkins Press, 1964.

Maass, Arthur, et al. Design of Water-Resource Systems: New Techniques for Relating Economic Objectives, Engineering Analysis and Governmental Planning. Cambridge, Mass.: Harvard University Press, 1962.

Margolis, Julius. "The Economic Evaluation of Federal Water Resource Development," American Economic Review, XLIX (March, 1959), 96-111.

Ruttan, Vernon. The Economic Demand for Irrigated Acreage. Baltimore: Johns Hopkins Press, 1965.

Thomas, Harold. "The Animal Farm: A Mathematical
    Model for the Discussion of Social Standards for Control
    of the Environment," Quarterly Journal of Economics,
    LXXVII (February, 1963) 143-48.

ABOUT THE AUTHOR

Harold A. Hovey has had varied experience in government planning and budgeting as well as in the presentation of budgets to the Congress. He was an employee of the Office of the Secretary of Defense during the installation of the McNamara-Hitch management and budgeting systems in the early 1960's. In 1962-63, he worked in the Bureau of the Budget's Office of Management and Organization before returning to the Defense Department. After leaving government service, he was employed by the National Association of Electric Companies, where he concerned himself with federal policies (including cost-benefit analysis) as they affected the electric utility industry. He is now a senior economist at the Battelle Memorial Institute in Columbus, Ohio.

Dr. Hovey, a graduate of Wabash College, received the Ph.D. and L.L.B. degrees from George Washington University, Washington, D.C. His previous book, United States Military Assistance: A Study of Policies and Practices, was published as a Praeger Special Study in 1965.